Talcott Parsons
ON INSTITUTIONS AND
SOCIAL EVOLUTION

THE HERITAGE OF SOCIOLOGY
A Series Edited by Morris Janowitz

TALCOTT PARSONS

ON INSTITUTIONS AND SOCIAL EVOLUTION

Selected Writings

Edited and with an Introduction by

LEON H. MAYHEW

105089

THE UNIVERSITY OF CHICAGO PRESS
Chicago and London

THE UNIVERSITY OF CHICAGO PRESS, CHICAGO 60637
THE UNIVERSITY OF CHICAGO PRESS, LTD., LONDON

94 93 92 91 90 89 88 87 86 85   2 3 4 5 6

Library of Congress Cataloging in Publication Data

Parsons, Talcott, 1902–1979
    Talcott Parsons on institutions and social evolution.

    (The Heritage of sociology)
    Includes index.
    1. Parsons, Talcott, 1902–1979.   2. Social action—
Addresses, essays, lectures.   3. Social institutions—
Addresses, essays, lectures.   4. Social systems—
Addresses, essays, lectures.   5. Social change—Ad-
dresses, essays, lectures.   I. Mayhew, Leon H.
II. Title.   III. Series.
HM22.U6P362   1982   306   82-4911
ISBN 0-226-64747-1 (cloth)   AACR2
        0-226-64749-8 (paper)

CONTENTS

PREFACE

This volume in the Heritage of Sociology series is introduced by a somewhat longer essay than most of the books in the collection. Talcott Parsons's work presents readers with almost legendary difficulties. Most of his important essays and books presume that the reader is familiar with his rather specialized vocabulary. Even when Parsons begins by defining basic terms, his special uses for words and his style of exposition strike many readers as forbidding. It seems appropriate to introduce this volume with an account of the basic tools of Parsonian analysis. I also try to interpret the larger themes of his work, providing a more or less chronological account of the development of his thought, his presuppositions, and his position on the ideological spectrum of social thought.

I am deeply grateful for the assistance Talcott Parsons provided in the preparation of this book. In the winter of 1978, Parsons taught a graduate course in Berkeley, and I was able to attend most of the meetings of this seminar. Shortly before his return to Cambridge in April of 1978, we had an opportunity to discuss plans for the present volume. I showed him an outline of the introduction and a tentative list of the selections I had chosen. We discussed my intention to focus on the theme of institutionalization and to depict the changes in his thought over fifty years as modifications in his approach to this concept. He agreed that this would be a useful expository device and appeared to accept the validity of my interpretation of his thought. Indeed, he was quite excited by this approach and offered to write an essay on institutionalization especially for this volume. Lamentably, his death a year later, in May of 1979, brought an end to this plan.

I do not mean to imply that my introductory essay has his official endorsement; he did not see the finished draft. Nor do I seek to make an official statement. Nevertheless, it is useful to report that Parsons viewed the main lines of this approach as true to his own conception of his life's work.

In the essay that he intended to write, he wished to parallel my own insistence that his sociology is essentially naturalistic. He was intrigued by the suggestion that the process of institutionalization was, in effect, a process of the survival of workable interpretations of social values; the idea converged with his own growing conviction that there is a precise analogy between the social process of institutionalization and the biological process of natural selection, a theme that I had, up to that time, missed in his work.[1]

I have not attempted a biographical account of the context and development of Parsons's thought. This ground has been well covered in his own essay "On Building Social System Theory: A Personal History,"[2] which I warmly recommend to readers who wish a more circumstantial history of his writings.

Had I wished to treat biographical themes, I would have stressed a brief period of intellectual ferment in 1954, during which Parsons discussed his Marshall Lectures (delivered at Cambridge University in November of 1953) with Neil Smelser. During these discussions a series of concepts crystalized in Parsons's thinking. The extension and elaboration of these concepts occupied most of his attention for the next twenty-five years. I must express my appreciation to Neil Smelser for his patient description of Parsons's first attempts at applying the four-fold functional scheme to the factors of economic production. Professor Smelser also recounted the rapid elaboration of this paradigm and Parsons's subsequent determination to follow through the implications of this analysis in as many sociocultural contexts as his fertile imagination would permit.

Thanks are also due to Gary Hamilton, Michael Hoffman, and Jonathan Mayhew, who gave the manuscript a close and helpful reading and provided a variety of forms of editorial assistance. Finally, Janet Mayhew must, as always, be thanked and praised for many hours of effort, innumerable contributions, and, above all, unfailing support.

Davis, California

TALCOTT PARSONS, 1902–79
A BIOGRAPHICAL NOTE

Talcott Parsons was born on December 13, 1902, at Colorado Springs, Colorado, the son of a Congregational minister who ultimately became president of Marietta College in Ohio. At Amherst College, Parsons emphasized philosophy and biology and contemplated a career in medicine. However, by the time of his graduation in 1924, he had already decided upon a career in social science; he immediately entered the London School of Economics, where he came under the influence of Bronislaw Malinowsky. In 1925 he moved to Heidelberg University, where the teachings of the late Max Weber were still influential, even though Weber himself had been dead for several years. Parsons earned a doctorate in economics from Heidelberg by writing a dissertation while undertaking an apprentice year of teaching at Amherst (1926–27) and was then appointed instructor in economics at Harvard. In 1931, still an instructor, he transferred to the newly formed Harvard Department of Sociology. His initial advancement was slow; he remained an instructor for five more years before achieving the rank of assistant professor and was not promoted to associate professor until 1939. The turning point in his academic stature was the publication in 1937 of *The Structure of Social Action*, an event which brought immediate and lasting renown to a then relatively obscure assistant professor.

From 1937 on, a steady stream of original and challenging essays and books brought Parsons increasing recognition—both honors (including several honorary degrees and memberships in honorary societies) and that special form of recognition that comes with being made an object of critical attacks from opposing points of view. By the early 1950s Parsons had clearly become the most distinguished, if also the most controversial, social theorist in the United States.

In the mid-forties Parsons was a central figure in the organization of an interdisciplinary Department of Social Relations at Harvard and became its first chair in 1946, serving in this position for ten years.

Parsons was a strong supporter of the professionalization of sociology and was a very active participant in the American Sociological Association, serving as president in 1949, for several years as secretary, and in 1965, as the founding editor of the association's professional publication, *American Sociologist*. He was president of the American Academy of Arts and Sciences from 1967 to 1971.

He remained at Harvard until his retirement in 1973 but extended his profound influence over successive generations of students and colleagues through extensive travel and through several visiting positions at such institutions as Columbia, Chicago, Cambridge, the Ford Center at Stanford, York University, and, after his retirement, at Rutgers, Pennsylvania, and the University of California at Berkeley. He died while on a trip to Germany on May 8, 1979.

INTRODUCTION

Talcott Parsons is regarded, by admirers and critics alike, as a major creator of the sociological thought of our time; some even claim he has been the most influential figure in the creation of academic sociology in the United States. Despite the universal recognition of his influence, his thought is not well understood. Perhaps we should not be overly surprised at this paradox, for his theories are often recondite, and many readers find his style opaque. I think there is a more substantial explanation of this paradox. It is precisely because Parsons has been so influential that he is so little understood. His work has been made to stand for orthodoxy. Hence, he is used as a straw man who is purported to assert one or another easily rebuttable proposition or simplistic theoretical stance, whereupon the heroic foe of orthodoxy demonstrates the absurdity of the "Parsonian" view and emerges as a victorious champion of an alternative, novel, and embattled position. Such polemics are unlikely to produce a rounded perspective on the supposed exemplar of orthodoxy. Yet many sociologists are trained almost entirely from such secondary sources.

Let me begin with a specific example. In 1943, Parsons published one of his most famous papers, "The Kinship System of the Contemporary United States."[1] This paper is most frequently remembered for its claim that modern, occupationally organized society is most compatible with familial arrangements of a conjugal form, in which the nuclear family is isolated from the larger circle of extended kin. A large body of subsequent research has demonstrated that considerable contacts with networks of extended kin do still occur in modern societies and are still used in various meaningful ways. Hence, Parsons is frequently cited as the author of a disproven theory.

Even without dwelling upon the dubious merits of the argument that continuing patterns of contact with extended kin disprove the *relative* isolation of the nuclear family, it is easy to show that in this instance Parsons's contribution, as it appears in patterns of references and citations, has become distorted. The relative isolation of the nuclear family in the United States was only the starting point of his argument. The aim of the 1943 paper was to suggest the structural consequences, including various social stresses and strains, of isolating the nuclear family from extended kin in other generations: isolation places a burden on family relations because the marital bond depends on emotional ties within the conjugal arrangement; adolescents experience strain because they must make an abrupt transition from intense dependency within the families of their youth to equally intense involvement in new families, which they must create. The expectations of the elderly for continuing support are undermined; the close structural correspondence of the male-dominated occupational hierarchy to the nuclear family—the "breadwinner" complex—leaves women without satisfying connections to productive activities. Parsons attributes such ideological complexes as romantic love, youth culture, and the culture of "glamour" to these strains. In short, he traces a host of problems and strains in twentieth-century culture to the impact in modern society of a dominant occupational structure that isolates the young, the old, and women from full participation. Parsons is occasionally cited to this effect, but a contemporary sociologist who stressed this aspect of his classic paper might well surprise those who accept the common opinion that Parsons's thought is conservative, incapable of recognizing social problems, and indeed, insensitive to humane issues.

Distortion of Parsons's thought is equally pronounced in accounts that purport to deal with his work as a whole, for again Parsons is often made to stand for orthodoxy, or for established sociology, even though it is questionable that his most original ideas have ever been warmly accepted in the sociological community. Whether one's image of Parsons is founded on skimpy and selective citations of his purportedly discredited propositions or on more substantial discussions of the allegedly inadequate (Parsonian) foundations of contemporary sociological thought, this image lacks prima facie validity. Nor are adulatory defenses (some of which stoutly support the vulgarized misattributions of the critics) likely to provide an adequate account; polemics do not lead to accurate representation and balanced appraisal.

While this essay is not intended as apology, I attempt throughout it to explicate Parsons on his own terms. Throughout his long productive career, Parsons worked within a definite set of programmatic aspirations for sociology. Very early in his work he made a set of strategic assumptions about the nature of society and sociological thought, and his subsequent writing develops the implications of this basic philosophical stance. From time to time he tried new means of elaborating his ideas, leading some critics to charge him with inconsistency or equivocation, but whatever ambiguities may have developed in the course of half a century of writing, the basic framework of Parsons's "action" perspective remained intact. That perspective (in its several incarnations) is best understood when approached with sympathetic appreciation of its goals.

Sociological Theory and the Action Frame of Reference

For twenty years, Parsons's most visible position in American intellectual life was as an importer and interpreter (and, perhaps, heir apparent) of European traditions of social thought. From the appearance of his translation of Max Weber's *Protestant Ethic* in 1930 to his edited version of portions of Weber's *Wirtschaft und Gesellschaft* in 1947,[2] the mainstream of his published work was devoted to translation, analysis, and exposition of major European thinkers. The high point of this work was *The Structure of Social Action*, published in 1937.[3] In this book, Parsons analyzed the writings of Marshall, Pareto, Durkheim, and Weber against the background of problems in the legacy of social thought as it had been formed by Hobbes, Spencer, Kant, Hegel, Comte, and others. Much of Parsons's other work in this vein is relatively forgotten, in some cases because it represents, in effect, working papers for *The Structure of Social Action*, but we should not lose sight of the extent of Parsons's preoccupation with this genre. From the appearance of his first article in 1928, a commentary on Sombart and Weber,[4] through the publication of his translations of selected portions of Weber's magnum opus in 1947, Parsons published some forty items. Of these, fourteen deal directly with the thought of various European writers, including (besides the quartet discussed in *The Structure of Social Action*) Sombart, Malthus, Comte, and Malinowsky.

During these twenty years, several other of Parsons's most famous and influential papers appeared, notably "The Professions and Social Structure" (1939), "An Analytical Approach to the Theory of Social Stratification" (1940), "Age and Sex in the Social Structure of the United States" (1942), and "The Kinship System of the Contemporary United States" (1943).[5] In these and other papers, Parsons pushed for the cause of *general* theory, trying to show that theoretical premises at the highest level of abstraction transform our understanding of concrete phenomena. Moreover, in these essays and in his interpretive work on other people's ideas, he began to suggest the direction that systematic theory might take, but extended work on abstract theory as such did not appear during this period. *The Social System* (1951), *Toward a General Theory of Action* (1951), *Economy and Society* (1956), and "An Outline of the Social System" (1961) were yet to appear.[6] Nevertheless, the main outlines of Parsons's approach to theory had clearly emerged.

Grand Theory

The first premise of Parsons's strategy for constructing a social science is that theory at the most abstract level is necessary and, in any event, inevitable. He describes himself as an "incurable theorist."[7] Facts cannot "speak for themselves, . . . the fact a person denies he is theorizing is no reason for taking him at his word and failing to investigate what implicit theory is involved in his statements."[8] In lecturing he was fond of quoting Alfred Marshall: "The most reckless and treacherous of all theorists is he who professes to let facts and figures speak for themselves."[9] Speaking to the Society for Social Research at the University of Chicago in 1937, Parsons put the matter forcibly and clearly:

> I must categorically disagree with the view that any empirical science can be developed to a high point without reference to generalized conceptual schemes, to theory.... In the first place our study of fact ... is always guided by the logical structure of a theoretical scheme, even if it is entirely implicit. We never investigate "all the facts"... but only those which we think are "important." This involves a selection among the possible facts. Now if we investigate carefully, though few empiricists do, what is the basis of this selection, it will, I think, uniformly be found that among the criteria of importance and the only ones of strictly scientific status is that of their relevance to the logical structure of a theoretical scheme.
>
> Secondly, few if any empiricists, being as they usually are truly imbued with scientific curiosity, are content simply to state bald discrete facts. They go beyond this to maintain the existence of relations of interdependence, causal relations.... Now I wish to assert that such an imputation of causal relationship cannot be proved without reference to generalized theoretical categories.[10]

In the same address, Parsons goes on to point out that since social affairs are so complex, and since we cannot in our theoretical formulations cope with more than a few variables at a time, sociological theory must necessarily be quite abstract in relation to the complex flux of on-going social life.

On the grounds that it is better to formulate explicit theory than to hide potentially examinable premises behind floods of superficially objective data, Parsons has always tried to specify his theoretical perconceptions, starting from the fundamental frame of reference of his analysis.

The Action Frame of Reference

All scientific statements, even the most purely descriptive statements of fact, occur within and imply a frame of reference.

Thus, for Parsons, a scheme describing bodies in space and time is the frame for classical physics and is an example of a "mode of general relations of the facts implicit in the descriptive terms employed."[11] A frame of reference is the starting point for analysis and is determined by the particular vantage point and purposes—the peculiar mode of abstraction the observer brings to his data. Parsons, from the beginning, employed the "action frame of reference." He conceives the raw stuff of the social sciences to be human action, that is, human effort expended in pursuit of goals. His program was enunciated in ringing, polemical terms in 1935 in the opening words of "The Place of Values in Sociological Theory":

> The positivistic reaction against philosophy has, in its effect on the social sciences, manifested a strong tendency to obscure the fact that man is essentially an active, creative, evaluating creature. Any attempt to explain his behavior in terms of ends, purposes, ideals, has been under suspicion as a form of "teleology" which was thought to be incompatible with the methodological requirements of positive science. One must, on the contrary, explain in terms of "causes" and "conditions," not of ends.[12]

The first step toward understanding Parsonian thought is to arrive at a thorough comprehension of this fundamental rejection of positivism. On one hand, action, as goal-directed, purposive conduct, can never be reduced totally to its conditions, to the environmental constraints that impinge upon it. On the other hand, action cannot be conceived as a mere smooth, automatic flow of successfully realized intentions; the world of causes and conditions does indeed exist "out there" as a set of exigencies to be used and overcome in implementing purpose. The action frame of reference implies the autonomy of all its constituent components: there are *actors*, who have *ends*, which they actively, creatively pursue in a world that provides both realistic obstacles, i.e., *conditions*, and realistic opportunities, i.e., *means*, of pursuing ends. None of the elements can be reduced to the others. It is Parsons's resolute refusal, within this means-ends schema, to waver toward either a realistic or idealistic pole that distinguishes his social thought. Through fifty years of writing, he coped with the problem of reconciling intentional and conditional elements within a single unified scheme; indeed, he asserts that the very tension between these elements is the object of social analysis:

> Action must always be thought of as involving a state of tension between two different orders of elements, the normative and the conditional. As process, action is, in fact, the process of alteration of the conditional elements in the direction of conformity with norms. Elimination of the normative aspect altogether eliminates the concept of action itself and leads to the radical positivistic position. Elimination of conditions, of the tension from that side, equally eliminates action and results in idealistic emanationism. Thus conditions may be conceived at one pole, ends and normative rules at the other, means and effort as the connecting links between them.[13]

In the means-ends schema, norms have special significance. All action involves alternative possibilities; accordingly, to avoid seeing action as utterly random, we must posit criteria for choice among alternatives. These criteria are called norms. Since Parsons refuses to suppose that norms can be derived entirely from realistic conditions—a supposition that would, in effect, deny the possibility of real choice—norms must be viewed as a product of the human creativity Parsons stressed at the beginning of "The Place of Values in Sociological Theory." Norms are derived from human aspirations and values; they flow from the ends side of the polarity of ends and conditions and, consequently, must be considered as intentional rather than conditional elements of human action.

Having established norms as independently variable components of the structure of social action, Parsons proceeds to develop sociological concepts—concepts of society and social structure—that emphasize the normative. It is necessary to stress that Parsons is not an idealist; he does not see the real substance of social life as emanating from "world spirits" or norms and values by any other name. However, he does insist on the theoretical significance of the normative; the idea of norms is as well grounded in the inherent structure of social action as the idea of conditions. Further, as we shall soon see, Parsons views the normative as a peculiarly *social* component, especially strategic for the sociologist.

For Parsons, the grounding of the normative in the very concept of action, as a necessary element of an action frame of reference, gives the study of norms a solid theoretical foundation. He is then led to the conclusion that the analysis of norms enjoys a critically important place in sociological theory, because the grounding of the normative in the action framework also makes possible a logical scheme for the conceptual elaboration of sociological variables. This argument is so central to Parsons's approach, especially in the two formative decades of his work, that its logical structure deserves more extended exposition. First, it will be necessary to develop the argument that norms have special importance in social life, an argument elaborated at length in *The Structure of Social Action*. Once this argument has been laid out, it will be possible to reproduce the second argument: that the logical position of social norms in the action frame of reference provides a basis, or theoretical scheme, for analyzing social structure and its functions. This second point is one of the principal lines of argument of Parsons's second major work, *The Social System*.

Norms and Social Integration

According to the argument set forth in the preceding section, the action frame of reference necessarily involves a normative element. If there is choice between alternative courses of action, we must either concede that action is random or that there are criteria for choice.

What might be the content of such criteria? Parsons starts by examining one possible criterion: the norm of rational efficiency. This norm calls for choice of the most economical and effective means to achieve any given end. Can a group achieve an ordered social life founded solely on the norm of rational efficiency? Parsons answers in the negative, claiming that Hobbes asked and answered this question once and for all in the seventeenth century. Hobbes pointed out that if individual choice is founded only on the rational calculation of utility, nothing will prevent some from deciding that others can be used as means to their own ends.

In such a state, life would be, in the famous phrase, "nasty, mean, solitary, brutish, and short."

Parsons labels as "utilitarian" those theories that start by assuming that conduct is (or ought to be) governed by the norm of utilitarian calculation. In this sense, Hobbes is a utilitarian, although theorists who so designated themselves did not emerge before the eighteenth century. Hobbes is taken by Parsons to be the prototypical utilitarian theorist; he starts with utilitarian assumptions and works them out to their logical conclusion—that ordered social life cannot be founded on rational calculation alone. There must be a normative framework to establish criteria of choice that will provide for social control of disruptive conduct. For Hobbes, these norms are taken to be the terms of the agreement, or social contract, whereby men mutually consent to accept a sovereign and the commands of this sovereign, that is, positive law. For Parsons this is a metaphysical solution, for it depends on the nonempirical concepts of the social contract. Metaphysical too are the theories of the more liberal utilitarians who, uncomfortable with Hobbes's authoritarian solution, sought to found normative order or law on mutual recognition of natural rights or on some other version of what Parsons calls "the postulate of the natural identity of interests."[14]

As a scientist, the sociologist must abjure all metaphysical explanation. Neither the existence nor the content of norms can be derived from philosophical speculation about the agreements of rational individuals. Norms must be studied naturalistically, as criteria that emerge to regulate individual choice in socially relevant ways. Social norms are not founded on rational calculation of individual interests. Whenever action involves more than a single individual, norms, considered as criteria of choice, must be responsive not just to the immediate interests of the actors but also to the exigencies of maintaining and coordinating their relations. By this argument, the function of social integration replaces the interests of individuals as the foundation of the normative element in action—a foundation that suggested to Parsons a strategy for sociological analysis.

If the contents of social norms reflect the exigencies of coordinating the relations of actors who have disparate and private interests, it ought to be possible to analyze systematically the problems these actors face; then from an analysis of these problems would flow an account of the intrinsic logic of the choices facing actors as they encounter each other, assess their own interests and ends, and formulate means of mutual adjustment. Such a scheme would quite naturally mesh with analysis of the requisites of organized social interaction. Thus, a system for classifying norms according to the basic problems facing all actors— based, that is, on the inherent structure of social action—would identify the normative problems associated with various problems of social integration. Sociological analysis would be supplied with a tool for interpreting social norms as indicators of underlying social problems. For example, actors must face the question of whether ends or means shall be paramount in a social situation. When attainment of immediate gratification is allowed to be primary, we may speak of an "affective" norm. When, on the contrary, a norm calls for subordination of immediate gratification to some more long-term end, we may call that norm "affectively neutral." The study of the social settings and contexts of affective and affectively neutral norms will provide an entrée to the analysis of how appetites and interests are both satisfied and regulated in groups—an important functional problem.

The elaboration of this strategy is one of the principal themes of *The Social System*. In the famous section entitled (rather formidably) "The Pattern-Alternatives of Value-Orientation as Definitions of Relational Role-Expectation Patterns,"[15] Parsons sets forth the "pattern variables" as the principal tools of structural analysis, outlining the derivation of these categories from the intrinsic logic of social action—the inherent dilemmas of choice facing actors. I shall not attempt to explain the pattern variables and their derivations in full detail. It is more important to emphasize their place in Parsons's basic approach to sociological thinking. First, because of its integrative significance in relating actors to one another, the normative element of action is considered the main social element and the element most interesting to sociologists. Second, as an element in the structure of social action, the normative can be approached within the action frame of reference, deriving the categories of analysis from the inner logic of this scheme. Specifically, the fundamental distinctions between the actor and the external situation and between means and ends form the basis for deriving the inescapable dilemmas of human choice. Third, since norms must regulate any ordered interaction between people, the normative order may be considered the basis of social structure. Finally, the implication of these premises is that the first task of sociological theory is construction, grounded in the action frame of reference, of a structurally relevant scheme for the analysis of norms—the pattern variables.

Institutionalization

According to the action frame of reference, actors pursue ends within the constraints of conditions, selecting normatively regulated means. The normative regulation of the means permits coordinated, integrated interaction to take place; so, indeed, does the normative regulation of ends. The next step in the argument is the assertion that normative integration will be more stable if the norms themselves become ends; that is, if actors come to want to obey norms. In a stably ordered social system, the action of the participants is regulated by norms that the actors have come to have a personal interest in obeying.

Notice that at this point something very interesting has happened to action theory. After Parsons has repeatedly insisted on the independence of ends and conditions—human ends cannot be reduced to or derived from the conditions of the situation—he seems to insist on a very close connection between ends and norms. In a stable social system, norms become attached to ends or even become ends in themselves. The process by which this comes about is called *institutionalization*. This is the key concept in Parsonian sociology.

Parsons's approach to the concept of institutionalization did undergo some changes in the course of his career. Much has been made of Parsons's apparent changes of position; he is said to have moved from a voluntaristic to a behavioral point of view; he is said to have become more "macrofunctional" in his late work. But through all these changes in emphasis—all by-products of the progressive elaboration of his system—one central theorem has remained at the very center of his approach to sociology: *The structure of social systems consists in institutionalized normative culture*. An explanation of this rather cryptic statement will provide a useful account of the fundamentals of Parsonian sociology. Moreover, if our explanation traces changes in the meaning of the key term "institutionalized," this account will effectively summarize the main lines of development and change in his work.

In Parsons's earlier writings, undertaken while working out the action frame of reference, the most elegant definition of institutionalization is "a linking of norms and ends—actors coming to seek conformity as an end." However, we should not lose sight of the more general implications and connotations of the term.

Any attempt to attribute ordering, regulatory power to norms must come to grips with the problem of how norms control conduct. Several answers are possible: norms can be backed by force; conformity can be induced by rewards; habits can correspond to norms; or actors can come to see norms as morally right. But it is not enough for the sociologist merely to enumerate various reasons why one might conform to norms. It is essential to understand how such conformity becomes patterned and routine in society, how persons come to expect certain conduct from each other, and how stable social patterns become supported by established, organized mechanisms. The process by which this happens—the process by which norms come to be routinized, established, and, so to speak, built into social organization—is what we call institutionalization. For any system of sociological thought, its concept of institutionalization provides a key to its stance on the complicated and vexed question of how ideal or normative elements—conceptions of right, of required appropriate conduct, of ideal expectations—are related to established patterns of power, realistic interests, and networks of bonds between people. Parsons's own conception of this process changed somewhat over the course of his career.

First Emphasis: Socialization

One means of institutionalizing norms is to "socialize" individual actors—to teach them to conform to norms habitually, willingly, and naturally, not from fear of punishment or promise of reward, but because an inclination to conform to given social norms is built into their socially formed personalities. This meaning of institutionalization is implied by the first, elegant definition provided above: "a linking of norms and ends—actors coming to seek conformity as an end." It is also the approach emphasized by Parsons in his earliest forays into the theory of institutions. In writing *The Structure of Social Action,* Parsons had been impressed with the convergence of several important European thinkers on the proposition that social action involves acting out the tendencies of personalities that have been socially formed and that this process is the key to ordered, socially regulated interaction. Thus, writing of Durkheim's theory of social restraint, Parsons asserts that Durkheim started from the position that constraint comes from desire to avoid external consequences and came later to understand that conformity rests on moral authority—a social category—and that moral authority works because the social life on which it is founded is "a constitutive element in the individual's own concrete personality." Thus, "he is not placed in social environments so much as he participates in a common social life."[16]

In *The Social System,* socialization is the major theme in Parsons's treatment of institutionalization. Social systems are said to be dependent upon cultural systems, which provide symbols, values, and norms, and also on personality systems, which provide motivation. Motivated attachment to cultural demands provides integration and stability for social systems. Hence, much of the analysis in *The Social System* is devoted to the problem of adequate motivation, especially, sufficient attachments to common values. Social integration occurs when motivational and cultural elements are brought together in an ordered system. The principal mode of bringing these elements together is internalization, "so that to act in conformity with [a value standard] becomes a need-disposition in the actor's own personality structure, relatively independently of any instrumentally significant consequences of that conformity."[17]

These abstractions can best be understood by considering a simple, idealized, fully integrated social system involving two actors. Each has certain expectations of what the other will do.

These expectations are derived from norms that both share, which in turn are founded on shared value standards. Both actors are, we presume, deeply committed to the value standards, motivated to conform to the norms, and will hence fulfill each other's expectations. Indeed, their attachment to the norms is so deep that the pattern of motivation may be said to be part of the motivational structure of the actors' individual personalities. Thus, John and Barbara, a married couple, might expect each other to help with washing the dinner dishes each evening. They share a value standard of mutual aid in domestic tasks, believe that an obligation to cooperative dishwashing is a valid implication of this value standard, and, because of their deeply rooted attitudes, gain great satisfaction from the activity. Given this state of affairs, we may expect stably ordered interaction.

Now, to reintroduce the more abstract terms, let us call the process by which John and Barbara learn to want to conform to the norm of mutual aid *socialization;* let us call the process by which the cultural ideal of domestic cooperation becomes constitutive of their personalities *internalization;* let us call the process by which the norm of mutual aid in dishwashing becomes established in their routine relations (because of their socialization) *institutionalization;* let us call the process by which order is thereby brought about *integration.* Finally, let us realize that as used here, these four terms—socialization, internalization, institutionalization, integration—are essentially different names for the same process! What we have here is a theory of social order that clearly stresses the importance of deeply rooted motivation to conformity with social norms.

We can imagine a different John and Barbara, who also wash dishes together every evening; Barbara's principal motivation is fear of physical abuse and John's is the hope of sexual favors. Now Parsons does not deny that such external motives play their part in social life, but he does claim that ordered, integrated social systems cannot, in the last analysis, be founded entirely on mutual utilitarian calculation. This conclusion was demonstrated, he thinks, by the founding fathers of social action theory discussed in *The Structure of Social Action.* Hence, the best strategy for systematic sociology is to explore the dynamics of systems of social order founded on the intrinsic, socialized motives of our first John and Barbara.

Although this approach to institutionalization seems quite simple (indeed I have deliberately oversimplified it), Parsons's treatment of socialization is complicated and subtle. The notion that institutionalization consists in socialization could create an extremely simple sociology. If we were to assume a flexible, pleasant human nature, easily shaped and molded to patterns of conformity, then, within the framework of this theory of institutionalization, stable and integrated social orders would not be problematic. If, on the other hand, human personality has exigencies of its own—if human nature is in some ways stubborn, resistent, aggressive, and recalcitrant—then social order is correspondingly difficult to understand. At the time that Parsons was particularly interested in personal socialization as the mechanism of institutionalization, he was also very interested in Freud. Hence, it is not surprising that for Parsons the latter, more problematic conception of socialization reigns: human nature includes strongly antisocial drives; the developing child resists motivation and, in later life, retains to a greater or lesser degree unresolved motivational problems and ambivalencies. Parsons, in working out a sociological account of human development, relied on Freud's sense of the refractory side of human personality, emphasizing the difficulty of socialization and hence the need for all sorts of social supports for developing and sustaining socialized conduct and for coping with the emotional stresses and strains that necessarily agitate even well-socialized adults. How, for example, do we ever learn to substitute remote, long-term, symbolic gratifications for the direct, immediate, palpable rewards on which initial socialization is always founded? How, in Parsonian pattern-variable terms, do we learn motivation to perform affectively neutral roles? Given that such neutral and instrumental roles are so pervasive in modern society, how can the social order survive the strain implied by widespread assignment to these roles—roles that require considerable emotional maturity? Adapting Freudian thought to his purposes, Parsons stresses the resolution of the Oedipal crisis as the prototypical learning of affectively neutral roles, and, recognizing the pitfalls of the Oedipal transition, he is on the lookout for all sorts of "reaction formations" or symptoms of strain and ambivalence in modern culture. To a greater or lesser degree, all forms of romanticism, from "youth culture" to agrarian conservatism to more sophisticated and intellectual manifestations of romantic attitudes, reflect Oedipal and post-Oedipal ambivalence about constraints on immediate affective gratification.

That human beings can be socialized seems to strike Parsons as not far short of miraculous. Given refractory human nature, various personal neuroses and their cultural analogues are to be expected. Accordingly, the perfectly integrated social system contemplated in the theoretical model does not exist in reality. Parsons repeatedly emphasizes this point. In view of his insistence on the necessary imperfections in all concrete instances of socialization and social integration—in view, indeed, of his repeated identification of such imperfections as sources of tension, strain, conflict, and change in society—it is ironic that Parsonian sociology is so frequently identified as an instance of the "oversocialized conception of man."[18] Parsonian actors are far from oversocialized conformists or social machines who automatically reproduce social orders in their conduct. An element of conforming conduct exists in any ordered social system. By the same token, elements of alienation exist in all social systems. There are always tensions and strains portending potential breakdown and change, tensions whose dimensions and directions can be anticipated within the framework of the theory of the social system, containing, as it does, an account of the typical, socially relevant resistances to socialization.

Second Emphasis: The Hierarchy of Control

At one stage in the development of Parsons's system of thought, institutionalization was viewed primarily as a problem of socialization, and accordingly, integrative strains were usually viewed as by-products of inadequate or ambivalent motivation. Nevertheless, even during this phase, Parsons was fully aware of the embedding of institutions in larger social patterns. In the 1950s the focus of the theory of institutionalization shifted from socialization to the grounding of institutions in the full panoply of the conditions of social organization. Inadequate motivation is more explicitly recognized as but one of several categories of failure of social control. Parsons came to see social control—the ordering of patterns of conduct by patterns of institutionalized values—as hierarchically organized. The interests of social actors are but one of the conditions of institutionalization and, by the same token, but one of the forces that through socialization can come to support stable institutions. These various forces and conditions are said to be hierarchically organized, in the sense that some are close to the ultimate conditions of action and others fall toward the intentional or value-oriented pole of action.

Parsons's interest in the broader aspects of institutionalization, though never entirely absent from his work, was already clearly apparent by 1949, the year of publication of "Social Classes and Class Conflict in the Light of Recent Sociological Theory,"[19] an interesting comment on class conflict and Marxian approaches to the study of stratification. In this essay, Parsons insisted that imperfect integration is not merely a matter of various random deficiencies of personal motivation. Paying tribute to Marx's recognition of the individualistic biases of the purely utilitarian conception of the problem of order, Parsons remarks:

> ... Marx represented a first major step beyond the point at which the Utilitarian theorists, who set the frame of reference within which the classical economics developed, stand. Marx introduced no fundamental modification of the general theory of human social behavior in the terms which this school of thought represented. He did, however, unlike the Utilitarians, see and emphasize the massive fact of the structuring of interests rather than treating them as distributed and random....
>
> ...The Marxian view of the importance of class structure has in a broad way been vindicated.[20]

These passages, which must seem extraordinary to those who have been taught to view Marxian and Parsonian approaches as radically antithetical, are of considerable significance in our attempt to come to grips with the theory of institutionalization. If "institutionalization" means the support of a normative order by a pattern of motivational interests, then no adequate theory of institutionalization can ignore the social patterning of interests that every normative order must confront. The essay proposes that class conflict is endemic in a modern society, and that this is intimately connected with several other features of social organization—the occupational structure of the economy (which attaches considerable social motivation to the pursuit of private gain), the structure of authority and political control, and the embedding of social relations in a web of kinship. By implication, we must conclude that all these forms of social structure must be brought into the theory of institutionalization. The theory cannot conceptualize disorder as mere failure to socialize individual tendencies to pursue selfish ends, however psychologically sophisticated our theory of selfishness. Rather, the theory must comprehend the full range of structural conditions of order and disorder. In order to move the theory in this direction, Parsons began to elaborate the conception of a "hierarchy of control."

The theory of the hierarchy of control restates in more elaborate terms Parsons's longstanding interest in the tension between the intentional (or normative) and the conditional elements of social action. In studying social systems, the most purely normative element is not individual intention but general values—human conceptions, in the abstract, of desirable types of social systems uncontaminated by compromises with practical problems of implementation. The complex system of norms—regulations, laws, expectations, etc.—by which concrete patterns of social life are regulated are said to be derived from higher-level, more general values.

The notion of derivation bothers some readers; it leaves the impression that Parsons supposes norms to emanate from values by some mystical process. Nothing could more completely distort the intent of his scheme. The point is that norms do not spring mechanically from values by an entirely logical process of specification. On the contrary, norms reflect both the values from which they are derived and also the realistic exigencies of the conditions of action—the realistic problems of making social action effective and coordinated. It is quite possible to render a naturalistic, processual account of derivation: actors, as they cope with the world and each other, face problems of coordinating their action, avoiding conflict, and getting things done. In coming to stable terms with each, they create regulative norms, drawing upon shared values as first premises for guidance. At the same time, the particular norms that emerge must also be practical; they must permit successful coping with the conditions of effective, productive effort. The process, as well as the resulting social order, can be viewed as exhibiting a hierarchy of control, with the most general normative elements controlling the development of lower-level, more specific elements—concrete obligations. At a still lower level, more realistic elements fix the conditions of normative development.

In the foregoing simplified exposition, I have reduced the hierarchy of control to three levels: values, norms, and realistic conditions. In Parsons's more extended analysis, several other levels are specified. The highest levels are cultural, including the ultimate "grounds of being," or basic philosophical propositions, from which values are derived. Within the social system, there are four levels: values, norms, collective goals, and roles. Each level is said to control the level below it and to constitute conditions for the level above it. Social systems must respond to conditions, but the direction of response depends upon what sorts of new institutionalized norms can gain legitimate acceptance within the framework of established value premises.

Implicit in this scheme is the idea that higher levels change more slowly than lower levels, or, alternatively, that pressures for change and other disturbances are handled by adaptive changes at the lowest possible level in the hierarchy. For a common-sense example, we might think of the increasing height of players as a challenge to the game of basketball. Tall players allow for new and very effective offensive strategies. If these new attacks cannot be countered with equally effective defensive strategies, it might be necessary to change the rules, in the first instance by outlawing specific moves—for example, guiding a teammate's shot into the basket from above the basket, "goal tending" as it is called. Secondary changes might involve more fundamental rules, such as increasing the width of the lane to the basket within which offensive players are not allowed to stand for long periods of time. Everything possible will be done within the framework of such rules before altering elements that are more constitutive of the game itself. The height of the basket, for example, is a profoundly constitutive element, an element in which players have deep investments. We might think of this example as a metaphor for social change generally, substituting more analytical categories of normative order for the more concrete components of this specific normatively regulated game.

Information and control. The hierarchy of control is for Parsons an explicitly cybernetic concept. At the top of a cybernetic hierarchy are informational elements which define and control lower-level elements of energy and matter. He makes analogies to such biological phenomena as the control of the genetic process by the information in the genes and the control of metabolism by the information provided by the molecular structure of enzymes. The capacity of information to define and direct is the key to appreciation of the controlling importance of relatively low energy factors in the social process. Advocates of the supposed domination of social life by economic production or power fallaciously suppose that because these factors are both necessary and characterized by overwhelming energy, they must determine the fabric of social life and control the direction of social change. This is a no more allowable inference than (to use other analogies of which Parsons was fond) to conclude that heaters control their thermostats, horses their riders, or the id the superego.

Components of institutionalization. In applying his analytical scheme to social life, Parsons came to speak of four hierarchically arranged components of institutionalization: specification, ideology, interests, and jurisdiction. These four components may be concretely illustrated by examining the conditions of institutionalization of a particular social value—racial equality—which is very much in the forefront of current problems of social integration in American society. For many years we have assumed that racial and ethnic tensions can be mediated by drawing upon the resources provided by commitments to the value of equality of opportunity. The institutionalization of equality of opportunity occurs at four levels:

1. *Specification*. If a social value is to be institutionalized there must be consensus in the population on the implications of the value for conduct. Consensus on an abstract value such as equality of opportunity is not enough; there must be agreement on the specific courses of action that the value demands. Is mere equal, "colorblind" treatment of everyone required, or is it necessary to undertake positive programs to aid historically excluded groups in the community? Who is responsible for implementing equality and what, exactly, are their responsibilities? Value traditions are formulable in alternative versions, and the shape of an established institution reflects the particular version that has become dominant in a population.

2. *Ideology*. If a social value is to be institutionalized, it must be supported by appropriate conceptions of the nature of the social world. Action is responsive not only to actual social conditions but to perceptions of conditions; therefore, patterns of belief within a population shape social institutions. For example, equality of opportunity will have one meaning if some groups in the population are considered to be innately subhuman, and quite a different meaning if accepted social ideology alleges the essential equality and valid potential of all groups and accordingly insists that all groups be viewed as candidates for full membership in the societal community, enjoying all the rights that community members take to be meaningful guarantees of effective opportunities.

3. *Interests*. Here we return to the concept of adequate motivation. Social values are institutionalized when patterns of interests are established which motivate actors to conform. However, in a macrosociological context, it is clear that the concept of adequate motivation is not to be confined to the problem of psychological motivation in individual actors; patterns of the established interests of organized groups are an equally important factor in institutionalization. Institutionalization may rest in large measure on the establishment of systems of rewards and sanctions, such as legal agencies or markets, that create networks of

interests upon which institutions rest. Thus, the emergence of real equality of opportunity may be supported by legislation, or by the economic costs of discrimination in an expanding economy, as well as by emotional or personal commitments to equal treatment. The concept of interests also leads to study of the organization, capacities, and growth of groups that have an interest in urging or resisting change.

4. *Jurisdiction.* The fourth element of institutionalization concerns the access of systems of social control to actors. Jurisdiction presumes sovereignty in the classical sense; that is, institutionalization ultimately requires physical control over a territorial area. In his schematic writing Parsons often emphasized the ultimate territorial condition of jurisdiction, but the concept must be viewed in a more inclusive and general way. In order to guarantee a normative order successfully, the agencies of social control must have physical access to nonconforming actors, but they must also have access to information about nonconformity. Furthermore, in any social system in which due-process legal protections are institutionalized, agencies of social control must have jurisdiction in the legal sense and access to sufficient information to establish legal proofs. Jurisdiction, like the other components of institutionalization, is not only a condition of institutionalization; it is one of the factors affecting the form of established institutions. The structure of an institutional order is affected by the character of the relevant activity, its accessibility to the organs of control, and the channels of and barriers to communication in the population.

The importance of jurisdiction is illustrated by the jurisdictional difficulties involved in all attempts to enforce equality of opportunity. Real opportunity implies a set of well-developed and readily available channels for individual growth and advancement within a complex array of social institutions and groups: schools, churches, business firms, neighborhoods, clubs, political groups, and many others. The implementation of equality of opportunity becomes quite difficult in the face of the many obstacles blocking access to these varied social arenas. The relative ease with which discriminatory acts can be disguised and the definitions of some institutional spheres as private tend to give attacks upon unequal opportunity a piecemeal and fragmentary character. Two decades of experience with the jurisdictional problems inherent in the concept of passive equal treatment led to more active specifications of the value of equal opportunity, especially the idea of affirmative action, which, by making compliance more immediately visible, improved jurisdictional access to noncompliance.

The four functions. The concept of a hierarchy of control provided a more macrosociological approach to institutionalization; the establishment of norms becomes a matter of regulating a range of systematic social conditions rather than inculcating psychological predispositions. Accordingly, Parsons's conceptual approach to social systems began to stress the logic of the basic attributes of all systems rather than the logic of the basic attributes of all social interaction. It is not that he abandoned the philosophical preconceptions of action theory; on the contrary, throughout his career he termed his work "action theory" and continued to insist on the first premises of this approach. However, he became more interested in working out paradigms for analysis of the larger systems within which interaction takes place. His emergent attention to macroanalysis, of which the concept of a hierarchy of control is one example, was founded on a new classification system that came to replace the means-ends scheme and the system of pattern variables as the foundation paradigm for his analysis. This new paradigm purports to derive four functional problems confronted by all systems—including systems of social action—from basic features shared by operating systems of all types. The four functional requisites are *adaptation,* or securing generalized resources for use in achieving the varied output goals of the system; *goal attainment,* or providing for the effective expenditure of resources in the pursuit of particular goals; *integration,* or providing for the coordination of the diverse elements and units within the system; and *latent pattern maintenance,* or maintaining the stability of the overall structural reference points and boundaries that define the system. These functions (which are often referred to by their abbreviations A, G,

I, and L) can be ordered according to the hierarchy of control, with pattern maintenance the controlling function at the top and adaptation the ultimate conditional element at the bottom.

A system is any set of interdependent elements that coheres into a self-regulating whole and is maintained by drawing resources from an environment. By this definition an organism is a system. So also is a human personality, if it has a set of stable and interconnected elements—e.g., traits, capacities, attitudes—and has both mechanisms for maintaining patterns of elements over time and the capacity to gain psychological sustenance through interaction with people and things. Similarly, human groups may be said to form systems when interactions between members come to have stable patterns of organization, which are maintained by drawing upon the resources that nourish group life. For example, following Parsons's account of the social significance of effective motivation, a personal inclination to conform to social norms may be said to sustain the system of group life.

The four functions virtually follow from the very concept of a system. If a set of elements can be considered to form a system (rather than a merely arbitrary subset of the parts of some larger whole), then there must be a boundary that demarcates the elements within a system from elements not properly considered a part of the system. There are therefore two sorts of relations or connections to be considered in the theory of systems: relations between elements internal to the system and relations between the system and its external environment. This distinction establishes the first dimension for classifying types of systematic functions.

The internal-external dimension is, of course, a reprise of Parsons's earlier notion of an actor in an environment recast in terms appropriate for discussing systems. (The action frame is more recast than abandoned!) Similarly, the second dimension—*instrumental* vs. *consummatory*—is the older distinction between means and ends reformulated in systematic terms. Systems are maintained by drawing upon and using resources; we may distinguish between the process of building up and storing resources for future use, instrumental functions, and the consumption or mobilization of resources for actual performance, consummatory functions. The cross-classification of these two dimensions produces four system functions: external-instrumental, external-consummatory, internal-instrumental, and internal-consummatory.

1. *Adaptation*. Adaptation is the external, instrumental function of systems. Adaptation is external in the sense that it involves relating the system to an environment and instrumental in the sense that it involves, not the actual pursuit of particular environmental goals, but the development of generalized means for pursuing a variety of future goals and for meeting a variety of environmental conditions as they change over time. The key word in this definition is "generalized." Systems increase their adaptive capacities by developing generalized mobile facilities that are uncommitted to any particular use. A system's mechanisms for generating and mobilizing productive energies and resources may be called the *economy* of the system.

2. *Goal attainment*. Goal attainment is the external, consummatory function—external in that it refers to achieving ends in relation to the environment, and consummatory in that it involves not the development of generalized instrumental resources but organization for the effective pursuit of particular system goals. In social systems these are collective goals. The key word in this definition is "effective." Social systems are well equipped for goal attainment when they have an organized capacity to control performances so as to bring them to bear on collective goals. In this sense, capacity for goal attainment refers to a system's ability to organize the effective expenditure of political energy. Energy is expended ineffectively when it is dissipated on diffuse goals or when it is diverted to internal power struggles. A system's organization for directing energies and resources toward collective ends may be called the *polity* of the system.

3. *Integration*. The third function is internal and consummatory. Whereas goal attainment and adaptation are problems in relation to an environment, integration requires relating the constituent units of a system to each other. Integration is a consummatory function in the sense that it involves, not the development of general facilities and resources for stability, but confrontation and solution of specific coordinative problems. In-

tegration may be defined as the prevention of mutual interference of the units of a system with each other. In social systems, such interference may arise from conflict, from the breakdown of mutual expectations, or from a lack of complementarity of performances; organizations for coping with these problems are sometimes referred to as the *community*.

4. *Latent pattern maintenance*. The final functional requisite is internal and instrumental. The principal resource for integration of the units within a system is consistency in the basic pattern of their relations. Hence, a system must have means of establishing and sustaining a stable structure. The idea that organisms have a tendency to maintain a normal state of internal stability through coordinated responses of organ systems that compensate for environmental changes is the basic biological concept of homeostasis. Application of the notion of homeostasis to social systems is very controversial and is especially reviled by those who argue that change is more basic than stability or that, at least, any nonconservative social theory must so assume. Nevertheless, the theory of social systems must posit mechanisms for maintaining structure; the very concept of a bounded system implies some stabilities of internal structure. After all, if every event within the system were entirely determined by and at the mercy of constant changes in the environment, there would be no basis for drawing a line around that particular set of elements and calling it a system: it would be an arbitrary assemblage of parts of some larger whole.

Having established that pattern maintenance is, by definition, a system requisite, Parsons goes on to assert that internal processes of integration take a fixed structure for granted; the structure is, as it were, a resource for integration. In social systems, he says (following the line of argument set forth in *The Social System*), the requisite of pattern maintenance is met through the establishment of processes to insure continuing commitment to general patterns of normative order. Stable values insure continuity in the normative order and in patterns of mutual expectations and provide a reference point for the inculcation of generalized commitment to the society. Parsons sometimes refers to the social organization that supports pattern maintenance within a social system as the *fiduciary system*.

Latent pattern maintenance is a defining and controlling, informational component of a social system rather than an operating component. In this respect it is different than the other three functional requisites. Parsons intends the modifier "latent" to imply this special feature of pattern maintenance: pattern-maintenance systems serve to define action, whereas the other three are aspects of ongoing action. It is interesting to note, by the way, that this conception of latency serves to underline how deeply process and action are built into Parsonian theory, especially in view of the common allegation that he eventually abandoned process and reified structure. In his final major published statement, "A Paradigm of the Human Condition" (1978),[21] he continued to stress that action is process and that structure is always defined through a process. Speaking of the proper placement of the "telic system" in the paradigm of the human condition, Parsons notes, "This placement seems to fit the criterion of 'latency' in the sense that whatever content may be imputed to the telic system is not overtly manifest at the action level but has to be defined, as it were, through processes of action."[22]

Systems and subsystems. The scheme of four functional requisites was originally developed in 1952 when Parsons, in collaboration with Edward Shils and Robert Bales, became interested in the convergence between the pattern variables and a scheme that Bales had worked out for studying social interaction and group processes in small, problem-solving groups.[23] Bales observed experimental groups going through phases as they coped with various problems of group functioning. Each group was assigned a certain intellectual problem to which they were expected to provide an agreed-upon group solution. Meeting this goal required the members of the group to develop resources of information and opinion and to bid for leadership in directing the group to use these materials in finding consensual solutions to their assigned problems. At the same time, aggressive expression of opinion and attempts to direct tended to undermine cooperation and the underlying commitment of the group's members. This often led to action intended to reaffirm the solidarity of the group. The basic ideas of the four-function scheme are all present in this approach to group process, or "phase-movement," in small, face-to-face groups. Parsons quickly became convinced of the generality of the paradigm and immediately applied the ideas to larger social institutions, first to the theory of social stratification and to the place of the family in industrial society and, subsequently (with Neil Smelser), to the economy and its relations with other institutions.[24]

It was originally possible to view the four concepts as applying either to four problems encountered by all social systems or as four corresponding phases of action that the members of groups undertake to confront those problems. At first, while he was seeking to articulate the scheme with the pattern variables, Parsons emphasized the action side, but very quickly he came to emphasize the problem side, calling the paradigm "the four functional imperatives" and applying it in a wide variety of contexts over the entire second half of his career. As Parsons himself put it much later, "This basic classification has remained with me for the more than fifteen years since it first emerged and has constituted a primary reference for all my theoretical work."[25]

The four-fold functional paradigm can be used, like the pattern-variable scheme, to classify normative orientations. According to the first premises of action theory, social values, being human creations, vary; systems of human value can start from one or another arbitrary body of premises. The four-function scheme establishes a way of introducing order to the range of variation of values. Value systems vary in the functions to which they accord primary importance. For example, American values give primacy to adaptation, allowing for a normative framework which, instead of commiting group members to predetermined collective goals, actually promotes flexibility, innovation, and the free play of individual and group interests. As interpreted by Parsons, our values stress "institutionalized individualism" and pluralism. Americans value the pursuit of individual interests within the framework of a normative obligation to develop the self in an individualistic but socially responsible manner; American values also encourage the development and maintenance of plural, autonomous centers of group life. These centers, be they cultural or religious groups, communities, or special interest associations, are not directly controlled or dominated by centralized authority; nor are they forced into rigid cultural conformity. They must, however, develop within the limitations set by the demand for underlying loyalty to the larger society. Institutionalized individualism and pluralism promote specialization and the development of social structures founded on institutionalized exchange. (This is an important theme in Parsonian sociology. We will have occasion to return to the topic of specialization and exchange in a subsequent section.)

The range of application of the four-function paradigm is indeed broad. I recall working as Parsons's teaching assistant in 1960–61; I was astonished when he began a course called "The Theory of Action" with a four-fold classification of the universe, a scheme which, after two decades of gestation finally found its way into print (in a refined and elaborated version) as "A Paradigm of the Human Condition." I was no less surprised the next term when, in a course on the sociology of religion, Parsons introduced a four-fold classification of the Trinity, with the fourth cell filled by *homo religicus*. Again, this scheme was ultimately revised and published as "Religion in Postindustrial America."[26]

Each of these diverse classificatory exercises fits into the larger Parsonian scheme in a determinate way. The key to this entire edifice of four-fold classification is found in the notion that each functional subsystem of a larger system is itself a system and, as such, has its own four subsystems; or, looking at the hierarchy from the other direction, each system is a functional subsystem of yet a larger system. Thus, the whole realm of organized action can be analyzed as a complex set of systems within systems within systems. For example, human action is organized within cultural (L), social (I), personality (G), and behavioral (A) systems; the social system has its fiduciary (L), integrative (I), political (G), and economic (A) subsystems; the integrative subsystem must itself meet the functional requisites of successful operation; so it has its own four functional subsystems, and so forth.

Differentiation and exchange. Parsons does not claim that all concrete action systems or social systems in fact contain a full panoply of separate specialized subsystems. The concepts are analytical rather than concrete. The claim is that, whether a system has or has not developed a bounded, specialized apparatus for dealing with a given functional problem, the problem must be dealt with somehow; it is therefore legitimate to speak analytically of, say, the integrative subsystem of a social system, whether or not the system has a clearly demarcated organization for dealing specifically with integrative problems. When a system does have specialized, systematically organized means for coping with its functional imperatives, we speak of *differentiation*. Because of the efficiency and effectiveness of specialization, there is a strain toward differentiation in all systems, and according to Parsons, this differentiation tends to occur along the functional lines analytically defined by the four-function paradigm. Hence, in highly differentiated social systems (e.g., modern societies), concrete subsystems develop—differentiated economies and polities, for example—creating a set of institutional arenas which correspond to the functional subsystems and sub-subsystems posited by the theory.

Institutionalized Exchange

Structural differentiation along functional lines has profound implications for the basic approach of action theory, especially for the problem of the integration of action. The old theorem of integration—the idea that social integration can be accounted for by the institutionalization of norms, which in turn, is accomplished by the socialization of actors—became more clearly inadequate; it became necessary to account for the integration of differentiated institutions with each other, and this problem of integration became the central concern of Parsonian theory. After the early 1950s, the problem of adequate motivation, though still relevant and still occupying a specific location in the overall panoply of systems within systems, was no longer dominant in Parsons's sociological theory.

Nevertheless, the definition of social structure as consisting in institutionalized normative culture remained the central premise of the theory. The theory still conceived the meshing of the mutual expectations of actors as problematic and still posited normative regulation as a critical and necessary element of this articulation. What changed is the basic image of normative regulation. A reader of *The Social System* might fairly conclude that norms guarantee consistent mutual expectations by defining specific courses of required conduct in some detail. Such a simple social system must be considered a special, limiting case, prototypical perhaps, and certainly easy to understand as the first step in an expository strategy; but in modern, differentiated societies, the integrative problem is one of organizing the relations of complex institutions, rather than merely coordinating the expectations of actors in face-to-face situations. In the macrosocial context, norms provide a framework rather than specific directions for conduct. Increasingly, Parsons came to see that framework as consisting primarily in a context for exchange: differentiated institutions are integrated by a sort of social metabolism in which each subsystem produces the resources necessary for other subsystems and receives in return the resources for its own functioning. It is the old paradigm of the division of labor and consequent process of exchange that had been the mainstay of utilitarian thought for centuries; but, following the critique of utilitarian concepts of exchange provided by Durkheim in *The Division of Labor*,[27] Parsons insists that exchanges, whether between individuals or between differentiated subsystems, must occur within a framework of institutionalized norms. The institutionalization of normative framework becomes the source of structure in this new conception of a highly differentiated social system.

Double Interchanges

Parsons's first and prototypical analysis of exchange between differentiated subsystems appeared in 1956 when, together with Smelser, he published *Economy and Society* as a contribution to the syntheses of economic and sociological theory. In an undifferentiated society, family households are also units of subsistence production and consumption. When differentiated economic enterprise, i.e., business firms, develops, it becomes necessary to integrate households and firms through the development of markets for labor and goods. Hence, a "double interchange" emerges between the economy (adaptive subsystem) and the basic unit-households of the system (the concrete structure corresponding to the pattern-maintenance function): members of households exchange their labor for wages and, in turn, exchange their wages for the products of business enterprise.[28] The market organization within which these exchanges occur cannot be taken for granted; it requires institutionalization of a normative framework, including occupational roles, the law of contract and property, and the medium of money, all of which are delicate and problematic. All exhibit a history of gradual establishment involving trial, error, and considerable intermittent conflict and breakdown.

The double interchange between L and A became the model for analyses of analogous interchanges between the other subsystems. A fully differentiated social system exhibits six sets of exchanges (L-A, L-G, L-I, I-A, I-G, G-A), each of which is accomplished through a double interchange comparable to the market for labor and goods, production and consumption. In *Economy and Society,* the interchanges between the economy and the other three systems were outlined, and subsequently Parsons proposed complex accounts of the other three sets of exchanges. He then went on to propose that a similar logic and approach could be used to illuminate the relations between the four levels of action itself: cultural, social, personal, and behavioral. In this way he established a logical program of analysis, founded on the notion that there are not limitless and amorphous connections between the systems of society but a fixed and determinate set of relationships, each of which has an analogous logic and structure, and each of which can be illuminated by the basic conception of an institutionally regulated market.

Economy and Society was a watershed in Parsonian thought. Conceived in a burst of creative energy in 1954 in discussions with Smelser, its basic paradigms provided a program for Parsons's next twenty-five years of theoretical work.

The Media of Exchange

As Parsons developed these various schemes of double interchanges, the idea of symbolic media of exchange came to play a key role in his analysis; his elaborate generalization of this idea provides the most striking and original element in his entire system of thought.

Consider again the case of the double interchange of production and consumption. One level of interchange involves relatively real entities—goods go to households and households contribute labor. The other level of exchange, the level that permits a high degree of flexibility and mobility, is symbolic. Monetary wages are paid to households, which households then spend, moving resources back to business firms. The second level mediates the first level and is clearly dependent on the institutionalization of money as a symbolic medium of exchange. This is not news. Parsons would hardly claim that he had made an original contribution in pointing out the role of money in permitting flexible economic exchange. The new and powerful idea is that money is an instance of a generic phenomenon and that there are other symbolic media that are very much like money in their capacity to allow flexible marketlike exchanges between the component institutions of society. The four media that perform this function within social systems are money, power, influence, and value commitments. Each of these terms has a familiar meaning in ordinary parlance. In order to call attention to various parallels to the phenomenon of money, Parsons must adopt special definitions provided by a new basic paradigm.

He starts with the idea that there are four ways in which actors can get others to comply with their demands: (1) *inducement,* or offering rewards; (2) *deterrence,* or applying negative sanctions; (3) *persuasion,* or offering reasons; and (4) invoking existing *commitments.* Each of these means of getting others to act is used daily in myriad concrete forms. A mother frowns at her misbehaving child (deterrence) who is crying because the mother will not buy a new game: "But the whole family can have fun with it," wails the child (persuasion); "And, besides, you promised" (commitment); "Be quiet and I will give you a candy bar" (inducement). All these are concrete and particular attempts to secure desired conduct from another; it is also possible to build a generalized capacity to invoke these various means of affecting others' conduct. If, for example, our illustrative mother has lots of money, she is in a position to offer a wide variety of rewards (presumably less expensive than the game in question) or even to give the child money—possibly to save toward buying the game later, for money has the special capacity of storing value—to buy whatever the child might want.

Money, then, is a generalized capacity of inducement. It has no value in its own right; the famous anecdote about lighting a cigar with a twenty-dollar bill makes sense precisely because the bill has more value in exchange than for the relatively trivial use to which a wealthy man might put it by way of conspicuous consumption. Money in the form of a credit balance in a bank account has not even this sort of trivial value in use. Although money has no value in its own right, it has a very considerable value as a symbolic message. As a symbolic token it measures the value of commodities, facilitates their exchange, and stores value over time. As a generalized capacity, money stores value rather than specific goods, thus maximizing capacity to acquire whatever specific goods will meet future exigencies. Of course, money stores value only as long as people believe in it. When people lose confidence in money, inflation occurs; people become less willing to accept a symbolic token because they fear that others will not accept it, and so on, in a vicious circle.

The classic theory of inflation attributes loss of value to an excessive quantity of money—more money than there are goods, or, in more sophisticated terms, "productive capacity." Such excess can occur only because, given the independence of money from the things it represents, it is possible to create money de novo. In a modern, complex economy, this is done primarily through the credit operations of banks, which lend money that they hold on deposit from others. Banks can accomplish this by the simple device of entering a credit to the account of the borrower, thus becoming, in a sense, insolvent; everything is fine unless all the depositors demand their funds at the same time. These credit operations serve to finance investment in new productivity which, if successful, sustains the ultimate base on which the stability of the medium depends. These, then, in broad outline, are the main features of a circulating medium of exchange: it is symbolic, it is a generalized capacity, it is free of commitment to particular use, it can be created, and it is subject to inflation and deflation according to people's confidence in how well it is backed by the real capacities that it symbolizes.

Power, Influence, and Commitment

Parsons's theory of media supposes that these features of money can be generalized: for each of the specific means by which actors seek to get each other to comply with their wishes, there exists a generalized capacity, organized by the social system, and symbolized by a medium with specific flexible capacities comparable to money.

Power. The generalized medium corresponding to deterrence is power. The notion of power as a generalized capacity to bind and direct others is not too far removed from ordinary usage of the word. But, for Parsons, who uses the word in a special sense to denote a symbolic phenomenon with particular capacities to mediate collective action, something more than generalized coercive capacity is implied: power involves the direction of others toward collective ends. Hence, it is the medium corresponding to the function of goal attainment. To cite Parsons's technical definition precisely, power "is generalized capacity to secure the performance of binding obligations by units in a system of collective organization when the obligations are legitimized with reference to their bearing on collective goals and where in case of recalcitrance there is a presumption of enforcement by negative situational sanctions."[29] Power, like money, is backed by complex social organization. Just as the value of money is dependent on the willingness of others to accept it, and the confidence on which the acceptability of money is founded is in turn based on the productive capacity of economic organization, so power is dependent on willingness of people to accept symbolic indicators of others' capacity to make binding decisions on behalf of the group, which in turn is founded on their actual capacity to achieve collective goals through central direction. Again, this capacity depends upon complex and effective social organization.

Power, considered in this special sense as a symbolic medium, involves a division of labor and a consequent need for integrative exchanges. Since organized capacity to achieve collective goals requires a division of labor between those who direct and those who accept direction, there must be something that these parties exchange in order to bind their differentiated roles. Those who direct make binding decisions (and take responsibility for their decisions) in return for the support of those who are directed. Support, however, is also an exercise of power in that it is conditional; those in control can be removed if they do not exercise their delegated direction in response to the group's demands for effective collective achievements.

This concept is strikingly reminiscent of the original formulation of the concept of civil power in secular thought—the idea of a social contract. The public gives up the right to exercise direct physical force on their own behalf in return for a (symbolic) promise that organized collective power will be exercised for the common good. When civil power does not or cannot deliver on these promises, the symbolic medium breaks down and the public withdraws allegiance, taking direct power back into their own hands.

However, Parsons goes substantially beyond the classical notion of a social contract. First, he insists that the implied contracts upon which power is founded require an institutional order outside all specific contractual exchanges; that is, power must be institutionalized. Second, he claims that power, being a generalized symbolic medium and free of commitment to particular, rigidly circumscribed contractual terms of support and demand, can be created and is subject to inflation and deflation according to the waxing and waning of public confidence in how well power is backed by the real capacities which it symbolizes.

An understanding of the exact mechanism by which power is created will clarify the basic logic of Parsons's conception of the creation of media and the consequent possibility of inflation and deflation as social processes. As long as those who direct collective action merely respond to the givens of their political situation, making ad hoc decisions in response to specific concrete demands upon them from the group, a fixed quantity of power merely circulates. But a holder of power may use that power to initiate long-run plans for the achievement of new and undemanded collective goals. If those goals are subsequently ratified by the group, which says, in effect, "Yes, do that," then the power holder has essentially created new political demands to back new collective decisions. This is called *leadership*, and by exercising leadership power can be created. It is possible, of course, that the leader will not be able to deliver. If a leader's decisions cannot be implemented within the limits of effective collective action, limits set by the actual political capacities of the system and its social organization, inflation occurs in the power market. People withdraw their support. Conversely, fear that a few political failures portend a collapse of collective effectiveness, can lead to a run on the power bank, with everyone demanding immediate delivery on all promises; this is a deflation of power caused by underconfidence.

Influence. Parsons refers to the generalized capacity to persuade as *influence*.[30] Again, a refinement of ordinary usage is employed. Parsons argues that what we mean by influential people, as opposed to rich or powerful people, is people who are believed because of who they are, without demand for full proof. Since we are talking about influence, not power, the ultimate grounds of persuasion must rest on the interest of those persuaded rather than on threats. Parsons argues that the ultimate ground of social persuasion, and thus of influence in this special sense, is common interest; that is, the influential person is believed because one accepts him or her as sharing a common aim. Would I lie to you? is the prototypical argument that lurks in the background of attempts to exert influence. A doctor offering a diagnosis to a patient provides a simple example of influence. Acceptance of the diagnosis rests on trust that the physician is not motivated by self-interest but by desire to protect the patient's interest. Further reflection indicates that the exercise of this sort of influence requires (like all the media) a normative, institutional framework in support of the reputation of physicians and of common understanding of the doctor-patient relation. Indeed, this very example hearkens back to Parsons's earliest attack upon the doctrine that modern societies are founded entirely on self-interest. The doctor-patient relationship and, more broadly, professional roles generally cannot be understood on this assumption. This was, as I have earlier suggested, the context for the original development of the scheme of pattern variables. But in the course of working out the notion of influence as generalized capacity to persuade through assertion and acceptance of common interests, Parsons develops a far more extensive counter-argument against the standard criticism of modern society. Far from being devoid of solidarities, modern society is elaborately woven together by the warp and woof of crisscrossing solidarities of all kinds based upon successful attempts to influence, each of which implies that a solidarity of common interest is accepted. Solidarities are also created by each recognition that a person whose influence is accepted speaks on behalf of a group.

The exercise of influence sustains and even creates solidarities. This is the key to understanding that the quantity of influence can, like the quantity of money, be expanded. When the members of groups accept the prestige of certain fellow members, conferring upon them the roles of leader and spokesperson, the groups come to have greater capacity to act as solidary entities and to symbolize the interests and demands of their members. This is done most effectively when leaders exaggerate the unity and solidarity of the groups they represent—exaggerate, that is, beyond the boundaries of what leaders could deliver if every member of the community asked for an accounting of whether a precise community of interests could be demonstrated, or demanded that each factual statement and promise be backed by concrete evidence rather than by the prestige of the leader. When group members begin to ask for such an accounting, deflation of influence has set in. The opposite process, the inflation of prestige, stems from claims to leadership far beyond the capacity of groups and their leaders to demonstrate actual underlying solidarities or common interests.

In sum, solidary groups are, as it were, formed on a species of credit. The daily process by which people ask for each other's trust through the exercise of influence is the process whereby groups are formed and sustained. To doubt the real solidarity underneath the rich associational life of a modern society is to participate in the deflation of the stores of influence by which its manifold diversity is articulated in the social relations between groups. To insist that only primordial and warmly emotional solidarity is real is comparable to claiming that only gold is money.

Commitment. Value commitments are also subject to generalization.[31] People may secure the compliance of others by calling their attention to the binding commitments they have made to carry out specific promises or to fulfill the expectations implied by allegiance to specific binding norms. Yet one hallmark of a modern society is the withering of diffuse, proscriptive norms. The normative order is more flexible and adaptable if people are committed to generalized conceptions of the right rather than to highly particularized definitions of righteousness. When people are willing to accept moral exemplars and custodians of virtue on the basis of confidence in these worthies' commitment to do whatever is right in the circumstance, we may speak of generalized value commitments. Such commitments constitute a medium comparable to money, power, or influence.

We have seen that each medium rests on a form of trust. In the case of value commitments the element of trust derives from Parsons's characteristic separation of the realms of value and realistic conditions. A commitment to "do right" could fail because of the realistic challenge presented by the world rather than from any lack of good will. If we accept the capacity of those responsible for interpreting and implementing fundamental values to adapt to complex exigencies with their integrity intact, we are accepting their value commitments. If we commit our own integrity to their hands by making them the custodians of our moral enterprises, we have accepted their value commitments as a medium of exchange. Once we have accepted their commitments, they are in a position to exert moral leadership comparable to the political leadership undertaken by those to whom we have delegated our power. Moral leaders—the prototypical exemplar being the so-called charismatic personality—can make new interpretations of the value tradition in order to articulate old values and new realities. In so doing, ethical traditions are transformed, often by the achievement of new levels of normative generality. When this happens, the quantity of commitment has been increased. On the other hand, when our moral leaders unwisely risk their integrity and compromise ours by undertaking promises to sustain values in the face of overwhelming situational conditions, an inflation of commitments has occurred. Deflation of commitments—sometimes referred to as "fundamentalism"—comes about when people become unwilling to accept moral leadership and refuse to participate in any venture other than direct implementation of their values in time-honored, habitual, specific ways.

Parsons, following Weber, would interpret the Protestant ethic in these terms. Religiously committed people came to accept disciplined and constructive activity in the secular world as entirely consistent with their moral integrity. Such a life could be just as fully sanctified as full-time ritual devotion. This transformation, which brought about the value generalization upon which the modern social order is based, was a consequence of the charismatic moral leadership of the Protestant reformers.

It is worth pausing at this point to remark how far removed Parsons's theory of media of exchange is from the static structuralism commonly attributed to him. The image of the oversocialized man, who merely acts out social structures automatically because the patterns of conduct required by these structures have become built into his personality, was a reasonable misinterpretation of action theory when institutionalization was seen as primarily a matter of socialization; but with the emergence of the idea that integration is achieved by the exchange of symbolic media within a general institutional framework, criticism of the Parsonian actor as oversocialized falls far wide of the mark. All of the media are indefinite: their institutionalization does not depend upon internalization of specific norms; rather it depends on generalized acceptance of the value of various media, so that these media can be used for a wide range of indeterminate purposes. In a market-organized society with well-developed media, one important source of the institutionalization of norms is people's interest in participating in exchanges within regulated marketplaces. Money, power, influence, and value commitments are available as rewards for normatively regulated participation in the institutional order.

The theory of media calls our attention to the fact that in a modern society normative regulation is relatively nonspecific. Integration depends upon a high level of trust in promises. An elaborate network of promises depends upon stores of confidence which are subject to inflation and deflation, both of which have implications for social change. Moreover, those who garner large stores of the symbols of these promises can mobilize them in innovative ways in pursuit of economic production, collective political aims, new social solidarities, and novel moral enterprises. The theory does not depict a static order; rather, it presents an explanation of how the dynamism of modern society is possible within the framework of an institutional order. It is consistent with Parsons's faith, evident from the beginning of his career, that modernity unleashes forces of creativity, individualism, large-scale enterprise, and productivity without moving us down an inexorable spiral toward either anarchy or totalitarian control.

Evolution and Modern Society

As Parsons developed a progressively elaborate account of the institutional foundations of modern, highly mobile societies, he became increasingly interested in how modernity evolved. In part, he was responding to the persistent criticism that his "structural-functional" theory could not account for social change; however, his interest in the evolutionary development of modern society in the West is deeply rooted in the sociological tradition and preceded the criticisms set off by publication of *The Social System* in 1951. Parsonian theory originated, we should recall, as a critique of unidimensional accounts of social evolution. He did not believe that modernity is a matter of unleashing private interests, the consequent destruction of community, and its replacement by new crass and bureaucratic ties. In view of these intellectual roots, it is not surprising that Parsons would wish to develop analytical tools for describing the historical growth of the rich panoply of modern social arrangements.

The key concept for describing evolutionary social change is the notion of differentiation. This is not in itself original: the concept has indeed been borrowed by social scientists from the inception of evolutionary biology in the nineteenth century. The concept of differentiation is, after all, the centerpiece of Herbert Spencer's sociology.

A definition of social evolution as the increasing division of labor—i.e., occupational differentiation—and the emergence of specialized organizations may be construed to imply that these new forms of social organization drive out and replace traditional forms. Parsons spent much of his career rebutting this construction. For Parsons, the differentiation of new forms is a separation of analytically distinct functions which historically have been fused in a single structural order. Both functions must continue to be performed in the new differentiated social order.

One of the purposes of the earlier scheme of pattern variables had been to demonstrate that the dimensions of normative classification are independently variable and not (as uni-dimensional schemes of social evolution suppose) a series of antitheses between modern and premodern norms. For example, according to the pattern-variable scheme, some norms—like those governing market bargaining—call for self-interested motivation. Other norms call for taking others' interests as primary. The norms governing doctors' relations with their patients provide the classic example. Parsons denied that self-interested conduct was simply taking over modern life. In all sorts of functional contexts, collectivity-oriented norms must operate, even in the most highly differentiated, complex, modern societies.

The separation of new functions from the traditional structures in which they were once embedded implies a need for reintegration of new elements with the larger society within which the process occurs. Older elements are not eliminated; they are reduced in scope, specialized, and brought into accord with newer special-purpose institutions. Given this general approach, it had long been incumbent on Parsons to explain the concomitant processes associated with differentiation—the processes which, together with differentiation, constitute social evolution. In 1961, he published "Some Considerations on the Theory of Social Change,"[32] a brief outline of four components of evolution, which he identified as differentiation, adaptive upgrading, value generalization, and inclusion.

Differentiation. Social differentiation is deemed an evolutionary process not only because it formally parallels the structural direction of biological evolution but because its consequence is also parallel: differentiation enhances adaptive capacity, the capacity of a system to control the environment and to adjust to environmental variety and change. Large-scale societies, which unite millions of people in complex, politically organized, and industrially supported groups, exhibit greater adaptive capacity than small, tribally organized groups founded upon kinship and a subsistence economy.

Parsons's basic hypothesis is that "ascription," here defined as the bonding of the performance of a particular function to a general purpose structure, prevents the highest possible level of performance of that function; specialized structures, organized around the exigencies and requirements of particular functions, are more effective. Hence, insofar as structural differentiation takes place along functional lines, each of the functions that sustain a system can become more effectively performed. This conception of the power of differentiation rests on the idea that the four functional requisites are, to a degree, incompatible. The dynamic implications of the four-function idea are not often appreciated by critics of Parsons. Yet, dynamic tension is deeply rooted in the scheme—indeed implied by the very definitions of the functions. The dimensions that define the functions are, after all, antithetical: emphasis on meeting immediate needs is not compatible with emphasis on developing uncommitted resources; nor can both internal and external problems be given priority at the same time.

I have made this point initially in very abstract terms in an attempt to convey the logical integration of functional and evolutionary theory, but the thrust of the theory is probably better conveyed by a more concrete and familiar example. Primitive societies tend to organize activities of a variety of functional types around a unitary if nonetheless complex structural nexus: kinship. Kinship ties define economic and political obligation as well as forming the basic matrix of solidary attachments. When kinship ties provide the solidary bondings of a society, there is great advantage in defining these ties as stable and relatively independent of short-run economic interests. The efficiency of economic systems, on the other hand, requires willingness to form and dissolve connections on quite practical grounds, without reference to emotional attachments to particular individuals. Hence, the differentiation of a specialized economy from embeddedness in a web of solidary kin relations increases the flexibility and mobility of economic organization and therefore increases the level of performance of the adaptive function. To return again to more abstract terms, the differentiation of an economic system frees resources from ascription, thus increasing their mobility and their wholehearted commitment to particular, specialized needs.

Adaptive upgrading. Whenever differentiation occurs, a concomitant process of adaptive upgrading is both permitted and required. Again, in the abstract terms of the general theory, differentiation frees the units of the system for higher levels of performance. This is, after all, the "goal" or advantage of differentiation in the first place; but the full advantage of this potential cannot be achieved if the units are not equipped with the capacity to achieve the new, higher levels of productive output. Hence, each new differentiation creates pressures for improving the capacities of contributing units. For example, a differentiated economy, with its variety of full-time, specialized roles, implies a high level of training and education in that people must perform these specialized tasks.

No doubt the reader will note that a pattern is beginning to emerge. Taking the four functional prerequisites one by one and treating increased capacity for performance as the goal (attainment function) of differentiation, Parsons proceeds to point out four positive, constructive aspects of the process of differentiation. Rather than viewing differentiation as an unmitigated modern horror, a process of dissolution of culture and community, of fragmentation of society and self, he looks at its functional benefits—starting with increased capacity for collective performance (G) and upgrading of the potential for individual contributions (A). In more common terms, this means a greater possibility that groups (including societies) can achieve what they want, more freedom for individuals to acquire knowledge and ability, and a greater likelihood that they will do so.

Value generalization. As differentiation proceeds, the fundamental normative structure of society must come to comprehend and to govern a wider variety of conduct. Freedom from ascription, mobility, and specialization all imply greater variety and hence a challenge to historic formulations of social values. The normative order must change to adjust to the new realities without leaving behind fundamental commitments on which the stability of the system depends. This is accomplished by value generalization, which is the pattern-maintenance (L) component of social evolution. Many social theories interpret the normative impact of modernization as either breakdown or total transformation, as if there were no continuity between what emerges and what went before. Parsons insists that the normal process of normative modernization can be described as a generalization of historic values. The social order can still be described as consisting in institutionalized values. As I noted earlier in outlining Parsons's theory of value commitments as media, moral leaders frequently function as reinterpreters of values, explaining to their followers that the new order represents not a loss of old truths, but a new means of implementing their deepest commitments. Denial of these claims is a form of deflation of the symbolic media by which the modern order is articulated. Such deflation is endemic in the ideologies of a changing order; as the distance from ultimate values to concrete conduct becomes ever more remote, conservative fundamentalists reject each new abstract conception for bridging the gap, insisting on more direct and immediate gratification of the urge for rectitude. According to Parsons, there is quite a bit of this sort of deflationary ideology in the reaction of intellectuals, including sociologists, to modernization. Change is often interpreted as breakdown or loss of traditional values rather than as an evolutionary transformation involving the reintegration of newly differentiated and very powerful social institutions.

Inclusion: A Third Stage of the Theory of Institutionalization

Differentiation spawns a variety of special-purpose organizations, associations, and other groupings. The articulation of these units with the larger society is problematic, especially as regards the alignment of loyalties to society and to its constituent groups. Parsons refers to the normative order through which this problem is addressed as the "societal community" and to the problem so addressed as "the problem of inclusion." In the first instance inclusion can be treated as a problem of reincorporating the specialized roles and groups that emerge in the processes of the differentiation of labor. For example, if occupational and familial roles are separated, a body of paid workers is created. The inclusion of these workers, in their roles as workers, is problematic and must be accommodated by one or another mode of inclusion, such as the institutionalization of norms that legitimize and regulate the sale of labor and define and protect the status of a paid employee. This sort of differentiation and inclusion can be treated within the framework of analysis Parsons had so far employed. However, as he continued to think about differentiation and about the actual course of historic social evolution, the problem of inclusion came to exhibit new dimensions that cannot be easily accommodated within the paradigm. In consequence, Parsons came (in effect) to view institutionalization from a new perspective, a perspective that implies certain fundamental alterations in the Parsonian perspective on the social system.

The primal social differentiation is the rending of the seamless web of kinship by establishing the social superiority of some lineages to others within a primitive kin-organized society. The radical equality of a ramified kinship system prevents a primitive society from developing the differentiated leadership that is prerequisite to mobilizing resources and energies in the pursuit of progressive, adaptive social policies—water projects, for example. Some concentration of power is necessary in order to line up wealth and efforts for collective projects. This implies the emergence of stratification. The fundamental equality of all the constituent kin groups of the society must be breached. Particular groups must come to control sufficient power and wealth to move and coordinate large-scale collective efforts. This, in turn, requires equally fundamental cultural change in order to explain and legitimate the special status of elite groups.

In the course of this development, a new elite culture emerges, designed both to enhance the prestige of the dominant class and to facilitate the technical tasks of "civilization." This new culture is founded upon literacy among a small group that is closely attached to the rulers. Parsons refers to the resulting social structure as a "two-class system": society is divided into (1) a socially organized elite, held together by ties of aristocratic kinship, patronage, and a common elite culture, and (2) the masses who are bound to the society in part by acceptance of formulae of legitimation and in part by their economic and political dependence on the elite. Stated in the more abstract terms of action theory, there has been a differentiation of culture and the social system. Culture no longer merely expresses an integrated social order; rather, it begins to develop autonomously within the elite group and to provide that elite with the cultural tools for effecting social change. With the emergence of military resources for conquest and expansion, a more radical separation of culture and society can take place in that a ruling elite can extend its political and economic hegemony over larger territorial areas, incorporating political rule over groups with radically diverse cultures. This intensifies the problem of normative inclusion, which can no longer be conceived as strictly a matter of deriving new normative conceptions from preexisting shared values, for shared culture can no longer be presumed.

Once culturally differentiated stratification has become an ingredient of the social order, inclusion becomes a critical problem and the dynamics of inclusion a major force for social change. Indeed, inclusion becomes such a dominant problem that adequate recognition of its significance implies reshaping of the theory of institutionalization. If the elite culture is not fully shared by the mass of the society, it is not possible to solve integrative problems by mere reinterpretation (or specification) of established social values. Inclusion of members of the society in the various social subsystems which sustain and promulgate the guiding values of the system becomes a necessary component of the process of evolution; inclusion becomes not just an element of evolution but a condition of institutionalization as well.

The institutionalization of normative order through inclusion of the entire populace within the societal community has proven quite difficult throughout the course of human history. It is not enough to propagandize or legislate. Inclusion in a societal community requires a wide variety of forms of concrete participation in supportive systems. Cultural roots run deep in the plural and primordial groups of society, familial, religious, and ethnic. Such basic loyalties need not be eradicated, but it is necessary to create new and more inclusive groupings with sufficient strength of loyalty and benefits of membership to motivate and sustain the values and norms of the larger society. In the modern context, the principal normative mechanism for facilitating inclusion in national communities is the concept of citizenship, a major theme in the democratic revolution, one of the revolutions by which the activities of larger and larger segments of the populace have become incorporated into the activities of national life. During the last fifteen years of his life, Parsons gave considerable attention to the social movements by which modern society has achieved the progressive inclusion of previously excluded populations: the industrial revolution, the democratic revolution, and, most recently, the educational revolution.[33]

These revolutions bring about new institutional forms that promote incorporation of various subgroups, cultural enclaves, and social strata into the life of the larger, unified society. Citizenship is one such institutional form; so are the modern legal system, the market system, bureaucratic organization, and collegial associations. These institutions have such great adaptive capacity as to suggest that they will ultimately dominate the social life of all modern societies, irrespective of their political ideologies. Within the framework of these institutions, formerly isolated and dependent populations are brought into more effective, normatively regulated participation in society—their capacities upgraded, their power increased, their range of opportunities expanded, and their loyalties strengthened. Thus, processes familiar to us as components of modernization are, for total societies, processes of institutionalization. Remembering the principal theorem of Parsonian sociology, we can also say that modernization, since it is a process of institutionalization, is also a process of social integration. The model of the totally integrated social system presented in *The Social System* is placed in clearer perspective. Concrete, historic societies are not integrated social systems. The integrated social system is a theoretical construct designed to illuminate the social forces unleashed by failures of integration; the model depicts not a historic or current state of affairs, but a theoretical account of the ultimate destination of the processes of social evolution—the state toward which the forces of modernization tend. From this perspective modernization is not the process of dissolution and disintegration described by so many social theorists. Since the process involves change, the people affected by it might well experience dislocations and losses. Hence, it is not surprising that descriptions of modernization as disintegration gain wide currency; but, viewed from the perspective of evolutionary theory, modernization involves the consolidation of larger and larger populations into more and more integrated social systems through the institutionalization of modern culture.

Elaboration and Consolidation:
Continuities

I have sought to summarize the movement of Parsons's thought by focusing on the changing meaning of institutionalization as he gradually moved from emphasis on the dilemma of the individual actor to the problems of modern macrosocial change. However, we should not lose sight of the continuities in his thought. The action frame of reference was never abandoned. The definition of social structure as consisting in institutionalized normative culture follows from the action frame of reference, and Parsons did not lose sight of this basic premise. He continued to assert that the institutionalization of normative culture integrates the social system. Normative culture—values—is a species of human intention; it is created by human thought and cannot be reduced to the realistic conditions of social life.

During the last decade of his life, Parsons sought to integrate the varied facets of his thought by generalizing and elaborating the concept of double interchanges mediated by generalized, symbolic media of exchange, extending the analogy of money and markets beyond the social system to the other levels of social action. Cultural systems, personality systems, and the behavioral system have, according to Parsons, their own differentiated components and generate their own symbolic media. In *The American University* (1973) and "A Paradigm of the Human Condition" (1978) he presents paradigms of symbolically mediated exchange throughout the entire system of social action.[34] The model provided by money, power, influence, and commitment is extended to such concepts as "intelligence," or the generalized capacity to implement cognitive values through knowledge and rational action, and "affect," or the generalized capacity for emotionally meaningful social involvement.

This panoply of concepts has been used extensively to elucidate contemporary social developments. For example, Parsons's extensive analysis of the contemporary American university is, in effect, a long essay on the idea that the university is an "intelligence bank." The participants in university life entrust their cognitive interests to the institution. Given sufficient commitments from their depositors, universities can increase the supply of intelligence in society. Inflationary and deflationary cycles can occur as faith in the universities' product rises and falls. True to the structural-functional roots of his thought, Parsons proceeds to analyze the structural and organizational requisites of successful intelligence banking, arguing that much of the institutional paraphernalia of university life is well suited to conserving and protecting its social functions.

A full account of the many intricate arguments by which Parsons's complete inventory of media and interchanges is constructed is well beyond the purview of this essay. The point to be made here is that this extended scheme helped to unify Parsons's lifework. By extending the basic concept of mediated exchange beyond the social system, Parsons found it possible to return to earlier themes in his work. He was able to reformulate his long-standing interest in the internalization of norms using the concept of mediated interchanges between the social system and personality. With a comprehensive, developed map of all the components of the system of action, identification of institutionalization with the socialization of the individual actor becomes impossible. The internalization of norms takes its well-defined place within a large array of interactions within and between the various levels of social action, each of which can be analyzed according to the general paradigm of exchange. Each phase in the development of the theory of institutionalization can be put in its proper place.

As I have suggested, throughout all this analysis, the action frame of reference remained intact: conduct was still conceived by Parsons as a pursuit of human purpose in the face of realistic conditions. From his first to his last writings, Parsons worked on the premise that sociological analyses must be grounded in both the ideal and the natural realms. In his last writings, he continued to display the urge to refine both the naturalistic and the idealistic elements of his paradigms. On the natural side, he began to explore the idea that the process of institutionalization is an analogue to natural selection in the biological world; on the idealistic side, he pursued a renewed interest in Kantian analysis, which provides a model to study the cultural ordering of the flux of experience.[35]

The pursuit of human purpose is collective. Parsons's lifework was to explore the implications of his early recognition that the action frame of reference must comprehend that actors achieve ends in both nature and society. From the beginning he saw that this could only be explained on the assumption that social life provides ordering frameworks; from the beginning he asserted that these ordering frameworks are normative in character— based on shared meanings, shared interpretations and understandings, shared values—from the beginning he recognized that collective action must always come to terms with the exigencies of realistic circumstance. He never lost sight of this basic model. Insofar as there is a notable change of emphasis over the five decades of development of his thought, it is his increasing recognition that ongoing adaptation to changing circumstance precludes social structures based upon predefined courses of action. The ultimate sources of ordered flexibility became the object of his search. More and more his conception of norms emphasized the establishment of a framework for exchange rather than the setting of rules for conduct. In the concept of exchange—exchange facilitated by generalized media—he found the key to understanding how orderly social life can be undertaken by people who are nonetheless free to create novel conceptions, to adjust to new conditions, and to pursue their own interests and their own self-expression.

An Appraisal

Perhaps it is too soon to assess the achievement and legacy of a body of work so recently completed. Even in his last years, Parsons continued to develop his version of action theory, not only refining and elaborating earlier schemes, but reconsidering and reformulating basic ideas. All too many of his critics have taken one or another phase of the development of his ideas as a final, fixed position which displays once and for all the essential Parsons, especially weaknesses and limitations that the critic alleges are inherent and inescapable in his fundamental approach.[36] For three decades, many critics have viewed *The Social System* as summarizing Parsonian sociology once and for all and have concluded that he views society as comprised of oversocialized persons, caught in a rigid and unchanging normative system—a tightly integrated system without structural conflicts and fully justified by consensus on basic values. No one familiar with the corpus of Parsons's work, especially his many essays and his extensive analysis of modernity—its historic roots, and its contemporary problems—could suppose that he had labored fifty years to produce such a naive conception of human conduct and association. I hope this introductory essay has made that point abundantly clear.

Yet this easily rebuttable, straw version of Parsonian thought persists in the literature, a fact that itself requires sociological explanation. Perhaps Parsons's own analysis of ideology will provide us a clue to understanding the strange fate of his thought in so much of the secondary literature on social theory. From Parsons's point of view, much of the criticism of his work is a species of what has been called in this essay "fundamentalism."

We must start by recognizing that his thought occupies a strategic position in contemporary ideological warfare. It is taken to be a bulwark of sociological orthodoxy and hence an ideology in support of established institutions—in a word, he is viewed as conservative. One cannot deny that some of Parsons's writing strongly supports particular established social institutions. For example, it is difficult to read *The American University* without sensing Parsons's deep loyalty to the elite American research university and his admiration for its mechanisms for supporting free and rational inquiry. In this instance his analysis seems vulnerable to the charge frequently leveled against functionalism: he appears elitist and undemocratic; special privileges seem to be justified by their essential contribution to the larger social good. (This is not to say, of course, that Parsons's analysis of the American university is incorrect or that his approach necessarily leads to this sort of conclusion in all instances.)

The change that Parsonian thought is conservative goes beyond individual instances of defense of established institutions; it is claimed that his approach is conservative at its very core. In order to extricate Parsonian thought from the tangle of ideology in which it has become caught, it is necessary to locate its political position. Parsons does take sides on the various perennial questions that pervade political thought and animate discussion of the moral predicament of modern civilization. But is his thought properly termed "conservative"? Such labels are obviously a matter of definition. If we mean by conservative "not radical," then Parsonian sociology is conservative. It does not follow the main lines of radical criticism as developed by contemporary Marxists and neo-Hegelian thinkers. In this regard, his thought is conservative in the sense that Roosevelt, the New Deal, and its ideological descendents are conservative. From a radical perspective, reformist political programs, which seek to incorporate and manage criticism and disturbance, are inherently conservative, counterrevolutionary movements designed ultimately to defend the status quo. The New Deal did not, however, seem conservative to self-proclaimed conservatives who attacked it as creeping socialism, as contrary to laissez-faire economic theory, and as disruptive of established social arrangements.

The example of the New Deal is apt, for the New Deal is a version of the very sort of liberalism that Parsons espoused and that permeates his basic stance on both theoretical and social issues. He was a modern liberal, akin to Roosevelt, to Adlai Stevenson, to John Kennedy. He did not approve of Herbert Hoover, Eisenhower, or Nixon. He was certainly not conservative in the sense that advocates of untrammeled private enterprise are. Indeed, for Parsons the sociological critique of laissez-faire economic theory constitutes the very foundations of the discipline. Nor was he a conservative in the literal sense of one who defends all established arrangements as desirable, or at least necessary. The antidemocratic version of conservatism is systematic defense of the restriction of privilege. Parsons was not a conservative by this criterion either; indeed, he was an ardent advocate of the extension of rights, opportunities, and participation to all social groups. As we have seen, the concept of institutionalization came ultimately to include the extension of opportunity as one of its essential components. Parsons was a conservative only in the sense that he, like other modern liberals, had faith that democratization can occur within the general framework of the established modern order. Radical reconstruction is not necessary; utopia, by definition, is impossible. In this limited sense, Parsons's thought is indeed conservative.

This is by no means a trivial conception of the term "conservatism." It is Parsons's passionate faith in modern society, his sophisticated attack on radical, alienated critiques, that explains his ambiguous position in modern social thought. On the one hand, his alignment with the liberal tradition cannot but be attractive in contemporary academic circles; on the other hand, his liberalism is so consistently founded on a critique of the ideology of alienated intellectuals that even many liberals must feel uncomfortable when they confront his unabashed defense of modern social trends. His work probes the liberal intellectual's own ambivalence about the contemporary world. This fact is, I think, at the root of much of the confusion, emotional rejection, and misplaced criticism that mars interpretation of Parsonian thought.

Parsons's faith in modern society in general and the American version in particular seems extreme, even naive, to some observers. The skeptics do not include only senior intellectuals and professional sociologists. During the early 1960s, I often heard Harvard undergraduates refer to his course on American society as "Every day in every way American society is getting better and better." In candor I must concede that Parsons's lectures on American society often seemed to present views somewhat akin to religious conviction. One could not but think that the individualistic, activist strains in American values—American emphases on striving, achievement, self-expression, the individual search for meaning, perhaps even salvation—were very close to Parsons's own "ultimate values." Certainly his efforts to trace these themes back to their roots in Protestant theology did not seem accidental. His regular assertions that American society had more capacity to correct wrongs, adjust to new demands, and achieve its own ideals than the critics of current social ills would have us suppose occasionally seemed almost to be affirmations of a doctrine of manifest destiny. The institutionalization of American values were to be realized by a process of sheer logical deductions. Sometimes Parsons was misunderstood: criticizing the intellectual underpinnings of an attack on a current social problem, he easily created the misimpression that the problem did not exist or did not need correction. Nevertheless, the strong faith that students perceived was there: he did defend modernity and the capacity of America to achieve a good society.

His confidence should not be lightly dismissed. However much it might have been consistent with his basic values and temperament, it was, after all, solidly grounded in a very sophisticated intellectual position. The very concept of confidence leads us right to the heart of Parsons's mature social theory. Students of *The Social System* might easily have concluded that consensus is the key condition of the integration of social systems. Parsons's later analysis also treats consensus on norms as an essential framework for social order, but he stresses that the ongoing functioning of the order itself is based upon confidence, trust, and faith.

All complex social organization involves delegation: we must rely upon others to produce the goods we use, to hold our money, to lead public affairs, to represent other groups to us, to teach us, and to assist us in our pursuit of health, equanimity, and integrity. Those who draw upon the "deposits" of others' confidence and trust can use these resources constructively to lead us. Yet there are always risks in giving up direct self-reliance and trusting our fate to others. Our confidence might be misplaced; those we have trusted might make mistakes or, worse, betray us. Our risks are intensified when those who hold our delegations themselves take risks, hoping that their actions will produce collective benefits in the long run. Yet they must take risks; we want them to. For only by acting confidently on faith can our economic entrepreneurs, our political leaders, and our moral interpreters avoid paralysis. This fact has a very important consequence: those who hold our delegations are always somewhat overextended. There can be runs on the bank in all areas of social life. Political leaders can be asked to deliver immediately on all their promises all at once; spokespersons for social groups can be asked to prove that they do in fact speak for what all the members of the group really want; educators can be asked to prove that their teachings will benefit all their students in immediate and concrete ways. For this reason, social criticism is intrinsically cheap. Since everyone is overextended, it is easy to prove that they are and to conclude that social life is a precarious sham: our money is not backed by gold and our solidarity is not backed by direct emotional bonds between individuals. Parsons chose a more difficult intellectual task. He tried to elucidate both how systems based on trust and confidence work and when they stretch thin and fail. He wanted to know what leads to the overextension of trust to the point that public confidence cannot be long sustained. There is such a thing as too much faith. He also wanted to know what leads to the contraction of trust, and to the consequent paralysis of social systems.

Given that endemic overextension is a condition of successful functioning, social systems are always somewhat vulnerable to the charge that the emperor has no clothes, especially because the emperor's nakedness is often quite easy to see. Social criticism is a necessary function in a modern society: critics help society to adapt to new circumstances; they prevent the sort of feckless overextension that is manifest in false and exaggerated claims by supporters of one or another special interest. On the other hand, social criticism can itself be exaggerated. Critics can, in an excess of zeal, underestimate the need for realistic confidence, even confidence in institutions which, strictly speaking, are overextended. Then the social critic can become a powerful force toward the destruction of the very faith upon which social arrangements depend—a special version of the so-called self-fulfilling prophecy.

What might be called overcriticism is quite tempting. Not only is it intrinsically easy, as I have suggested, but there are also powerful emotional motives for "deflationary," fundamentalist criticism. Trust betrayed is a profoundly unsettling experience. From a Parsonian (and Freudian) point of view, socialization requires the development of mature trust. We learn in childhood that we must often renounce immediate emotional gratification in the interests of long-run benefits. We learn to accept (in Parsonian terms) affectively-neutral roles on the assumption of a trade-off for future emotional rewards. Since the scales of earthly justice are never quite true, we are left with a sense that society has not fully paid its debts. This common human experience predisposes us to latent, regressive tendencies to wish to take the world back into our own hands—to renounce our trust in the remote and uncertain institutions by which modern society is sustained. Parsons believed that a great deal of contemporary social criticism has deep roots in this sort of regressive mistrust. Accordingly, it is not surprising that his own vision of modern social life should counterpose an image of a society based upon confidence in the long-run viability of complex delegations of our fate to others, and it is also not surprising that this vision should be viewed by romantic social critics as a betrayal of our deepest human needs.

The Olympian Perspective

Parsons adopted an Olympian stance. He seemed driven to pursue ever more abstract and generalized theoretical formulations, broader historical perspectives, more fundamental first premises, more objective interpretations. If he were summarizing his contribution, he would not emphasize political and ideological elements as I have done. He viewed himself as an objective social scientist; not an ideologist. In his own eyes he was free of ideological bias because he founded his analysis on broadly conceived, disinterested, dispassionate investigation of the conditions of social order and social change and confirmed his conclusions through the test of broad comparative and historical analysis. He developed his theories by continuous elaboration of their inner logic, not by adapting to fashions in thought.

Ironically, this Olympian predisposition nurtured his most important limitation as a social scientist. The legendary unintelligibility of Parsons's writing, which has caused humanistic critics to use his style as a didactic example of all that is wrong with "social scientese,"[37] stems in large measure from an uncompromising drive to state abstractions correctly. Correct as his statements may have been in the context of his own logic of intellectual development, to readers not versed in his concepts, his writing often conveys an Olympian disregard of the human needs of the reader and the humane significance of his ideas.

Perhaps unintelligibility to the lay public could be more easily forgiven if his writings were more accessible to professional social scientists. Some social scientists can no doubt be countercharged with ideologically motivated, willful desire to misunderstand and distort. C. Wright Mills's famous "translation" of certain passages in *The Social System,* which has played an important part in sustaining a false, straw-man version of Parsonian thought, is a case in point.[38] Nevertheless, other social scientists, starting with good will and high expectations, cannot understand Parsons in a very fundamental sense: they cannot make sufficient sense of his writing to formulate testable hypotheses that might move empirical social science forward. If other social scientists cannot establish a sufficiently clear reading of one's writings to do further work based on the same concepts, interpreted in the same way, referring to the same phenomena, then the cumulative impact of one's work will be severely limited. Again, this limitation stems less from his sometimes inpenetrable style than from the level of abstraction at which he chose to work. In consequence, many professional social scientists will find his work more valuable for its general perspectives, its suggestive ideas, and its penetrating insights than as a developed system of science.

The charges made against the substantive content of Parsons's work can also be traced to the lofty perch from which he studies social life. The two most common allegations against his approach are that it neglects conflict and that it neglects change. I think these charges can be viewed as responses to Parsons's habit of always placing conflict and change in the context of a higher order of stability. In this introductory essay, I have sought to emphasize this aspect of Parsons's approach and to show that it is, in fact, an approach to the study of change, not a neglect of change.

Radical sociologists assert that only a dialectical approach can insure that tension, conflict, and change are given due attention. Other, less ideologically motivated critics reason that the homeostatic assumptions of action theory, with its emphasis on stable normative frameworks, inherently emphasize the conditions of stability rather than the forces of change. In its most sophisticated version, this position is based upon a recognition that it is one thing merely to recognize that forces of disruption and change are endemic in social systems and quite another to have a systematic theory of the typical sources and forms of these forces. Parsons's early account of the Hobbesian approach to the problem of order merely assumes that all sorts of disruption are all about; hence, it is necessary to have a theory accounting for how stability and integration are possible in the face of the obviously precarious nature of social order. His use of Hobbes as a starting place made him vulnerable to the charge that he ignored the forces of conflict and change. In his early writing, he seems to assume conflict as an abstract category and to focus his attention on theory about institutional means for preventing and resolving it. Parsons subsequently recognized this problem. Indeed, he understood that Marx added a deterministic element to the utilitarian scheme by providing an account of the specific structure of conflict in capitalist society. Marx recognized that sociological theory could not start with an abstract notion of conflict as a "war of all against all"; the conflict that regulative structures are called upon to control has an explainable structure of its own. It is not all against all, it is group against group.[39]

At several points I have stressed that the theoretical apparatus that Parsons ultimately developed contains ample resources for dealing with tension and change. In fact, it is not too much to say that it is possible to reformulate the four-fold function paradigm as a specifically dialectical scheme. I have noted that the mutual incompatability of the four functions is a source of tension in social systems. Bales's account of changes in the character of interaction in small groups over time is a remarkable example. The members of small task groups find that work toward completing the group's assigned task leads to social and emotional tensions. Task-oriented activity entails disagreements and attempts to direct the activity of others. It becomes necessary to reduce tensions and mend fences, but attention to these problems makes group members uneasy about failure to deal with their collective task. It does not take much imagination to see that this account could be recast as a dialectical process involving inherent contradictions between integration and goal attainment. The scheme would account for the structure of conflict and change in the group, for the structure of conflict is built into the interests that group members have in the fulfillment of group functions. In short, the four-function paradigm provides insights into the specific structural sources of strains in social systems.

Parsons's analysis of the media of exchange provides all the more reason to view his theory as well equipped to deal with tension and change. The inherent overextension of the media makes every social system inherently vulnerable to particular types of breakdown. The theory allows us to explain why specific persons in specific structural locations have an interest in promoting the inflation or deflation of each of the media of exchange.

Why then, in the face of Parsons's obvious interest in social change and his development of theoretical concepts with obvious implications for analysis of the structure and consequences of conflict, do some observers persist in finding a static bias in the theory? Ideological considerations, to which I have already alluded, partly explain this situation. But the paramount explanation must refer again to Parsons's basic stance. His fundamental intellectual strategy—a strategy consistent with his deepest predilections—is to adopt a sufficiently broad perspective to see the long-range, high-order stabilities, especially stabilities in the fundamental values and norms that constitute the institutional structure of society, within which lower-order conflicts and changes are contained. To the critic, this approach seems to assert that integration and stability are somehow more fundamental than conflict and change. Parsons's strategy seems to dismiss or trivialize accounts of turmoil by persistently placing them in some larger context. For those willing to adopt with Parsons a broad perspective, his apparent emphasis on stability is illusory; in fact, it can even be seen as a strategy for the study of change.

For those who prefer broad perspectives, Parsonian analysis—grounded on first premises regarding the nature of human conduct, fertilized by incorporation of diverse points of view ranging from Freud to Weber, nurtured by sweeping historical study, animated by concern for the most fundamental humane, political, and social problems, and thrust forward by a courageous will to generalize specific theoretical insights—will long remain an intriguing and compelling approach to understanding the modern world. Parsons's ideas will be least attractive to those he refers to as pessimistic intellectuals:

> Widespread pessimism over the survival of modern society is closely linked to doubts, especially among intellectuals, about the actual viability of modern societies and their moral right to survive without the most radical changes. Indeed, it is often alleged that modern society is "totally corrupt," can be cleansed only by total revolution, and is ripe for it.[40]

His work will be most appealing to those who accept his conclusion that

> from a broad comparative and evolutionary perspective, the more "privileged" societies of the later twentieth century have to an impressive degree ... successfully institutionalized the more "liberal" and "progressive" values of that time.[41]

He will be appreciated by those who share his conviction that "the sociologist of the twenty-first century will discern just as many factors of continuity with the past as we can now discern with the nineteenth century and, of course those previous to it."[42] In Parsons's own technical terms, acceptance of his vision of contemporary society is ultimately a matter of whether one accepts his value commitments—his moral leadership—or whether one believes that there are no interpretations of our obligations to modern society that will allow us to survive with our values intact.

I. SOCIOLOGICAL THEORY AND THE ACTION FRAME OF REFERENCE

"The Role of Theory in Social Research" (1938) analyzes the inescapable importance of general analytical theory in sociology. Throughout his career, Parsons devoted himself to developing general and abstract theories of human society and conduct. Originally published in 1935, "The Place of Ultimate Values in Sociological Theory" committed Parsons to a voluntaristic perspective, emphasizing the role of creativity and will in human conduct. Although he later developed somewhat more deterministic models of action, he remained a voluntaristic theorist in that he denied that the symbolic, cultural regulation of action could ever be reduced to its physical and biological conditions. "The Action Frame of Reference," "Hobbes and the Problem of Order," and "Rationality and Utilitarianism" are brief selections from Parsons's seminal *The Structure of Social Action* (1937). In these passages we see how he came to define the problem of order as the central riddle of any sociological theory that takes voluntary action as its starting point. In *The Social System* (1951), Parsons elaborated his solution to the problem of order, emphasizing the importance of normative regulation. "Pattern Variables" is a selection from this work; it represents an early attempt to derive categories for the analysis of social structure from the inherent logic of the action frame of reference.

1

THE ROLE OF THEORY IN SOCIAL RESEARCH

Some will perhaps consider it presumptuous for one who has come to be known primarily as a theorist to talk about empirical research. I have done some work in the latter field and hope to make some contributions to it before many years. But apart from that I can perhaps but cite a statement of which Max Weber was fond, "In order to understand Caesar it is not necessary to have been Caesar." So perhaps it is possible for one who has not been quite so completely immersed in empirical research as some of you, but who has nevertheless been a good deal concerned with certain of its problems, to help illuminate them.

I should, however, like to make myself clear in advance. The current state of sociological science is not such that anyone is entitled to dogmatize with an air of canonical authority. To my mind the only hope of reaching that fundamental unity of outlook and purpose which I think almost all of us feel should actuate the workers in a field of science, is to attempt seriously, objectively and respectfully to learn from each other's work, thought and experience. It is my very strong conviction that, if the current situation be approached in this spirit, and the *trouble* taken to get to the bottom of other people's problems, there will turn out to be far more unity on fundamentals than appears at first sight.

What I can do on an occasion like this seems to me to be to present to you with due humility for your consideration a few of

Reprinted by permission with deletions from "The Role of Theory in Social Research," *American Sociological Review* 3 (1938):13–20.

the results of my own thinking about and experience in sociological work.

Practically all competent observers are, I think, agreed that there is a basic difference in the situation in such sciences as physics and chemistry, and those in the social group, particularly sociology. I do not mean to deny that the former group have their crucially important unsolved problems and areas of controversy. These, however, occur either on the frontiers of the technical part of the science itself or in the field of the interpretation of the broad significance of its results as a whole. But there is a very substantial core of material on which there is entirely general agreement. What should go into the more elementary courses in these fields is not in controversy. Moreover this common core is not only a body of discrete miscellaneous facts—it is closely integrated with a logically elaborated body of theory, much of which, like the fundamental equations of dynamics in mechanics, is stated in a highly generalized form.

When we turn to the social field we find a very different situation. Most of our controversial problems seem to be not on the periphery but at the very starting points of the field. There is widespread feeling that we must settle the deepest current controversies before we can do *anything*. This at least seems to be true of those who feel the need to reach high levels of generalization. This feeling of fundamental uncertainty is vividly brought out by the controversial nature of the content of elementary courses.

It is scarcely possible to consider this situation without being struck by what is both one of the most conspicuous and, to me, one of the most disquieting features of the current situation. That is, there is a tendency to the development of a very deep hiatus between the more empirically and the theoretically minded workers in the social science fields.

I do not mean merely that there is a good deal of division of labor, as I am told there is in physics, between men whose work is primarily in the laboratory and those who work only with reports of laboratory results, pencil and complicated mathematical formulae. It is rather the tendency to a complete divorce, a mutual repudiation of the legitimacy of each other's work and interests, which is disquieting. Certain of the empirically minded are not merely not interested in attempting to contribute to theory themselves, they are actively anti-theoretical. They consider any work in theoretical fields as positively pernicious and contrary to the canons of science. It is speculation, sterile dialectic, metaphysics or even mysticism.

On the other hand, many of the persons best known as theorists have not only not themselves made distinguished empirical contributions, they have often given the impression of not caring very much at least about the kind of empirical work which the empiricists have done, of having rather a sovereign disdain for the arduous difficulties of the empirical fields.

I do not propose to dwell mainly upon the shortcomings of the empirical schools. A very large part of the difficulty seems to me to lie on the theoretical side of the controversy. Many features of our theoretical traditions seem to me seriously to have inhibited the potential usefulness of theory for empirical research. One important reason why the empiricists have tended to be anti-theoretical is that they have, often rightly, seen much to object to in the particular brands of theory they have had held up to them.

But before going further into these questions it is necessary to state certain premises which seem to me fundamental, even though they imply a drastic repudiation of certain forms of empiricist position. Sympathy with a person's motives and feelings in a situation does not necessarily imply endorsement of the position he takes.

In these terms I must categorically disagree with the view that any empirical science can be developed to a high point without reference to generalized conceptual schemes, to theory. The process of the growth of scientific knowledge is not a process of accumulation of discrete discoveries of "fact." In the first place our study of fact, however little we may be aware of it, is always guided by the logical structure of a theoretical scheme, even if it is entirely implicit. We never investigate "all the facts" which could be known about the phenomena in question, but only those which we think are "important." This involves a selection among the

possible facts. Now if we investigate carefully, though few empiricists do, what is the basis of this selection, it will, I think,
uniformly be found that among the criteria of importance and the
only ones of strictly scientific status is that of their relevance to
the logical structure of a theoretical scheme.

Secondly, few if any empiricists, being as they usually are truly
imbued with scientific curiosity, are content simply to state bald,
discrete facts. They go beyond this to maintain the existence of
relations of interdependence, causal relations. It is stated not
merely that the steam railroad was developed and certain kinds of
industrial developments took place, but that without the invention of the railroad these developments *could not* have taken
place—that the invention of the railroad was a causal *factor* in
industrial development.

Now I wish to assert that such an imputation of causal relationship cannot be proved without reference to generalized
theoretical categories. If it is asserted, the assertion is logically
dependent on these categories whether they are explicit or implicit.

If this be true, the alternative for the scientist in the social or
any other field is not as between theorizing and not theorizing, but
as between theorizing explicitly with a clear consciousness of
what he is doing with the greater opportunity that gives of avoiding the many subtle pitfalls of fallacy, and following the policy of
the ostrich, pretending not to theorize and thus leaving one's
theory implicit and uncriticized, thus almost certainly full of er-
rors.

This assertion of the inevitability of theory in science naturally
cannot be proved on this occasion. The next best thing is to cite
authority. Alfred Marshall was an economist who so far as I know
has hardly seriously been accused of tender-minded disregard for
fact. In an address at the University of Cambridge he made a
striking statement which exactly expresses my feeling: "The
most reckless and treacherous of all theorists is he who professes
to let facts and figures speak for themselves."[1] If Marshall stated
this point in a most striking form, I think Max Weber may be said
definitely to have proved it. It was one of his greatest method-

ological contributions definitively to have refuted the claims of the German Historical Schools that it is possible to have valid empirical knowledge of causal relationships with no logical implication of reference to generalized theoretical categories.

But if generalized theory is essential to science, it does not follow that anything and everything which goes by that name is of equal value. Quite the contrary, there is much to object to in a great deal of what has gone by the name of sociological theory. Empiricists are, as I have said, right in repudiating much of current theory though that does not justify them in extending this repudiation to all theory in principle simply because it is theory.

Indeed, that there is something wrong with current social theory seems to me to be clearly indicated by the fact that there is such drastic lack of agreement and that most people who write and talk about it feel impelled to divide theorists up into "schools" which, it goes without saying, are mutually incompatible so that a person who agrees with one school in almost any respect, must by definition oppose all other schools in all respects.

This deplorable situation seems to me in large measure due to a failure to distinguish adequately the various conceptual elements which either go to make up, or have become associated with, what are generally called theoretical structures in science, particularly in social science. I should like to distinguish three classes of such elements and put forward the thesis that much of the difficulty is due to modes of conception of and undue emphasis on two of them, resulting in distortion of the significance and role of the third.

1. No science develops in a vacuum, either intellectual or social. The scientific content of an intellectual tradition is always closely interwoven with elements of a different character. So far as these elements are conceptually formulated, they may be called for present purposes philosophical elements. The problem of the relation of scientific and philosophical ideas intermingled in the same body of thought has been a prolific source of trouble in social as in other science.

With regard to this problem thought seems to have tended

strongly to get itself into a dilemma: One horn of the dilemma is the view that the scientific and philosophical components of a body of thought must necessarily be bound rigidly together in a single completely determinate system. The inference is that a body of scientific theory, if it is logically coherent, is simply an aspect of a philosophical system and none of it can be accepted without accepting the system as a whole. Thus the critics of classical and neoclassical economic theory have often held that acceptance of the theory for even the most elementary purposes implied the acceptance of the whole rigid philosophical system, extreme rationalism, psychological hedonism, utilitarian ethics and the rest. Conversely it has often been held that it was impossible to be confident of even the most elementary theoretical proposition, such as that the value of money is an inverse function of its quantity, without first settling definitively all the problems of the complete philosophical system on which it supposedly depends.

There is a very widespread and justified feeling that philosophical theories cannot claim the same order of objectivity and verifiability as the propositions of empirical science. Hence it is not surprising that people who disliked these implications should, without questioning the premises on which they rested, attempt to evade them by repudiating theory altogether. After all, to be responsible for a complete philosophical system, once the first innocent step in theoretical reasoning is taken, is a rather terrifying prospect. In this dilemma my sympathies are definitely with the empiricist.

But I cannot accept the dilemma. In my opinion the whole thing rests on a serious misconception of the relation of scientific theory to philosophy. I do not believe either that scientific theory has no philosophical implications, or that it involves no philosophical preconceptions. They cannot, in that sense, be radically divorced. But at the same time it does not follow that they are rigidly bound together in the sense this dilemma implies. On the contrary, though they are interdependent in many subtle ways, they are also independent. Above all it is perfectly possible for a scientist, even a theorist, to get ahead with his work without worrying about a philosophical system in general, but only considering philosophical questions one by one when and as they directly impinge on his own scientific problems. Indeed, this false dilemma is the principal source of the charge that theorizing is necessarily "metaphysical" and has no place in science.

Please note, I do not say that scientific theory should never concern itself with philosophical problems. But I do say that its burden can be enormously lightened if it divests itself of unnecessary philosophical concerns; and it can do this to a far greater extent than is generally believed, especially by empiricists.

2. The second type of conceptual element involved in bodies of theory which I wish to discuss is one which falls within the competence of science strictly construed, is hence not philosophical, but has, I think, received quite undue prominence especially in sociology. This is the element of what may be called "broad empirical generalization." Examples are such propositions as "the course of social development as a whole follows a linear evolutionary course," or "social processes are in the last analysis determined by economic (or geographical, or racial, etc., etc.) factors." Such "theories" embody a generalized judgment about the behavior of, or causes in, a hugely complicated class of empirical phenomena. They are analogous to such judgments as "the physical universe as a whole is running down."

Indeed it is in terms of such views, if not their philosophical positions, that sociological theories are usually classified. We have evolutionary vs. cyclical theories, economic, biological, religious interpretations.

Here again we find a dilemma. For we may well ask, how are propositions such as these to be *proved?* Where are the specific observations, the patently rigorous reasoning? If the proof is as cogent as their proponents claim, why the warring schools? Why cannot people be brought to agreement? The empiricist quite understandably begins to suspect it is because there isn't any such evidence, or is woefully inadequate to the conclusions. Hence so far as theory in general is identified with this kind of thing, it is held to be "speculative," only for people who have not absorbed the discipline of scientific caution, of asserting only what they can demonstrate. Here again my sympathies are with the empiricist. I do not think the great majority of propositions of this order have been or are capable of being rigorously demonstrated. Critical examination of them will reveal scientific defects of one kind or another.

3. So, if scientific theory in the social field consisted only of these two classes of elements, there would be much reason to follow the empiricist's advice and eschew it altogether. But I am confident that this is not the case, there are other elements as well which the usual empiricist indictment is prone to overlook, what I should like to call generalized analytical theory. This it is which seems to me to be the most important kind of conceptualization in the physical sciences.

Empiricists are often fond of maintaining that they emulate the physical sciences. It is my suspicion that they are able to make this claim partly because analytical theory has in such fields become so completely integrated with empirical research that it is completely taken for granted—no one feels it necessary to talk about its role because it seems obvious. After all, mathematics in its application to physics *is* theory.

Analytical theory in the sense in which I mean the term here, is a body of logically interrelated generalized concepts (logical universals) the specific facts corresponding to which (particulars) constitute statements describing empirical phenomena. Use of this concept in empirical research inherently tends to establish logical relations between them and their particular content (values) such that they come to constitute logically interdependent systems. Correspondingly the phenomena to which they apply come to be viewed as empirical systems, the elements of which are in a state of mutual interdependence.

Much the most highly developed analytical system in this sense in the social field is economic theory. Indeed, economists alone have among social scientists been steeped in an analytical system. But precisely because of the difficulty of clarifying the relation of this analytical system both to empirical reality itself and to the other types of conceptualization just discussed, even economics has not been spared an empiricist revolt, the institutionalist movement, which, though probably now passing, has in this context done a great deal of damage and threatened to do more.

Indeed, one important reason for the apparent backwardness of analytical theory in the social sciences is the greater formidability of these difficulties here as compared with the physical sciences. Those concerned with ordinary biases and with the often difficult distinctions between scientific and philosophical considerations I shall leave aside. But two others are of such great importance that I should like to say a few words about them: (1) Even in mathematical terms it is difficult to handle a system involving more than a very small number of variables. Where for various reasons mathematical treatment is excluded, as it is in most of the social field, or severely limited as, I think, it is in all, there is a very strong impetus to simplification of problems by dealing with only a few variables in a system.

This inevitably implies that analytical theory in the social field is highly abstract. For the values of the variables of such a system state only a very limited number of facts about the concrete phenomena to which it applies. It is very seldom that other elements are sufficiently constant within any very wide range of variation of these variables so that trustworthy interpretation and prediction can be based on the laws of this analytical system alone. It needs to be supplemented by considerations involving the others as well. This is one of the most important reasons for the unsatisfactoriness of proceeding directly to broad empirical generalization. The case of some of the deductions from economic theory is an extremely vivid one. The facts relevant to any system of analytical theory are *never* all the facts knowable about the phenomenon in question, and only part of these are the values of variables. (2) A variable is a logical universal or combination of them. Its "values" are the particular facts which correspond to this universal. These facts are or can be obtained in one and only one way—by empirical observation. But it is the essence of the ordering function of theory that any old facts, however true, will not do, but only those which "fit" the categories of the system. What facts it is important to know are relative to the logical structure of the theory. This is not to be understood to mean that theory should dictate factual findings, but only the definition of the categories into which the findings are to be fitted.

Precisely here is one of the crucial problems of the relation of theory to empirical research. For theory to be fruitful it is essential that we have research techniques which provide the right kind of facts. There is, indeed, evidence that this is one of the most serious difficulties, that a great deal of current research is producing facts in a form which cannot be utilized by any current generalized analytical scheme. This is a very complex problem. I can comment on only one phase of it.

One important group of social empiricists is particularly partial to measurement. They point out the extreme importance of measurement in physics and conclude that only so far as its facts are the results of measurements can sociology claim the status of a science. I do not wish to depreciate the value of measurement wherever it is possible, but I do wish to point out two things: First, the importance of facts is relative to the way in which they can be fitted into analytical schemes: measurements are fundamental to physics because many of its variables are such that the only facts which make sense as their values are numerical data. But numerical data are far less scientifically important until they can be so fitted into analytical categories. I venture to say this is true of the vast majority of such data in the social fields.

Second, measurement as such is not logically essential to science, however desirable. Measurement is a special case of a broader category, classification. It is logically essential that the values of a variable should be reducible to a determinate classification. But the classification they admit of may be far more complex than the single order of magnitude which measurement requires. Where nonmetrical, even nonquantitative data can, with the help of such classification, be made to fit directly the logical structure of an analytical scheme it may be possible to establish relations of crucial importance which any amount of numerical data lacking such analytical relevance could not bring out.

In conclusion I may state schematically what seem to me to be the principal functions of analytical theory in research.

1. In the vast welter of miscellaneous facts we face it provides us with selective criteria as to which are important and which can safely be neglected.

2. It provides a basis for coherent organization of the factual material thus selected without which a study is unintelligible.

3. It provides a basis not only of selection and organization of known facts, but in a way which cannot be done otherwise reveals the *gaps* in our existing knowledge and their importance. It thus constitutes a crucially important guide to the direction of fruitful research.

4. Through the mutual logical implications of different analytical systems for each other it provides a source of cross fertilization of related fields of the utmost importance. This often leads to very important developments within a field which would not have taken place had it remained theoretically isolated.

Finally, it may be asked, have the social sciences outside of economics any analytical theory at all to use? Must we not remain empiricists through sheer lack of anything else to turn to? I do not think so. I believe there is far more analytical theory in use than many of us realize. We have been, like Molière's hero, speaking prose all our lives without knowing it. Moreover, in a work recently published[2] I have traced a process of development of analytical theory of the first magnitude including, I believe, a demonstration of its fruitfulness in empirical research. I am convinced that investigation would show that the ramifications of this development reach far beyond the limited group of workers with whom I have explicitly dealt.

My closing plea is then: Let us take what we already have and both use it to the utmost and develop it as rapidly as we can. Let us not either through failure to understand what it is that we have or through disillusionment with its very real shortcomings, throw it overboard to the tragic detriment of the interests of our science. If it is used and developed through the intimate co-operation of empirical and theoretical work, I am very hopeful for the future of sociological science.

2

THE PLACE OF ULTIMATE VALUES IN SOCIOLOGICAL THEORY

The positivistic reaction against philosophy has, in its effect on the social sciences, manifested a strong tendency to obscure the fact that man is essentially an active, creative, evaluating creature. Any attempt to explain his behavior in terms of ends, purposes, ideals, has been under suspicion as a form of "teleology" which was thought to be incompatible with the methodological requirements of positive science. One must, on the contrary, explain in terms of "causes" and "conditions," not of ends.

Of late years, however, there have been many signs of a break in this rigid positivistic view of things. The social sciences in general have been far from immune from these signs, and in sociology in particular they have combined to form a movement of thought of the first importance. One main aspect of this movement has been the tendency to reopen the whole question of the extent to which, and the senses in which, human behavior must or can be understood in terms of the values entertained by men. In the present essay I wish to attempt a formulation of the kind of conception of human action which I take to be implied in some of these recent developments of sociological theory. In particular, what is the status in that conception of the element which may provisionally be called "ultimate values"? I shall not attempt here to trace the process by which this conception of human action has been built up, but merely to outline the conception itself.

Reprinted by permission from "The Place of Ultimate Values in Sociological Theory," *International Journal of Ethics* 45 (1935):282–300.

One of the most conspicuous features of the positivistic movement just referred to has been the tendency to what may be termed a kind of "objectivism." Positivism, that is, has continually thought in terms of the model of the physical sciences which deal with an "inanimate" subject matter. Hence the tendency has been to follow their example in thinking of a simple relation of observer to externally observed events. The fact that the entities observed, human beings, have also a "subjective" aspect has a tendency to be obscured, or at least kept out of the range of methodological self-consciousness. The extreme of this objectivist trend is, of course, behaviorism which involves the self-conscious denial of the legitimacy of including any references to the subjective aspect of other human beings in any scientific explanation of their actions. But short of this radical behaviorist position, the general positivistic trend of thought has systematically minimized the importance of analysis in terms of the subjective aspect, and has prevented a clear-cut and self-conscious treatment of the relations of the two aspects to each other.

Of course the results of analysis of human behavior from the objective point of view (that is, that of an outside observer) and the subjective (that of the person thought of as acting himself) should correspond, but that fact is no reason why the two points of view should not be kept clearly distinct. Only on this basis is there any hope of arriving at a satisfactory solution of their relations to each other.

End and value are subjective categories in this sense. Hence it is not surprising that the objectivist bias of positivistic social thought should tend either to squeeze them out altogether or to militate against any really thoroughgoing analysis of them in their bearing on action. For the same reasons the present attempt to present at least the foundations of such an analysis must be couched mainly in subjective terms. The implications of the analysis for the objective point of view can at best be only very briefly indicated.

There seems to be no evading the fact that the subjective analysis of action involves in some form the schema of the means-end relationship. We must be careful to avoid any arbitrary assumption that this schema can exhaust the subjective aspect, but for various reasons it is the most favorable starting-point of such an analysis. Hence, after some introductory definition of concepts, the second part of this essay will be concerned with an outline of the principal elements of action so far as it can be understood in terms of the means-end relationship, and with the main sociological implications of this analysis. Then, in the following parts we will proceed to a consideration of the possible relations of this schema to other aspects of the subjective, and in turn the sociological implications of these.

I

It is necessary in following out this program to point out an ambiguity in the concept of "end" which may cause serious confusion. One possible definition would be the following: An end is the subjective anticipation of a desirable future state of affairs toward the realization of which the action of the individual in question may be thought of as directed. The thing to note is that this definition makes the "real" reference of an end—that is, the future state of affairs—a *concrete* state of affairs. But only *some* of the elements in that concrete state of affairs can be thought of as being brought about by the agency of the actor. Part of it consists of a *prediction* of what the future state of affairs will be, independently of his action. Thus, if I say it is an end of my present action to take a vacation in New Hampshire next summer, the concrete state of affairs I anticipate—vacationing in New Hampshire in the summer—will, if the end is realized, only to a certain extent come about through my own agency. The fact that it is *I* who does it will, to be sure, be attributable to that factor—but the geography of New Hampshire and the fact that it is summer will not be my doing—I merely predict, on the basis of my knowledge of the circumstances, that the former will remain substantially the same as now for another year, and that the cycle of the seasons will, by July, have brought summer in place of the present fall weather.

Ends in this sense may be called *concrete* ends. Our concern in this discussion is not, however, with concrete ends, but with ends as a *factor* in action. That is, it is with the prevision of a future state of affairs *in so far as* that future state is to be brought about through the agency of the actor—it is the alterations from what his prediction, if accurate, would yield as the future state without his agency which constitutes the end. Thus I can "see" New Hampshire next summer without my vacationing there. I can also "see" myself at that future time not in New Hampshire, but, for instance, perspiring over my work in Cambridge. It is the peculiar elements of *myself, vacationing* in New Hampshire, which may be considered my end. Thus, ends in this discussion will be used as an analytical category—a *factor* in action, and this sense of the term will be implied throughout unless otherwise stated. It is highly important not to confuse it with the concrete reality I have referred to.

If the means-end relationship involving this sense of the term "ends" is employed in this analysis, it is clear and should be pointed out at the outset that the whole analysis involves a metaphysical position of a "voluntaristic" character. That is, the analysis has empirical significance and is more than a mere exercise in logic only in so far as subjective ends in this sense do actually form an effective factor in action. This postulate a materialistic metaphysics would roundly deny. The metaphysical implication of the analysis is, however, thus far only negative—at the pole of materialism it ceases to have empirical meaning. But on the other hand, short of that pole, the analysis by itself does not beg the question of the quantitative empirical importance of the factor of ends. So long as it is not negligible, we may go ahead with a good conscience. But in so far as positivistic social theory has involved a genuinely materialistic metaphysics (which I believe it very generally has), it has quite rightly shied away from this type of analysis. For it, "ends," in so far as they exist at all, must be epiphenomena. Hence the importance of the foregoing distinction. Some concrete ends *may* be epiphenomena to us also, but to postulate this of the *factor* ends in general is naturally a contradiction in terms.

Before entering on an analysis of the means-end relationship itself, one more preliminary question should be called attention to. The means-end schema is, in type, at the rationalistic pole of the analysis of action. An end is thought of as a *logically formulated* anticipation of certain elements in a future state of affairs, and the relation of means to end is thought of as based on knowledge of the inherent connections of things. This is, in its type form, a *scientific* statement couched in the conditional, or, as it is sometimes put, the virtual form. That is, *if* I do certain things, bring about certain conditions, I will achieve my end. But this rational schema of the relation of means and ends is not to be arrived at by empirical generalization from the crude facts of experience. It is not only an analytical schema, but one of a peculiar sort. What it formulates is a *norm* of rational action. Its empirical relevance rests on the view, which I believed to be factually borne out, that human beings do, in fact, strive to realize ends and to do so by the rational application of means to them. This involves what I just called a "voluntaristic" conception of human action. Neither the knowledge of the relation of means and end on which action is based nor the application of that knowledge comes automatically. Both are the result of effort, of the exercise of will. Hence the probability that concrete action will only imperfectly realize such norms. Ignorance, error, and obstacles to the realization of ends which transcend human powers will all play a part in determining the concrete course of events. While, on the one hand, the concept of action itself has no meaning apart from "real" ends and a rational norm of means-end relationships (it dissolves into mere "behavior"), on the other hand it equally has no meaning apart from obstacles to be overcome by effort in the realization of the norm. The concepts built up on the basis of the means-end schema are thus not empirical generalizations but, to use Max Weber's term, "ideal types." But, precisely in so far as this voluntaristic conception of action holds true, they are indispensable to the understanding of concrete human affairs.

I have said that the rational norm of action implied in the means-end schema constitutes a *scientific* statement in conditional form. Indeed, in so far as it has been concerned with the subjective aspect of human action, the whole of modern social theory revolves about the question of the relation of science and action: In what sense and to what extent may action be thought of as guided by scientific knowledge?

It should be clear that the creative, voluntaristic element which we have found to be involved in the factor of ends precludes action ever being *completely* determined by scientific knowledge in the sense of the modern positive sciences. For the business of science is to understand the "given"—its very essence is a certain objectivity, that is, an independence of the "facts" from the will of the scientist. In action, therefore, the element of scientific knowledge may have a place in imparting accurate understanding of the conditions in which action takes place—and in forecasting the results of such conditions whether independent of the actor's agency or not.

But *ends* are not given in this sense—they are precisely the element of rational action which falls outside the schema of positive science. Indeed, many positivistic theorists, by trying to think of rational action as the type *entirely* determined by scientific knowledge, and attempting thus to fit ends into the scientific schema, have in fact squeezed out the *factor* of ends altogether. For concrete ends could only be scientific facts in so far as they constituted scientific predictions from present and past facts. The creative element has no place. But although we must reject this narrow interpretation of rational action, nevertheless the scientific schema is basic to what is historically (in terms of the history of modern thought) the main type of means-end relationship—what I shall call the *intrinsic* relationship. It is that which can be analyzed in terms of scientific knowledge (or its common-sense predecessors), with the one exception of the *determination* of ends.

The factor of ends may be fitted into this schema in the following way. Though what concrete ends should be striven for cannot be determined on the basis of scientific knowledge alone, once the end is given the means to its attainment may be selected on that basis. Moreover, though an end cannot itself be determined by scientific knowledge, the fact or degree of its attainment may, after the time to which it refers has arrived, be verified by scientific observation. In so far as this is true of an end, I shall refer to it as an empirical end. Then action is rational in terms of the intrinsic means-end relationship in so far as, on the one hand, its ends are empirical, and on the other, the relations of means and ends involved in it are the intrinsic relations of things as revealed by scientific knowledge of the phenomena. Once he knows the end, the rationality of such action can be judged by an external observer, both before and after its completion, in terms of his own scientific knowledge. Deviations from the rational norm will be explicable in one or more of three sets of terms: ignorance of intrinsic relationships, lack of effort, or presence of obstacles beyond the power of the actor to remove, whether they be obstacles in the actor's own constitution and character or in his environment.

But does this type exhaust the logical possibilities of the means-end relationship? By no means! First, as to ends: Here it is necessary to enter into definitely philosophical questions. What is the implication of what I have called the creative character of the factor of ends, and hence of the impossibility of fitting it, for the actor, into the category of facts of the external world? It is, I think, a negation of the positivistic view that the "realities" which can be studied by empirical science are the sole realities significant for human action. I have purposely defined ends in terms of a vague phrase, a future "state of affairs." It is now necessary to define more closely what the phrase means.

It is clear that in so far as an end is, in the foregoing sense, an empirical end, the future state of affairs is to be thought of as a state of the scientifically observable external world. But there is a certain difficulty in thinking of this as alone involved. For the ends of action are not, in fact, to be based on the mere arbitrary whims of a once popular "libertarian" philosophy. Overwhelmingly the realization of the ultimate ends of action is felt to be a matter of moral obligation, to be binding on the individual—not, to be sure, in the sense of physical necessity, but still binding. The ubiquity of the concept of duty is perhaps sufficient proof of this.

But whence this sense of binding obligation? The source of specific moral obligations cannot be derived from the empirical properties of "human nature" as revealed by scientific psychology—for this is part of the same external world as the environment—the subjective point of view is that of the *ego* not of the body, or even the "mind." Psychology may reveal man as a creature who obeys moral obligations—but not as bound by his nature to *one* particular set of such obligations. Moreover, this explanation would violate both the inner sense of freedom of moral choice, which is just as ultimate a fact of human life as any other, and its consequent moral responsibility. In fact, a psychological explanation of moral obligation really explains away the phenomenon itself. Finally, also there is a very large body of empirical evidence indicating that specific moral values are not completely correlated with "human nature."

If this explanation is rejected, it seems to me that there is only one other avenue left open. The world of "empirical" fact must be only a part, only one aspect, of the universe in so far as it is significant to man. The "external world," i.e., that of science, is as it were an island in a sea the character of which is something different from the island. Our relation to the other aspects of the universe is different from that of scientist to empirical facts. It will be noted that all these characterizations are negative—it is something transcending science.

The ultimate reason, then, for the causal independence of ends in action, the fact that they are not determined by the facts of human nature and environment, is the *fact* that man stands in significant relations to aspects of reality other than those revealed by science. Moreover, the fact that empirical reality can be modified by action shows that this empirical reality, the world of science, is not a closed system but is itself significantly related to the other aspects of reality.

Now it has been stated that the concept of end involves logical formulation. Does this mean that empirical ends are the only possible ones? While our logical formulations of non-empirical reality differ from those of empirical reality—that is, are not *scientific* theories—they exist none the less. They are metaphysical theories, theologies, etc. Now such theories may be thought of in relation to ends in two ways: They may constitute the terms to be used in justifying empirical ends; this is, in fact, an empirically important case. At the same time, however, they may lay down, as desirable, ends of action altogether outside the empirical sphere—that is, ends the attainment of which cannot be verified by empirical observation. Such an end is, for example, eternal salvation. This class, the attainment of a "state of affairs" outside the realm of empirical observability, I should like to call "transcendental ends."

We may then put the situation somewhat as follows: Ultimate

empirical ends are justified to the actor in terms, not of scientific, but of metaphysical, theories. He may, however, by virtue of his metaphysical theories pursue not merely empirical but also transcendental ends. It is conceivable that there should be a system of empirical ends justified directly by a metaphysical theory without reference to transcendental ends. That is the case, for instance, with the ideal of socialism—it refers to a desired future state of affairs in this world only. But in general such a metaphysical theory at the same time enjoins transcendental ends. Whenever that is the case, empirical ends are also present; otherwise there is no relation to action as an empirical reality. The relation will in general be such that a transcendental end is thought logically to imply as a means to it a given empirical end.

One further distinction in the realm of ends remains to be made. Some empirical ends refer to a state of affairs differing from the merely predicted state by more than a changed state of mind of the actor. On the other hand, one may think of the actor as attempting to attain only a subjective state of mind—happiness, for instance. In these terms I should like to distinguish "objective" empirical ends from "subjective" empirical ends. The attainment of both is verifiable, but in different ways. This is to assume, as we do throughout, the anti-behaviorist position that scientific observation of an individual's subjective state of mind is possible and valid. It is necessary, of course, to distinguish an altered state of mind as a *result* of action from its rôle as an end. "Happiness" or "satisfaction" may be thought of as, in general, a result of the attainment of objective ends—empirical or transcendental. But on occasion it is thought of as an end in itself—whether attainable or not is another question.

The attainment of a transcendental end should not be thought of as that of a state of mind. What is true is that the only empirical evidence we have of its attainment is *through* the statements and the state of mind of the individual actor. Religious persons may state that they are saved, or that they have attained Nirvana. Scientifically, such statements are not verifiable. But we may verify that persons who *believe* they have attained such a transcendental end do *in fact* typically attain certain subjective states of mind.

Now to return to the element of means. We have given as the kind of means involved in the scientific norm of rational action those which are *intrinsically* related to their ends. This relation is a normative type which may be further defined as follows: The relation between end and means is intrinsic in so far as the employment of a given combination of means will bring about the realization of the end by processes of scientifically understandable accusation. There is, however, a large category of means employed in human action of which this is not true. From the point of view of a scientific analysis of the relation of means and end, the connection is arbitrary—therefore from the scientific point of view the action is "irrational." In so far as this arbitrary relationship is not due merely to ignorance, i.e., inadequate scientific insight, but to a definitely non-scientific "ritual" attitude toward the means, I should call this a symbolic means-end relationship. It is possible that there are other types of means, but for present purposes I shall limit myself to the two categories of intrinsic and symbolic.

II

Having detailed the principal types of elements of the means-end relationship, we may now proceed to inquire into their interrelationships in *systems* of action. We may start with the intrinsic means-end relationship. This may be thought of as constituting a "chain" of such relations. At one end will be those elements which are ultimate means or conditions of action but not, from any point of view, ends. These will, on analysis, turn out to constitute the two categories of heredity and environment—the cosmic and bio-psychological factors of human life. Positivistic social theories always attempt to elevate these into the sole factors and thus, as we have noted in another connection, squeeze out that of ends. Action, whether rational or not, is thought of as a process of adaptation to these factors.

At the other end of the chain is the factor of ultimate ends, which are, looked at in intrinsic terms, ends in themselves and not means to any further ends. The ultimate ends of the *intrinsic* chain must, it is apparent, be empirical ends, but may be either objective or subjective. The existence of such an element of ultimate ends is a logical necessity for any view which allows a place as a real factor in action for ends in any sense whatever.

In between these two extremes with indefinite possibilities of ramifications will be an "intermediate" sector of the intrinsic means-end chain. These elements are both means and ends at the same time—ends when looked at from "below," e.g., from means to end; means when looked at from "above," from end to means. This intermediate sector can be analyzed, it seems to me, into three subsectors—the technological, the economic, and the political, respectively. The technological element exists, in so far as action is concerned, with the choice and application of means for a single end in abstraction from others. The economic element enters when the question of the alternative uses of scarce means for different ends arises. The economic problem is essentially that of the allocation of these scarce means as between alternative uses in terms of the relative urgency of the ends—that is, of marginal utility.

Finally the political element is specifically concerned with the relations of individuals to each other as potential means to each other's ends. It is present in so far as authority over others and control of their actions for one's own ends is secured by means of coercive power. The state is the focus of the political element because it is the association which attempts to regulate the power-relationships of the community in the general interest, partly by its monopoly of the *legitimate* exercise of physical coercion.

The standard of rationality applicable to the intermediate sector of the intrinsic means-end chain is that of efficiency. It is a matter of the intrinsic adaptation of means quite apart from other considerations.

Now we must return to the factor of ultimate ends, which is our main concern. So far nothing has been said of the relation of ultimate ends to each other. One possible view is that they form a random plurality, with no connections whatever. The element of order in human action would then be restricted to the relations of means to these ends. This has been, indeed, the position implicit in at least certain trends of utilitarian thought. There are, however, cogent reasons for rejecting it.

Taken first on the individual level, reflection will show that this doctrine is fatal to the conception of rational choice, which is in turn essential to the whole voluntaristic conception of action put forward here. For a choice between ends implies that they are related to each other, that they are true *alternatives* in terms of a wider system of principles. It is, indeed, no wonder that utilitarianism shows such a strong tendency to slide off into some form of positivistic determinism, for once rational choice is eliminated in this fashion there is nothing left to determine action but biological and psychological drives. It can safely be concluded, then, that precisely in so far as the action of an individual is guided by rational choice, its ultimate ends are to be thought of as constituting an integrated system. Rationality of action for an individual implies just as much the working-out of such a coherent system of ends as it does a rational selection of means.

But then is it not conceivable that though individuals must be thought of as acting in terms of such integrated systems of ends, the systems of different individuals should, within the limits of biological survival at least, be thought of as varying at random? It is, indeed, *logically* possible but not, I think, empirically. For such a statement there are two kinds of evidence. In the first place it may be argued in general and abstract terms that this random variation of systems of ends would be incompatible with the most elementary form of social order. For there would be no guaranty that any large proportion of such systems would include a recognition of other people's ends as valuable in themselves, and there would thus be no necessary limitation on the means that some, at least, would employ to gain their own ends at the expense of others. The relations of individuals then would tend to be resolved into a struggle for power—for the means for each to realize his own ends. This would be, in the absence of constraining factors, a war of all against all—Hobbes's state of nature. In so far, however, as individuals share a *common* system of ultimate ends, this system would, among other things, define what they all held their relations ought to be, would lay down norms determining these relations and limits on the use of others as means, on the acquisition and use of power in general. In so far, then, as action is determined by ultimate ends, the existence of a *system* of such ends common to the members of the community seems to be the only alternative to a state of chaos—a necessary factor in social stability.

In addition, there is much empirical evidence that such systems of ultimate ends exist and play a decisive rôle in social life. This evidence is derived from many sources. One is the comparative study of actual historical societies and their functioning. Thus Greek society would appear to be scarcely understandable without reference to the peculiar conceptions of what human relations should be, centering about the idea of the *polis*. So much were these values common to all Greeks that persons who did not share them were unhesitatingly stigmatized as barbarians, and their values dismissed from serious consideration. Similarly in the Middle Ages with the values clustering about the church. Another very impressive source of evidence derives from the study of the processes of child development which brings out the enormous importance in the formation of individual personality of the child's "socialization" in terms of the values of the group. But perhaps the most impressive evidence of all is Durkheim's empirical demonstration that even the modern individualism to which the utilitarians have pointed as the main confirmation of their thesis involved highly important *common* values, centering, above all, in the common ethical valuation of individual personality as such.

It is advisable, though it should scarcely be necessary, to point out once more that we are merely arguing for the necessity of assuming that a common system of ultimate ends plays a significant part in social life. We are not arguing that the concrete reality may be understood completely, or even predominantly in such terms. Nor that the *common* system exhausts the genuinely ethical element. Thus, criticisms to the effect that there was in the Middle Ages anti-Christian action or sentiment, or that, after all, Socrates resisted the populace of Athens on ethical grounds, are not relevant unless the critic can prove not only that phenomena not fitting into this scheme *exist* but that those formulated in the scheme do not, which is an entirely different matter.

If the place for a common system of ultimate ends be granted, a further question arises: Is there inherent in our relations to nonempirical reality only *one* such system, are we in the normative sense subject to a unitary Law of Nature or not? Almost all philosophers have pictured the scheme of values they themselves formulated as the one ethically possible one. I do not propose even to attempt to enter into the philosophical question at issue. It is quite possible that there "is" only one such system. On the other hand, looked at empirically, which is, after all, the point of view of sociological science, this would seem to be a dangerous assumption. For the first thing that strikes the observer of values in history is the very great diversity of such systems. To take only one instance, the values embodied in the Indian doctrines of Karma and Transmigration and the empirical ends associated with them seem utterly incompatible with those inherent in our Western individualism. The former yield a direct sanction of caste; whereas caste is utterly unacceptable to even the highest of our high Tories. The safest procedure for sociologists would seem to be to take this historical diversity of value-systems as a starting-point, first to attempt to determine what are the ultimate value-systems relevant to understanding action in a given society at a given time. From that starting-point, then, it is quite legitimate to proceed to attempt to discover relationships between such systems—to classify them according to types, to establish genetic relationships. But all this should be done with the greatest of care to avoid the common fallacy of reading arbitrarily into the facts a tendency to the ultimate realization of the investigator's own particular values. The fallacy is, of course, only too prevalent. It may be said to be involved in virtually every current doctrine of social evolution and progress.

We may now consider the modes in which the ultimate common system of ends is related to action in the intrinsic means-end chain. There are, I think, two modes. Either an ultimate end is also the immediate end of a given train of action or it is not. In the former case the logical situation is very simple—it is merely a matter of an ordinary means-end relationship. Its rationality is to be judged by the ordinary standards of efficiency once the end is given. The standard of efficiency is, of course, applicable only in so far as the end is an empirical end; but this may in turn be derived from a system of transcendental ends. But the strategy, for instance, of a general in a religious war is to be judged in exactly the same terms as though the sole aim of the war were aggrandizement. Such a coincidence of ultimate with immediate ends occurs generally at times of critical decision—for individuals, societies, and social movements.

But most of our action is not directly concerned with critical decisions between conflicting ultimate ends. It is rather a matter of the pursuit of immediate ends which may be removed by a very large number of intermediate links from any system of ultimate ends. The miner mining coal, to smelt iron to make steel to make rails, etc., is contributing to railway transportation, but at a point very far removed from the question of the ultimate value of railway transportation. These very facts of the remoteness of such action from ultimate ends, of the latency of such ends in relation to it, create a problem of control. There would, to be sure, be no such problem were the rationality of action automatic. But such is not the case. This is true neither of the rational formulation which transforms what may be called "value-attitudes" into specific ultimate ends, nor of the knowledge of relation of means to these ends, nor finally of the actual application of this knowledge to action itself. The voluntaristic conception of action implies that there is resistance to the realization of the rational norm—partly the resistance of inertia, partly that of factors which would tend to divert the course of action from the norm. We will not here inquire into what these factors are—merely call attention to their presence.

This problem of control tends to be met by the subjection of action in pursuit of immediate non-ultimate ends to normative rules which regulate that action in conformity with the common ultimate value-system of the community. These normative rules both define what immediate ends should and should not be sought, and limit the choice of means to them in terms other than those of efficiency. Finally, they also define standards of socially acceptable effort. This system of rules, fundamental to any society not in the state of "active religion," is what I call its institutions. They are *moral* norms, not norms of efficiency. They bear directly the stamp of their origin in the common system of ultimate ends.

The question of the modes in which institutional norms become enforced on individual actions is a complex one and cannot be entered into here. Suffice it to say that there are two primary modes, first, by the inherent moral authority of the norm itself due essentially to its derivation from the common system of ends to which the individuals obeying it subscribe. Second, there is the appear to interest. That is, conformity to the norm may, apart from any moral attitude, be in the given concrete situation a means to the realization of the actor's private ends apart from the common value-system. This type may in turn be divided into two main types—where conformity is due to the positive advantages attached to it—as social esteem, and where it is due to a desire to avoid the unpleasant consequences of non-conformity—its sanctions.

Thus to sum up—the analysis of the intrinsic means-end chain yields the necessity for the existence of a class of ultimate ends which are not means to any further ends in this chain. Partly a priori and partly empirical considerations lead to the view that these ultimate ends do not occur in random fashion, but that both in the case of the individual and of the social group they must be thought of as to a significant degree integrated into a single harmonious *system*. In the case of the social group, which mainly interests us here, this is to be thought of as a system of ultimate ends held in common by the members of the group. In so far as these common ideal ends concern, directly or by logical implication, the relations of members of the group to each other, the norms of what these relationships are thought should be are understandable in terms of the common system of ultimate ends.

This common system may be thought of as related to the rest of the intrinsic means-end chain—above all, the intermediate sector—in two main ways. In the first place the immediate end of a particular concrete complex of actions may be, in this sense, an ultimate end. In the second place the actions in pursuit of non-ultimate immediate ends may be thought of as governed by normative rules, institutions. Institutions may be classified as technological, economic, and political, according to what elements of the intermediate chain they govern.

Because of the great intricacy and subtlety of the possible

relationships between action and moral rules, it is primarily, in connection with the institutional aspect of ultimate ends that the important sociological problems arise. The theory of institutions will indeed form one of the most important, as well as difficult, branches of sociological theory. But in order to see its rôle in perspective, it is necessary to place it in terms of a coherent scheme of the elements of action, as we are attempting to do. It is this which has, more than anything else, been lacking in previous attempts to formulate a theory of institutions.

3

THE ACTION FRAME OF REFERENCE

It has been seen throughout the study that it is necessary to distinguish two different levels on which the schema of action with all its main features may be employed; these have been called the descriptive level and the analytical level. Any concrete phenomenon to which the theory is applicable may be described as a system of action, in the concrete sense. Such a system is always capable of being broken down into parts, or smaller sub-systems. If breakdown, or analysis, is followed far enough on this plane, it will eventually arrive at what has been called the unit act. This is the "smallest" unit of an action system which still makes sense as a part of a concrete system of action.

Though this unit act is the ultimate unit which can be thought of as a subsystem of action it is still not, from the point of view of the theory of action, an unanalyzable entity but is complex. It is to be thought of as composed of the "concrete" elements of action. It takes a certain number of these concrete elements to make up a complete unit act, a concrete end, concrete conditions, concrete means, and one or more norms governing the choice of means to the end. All these concepts have been discussed before and there is no necessity to repeat. It need only be noted that while each of these is, in a sense, a concrete entity, it is not one that is relevant to the theory of action unless it can be considered a part of a unit act or a system of them. A chair is, for instance, in a physical context a complex of molecules and atoms; in an action context it is a means, "something to sit on."

It is essential to distinguish from the concrete use of the theory of action, in this sense, the analytical. An end, in the latter sense, is not the concrete anticipated future state of affairs but only the difference from what it would be, if the actor should refrain from acting. The ultimate conditions are not all those concrete features of the situation of a given concrete actor which are outside his control but are those abstracted elements of the situation which cannot be imputed to action in general. Means are not concrete tools or instruments but the aspects or properties of things which actors by virtue of their knowledge of them and their control are able to alter as desired.

The fundamental distinction of these two different applications of the theory of action raises the problem of their relations to each other. This may be put most generally by saying that they involve a common frame of reference. This frame of reference consists essentially in the irreducible framework of relations between these elements and is implied in the conception of them, which is common to both levels, and without which talk about action fails to make sense. It is well to outline what the main features of this frame of reference are.

First, there is the minimum differentiation of structural elements, end, means, conditions and norms. It is impossible to have a meaningful description of an act without specifying all four, just as there are certain minimum properties of a particle, omission of any one of which leaves the description indeterminate. Second, there is implied in the relations of these elements a normative orientation of action, a teleological character. Action must always be thought of as involving a state of tension between two different orders of elements, the normative and the conditional. As process, action is, in fact, the process of alteration of the conditional elements in the direction of conformity with norms. Elimination of the normative aspect altogether eliminates the concept of action itself and leads to the radical positivistic position. Elimination of conditions, of the tension from that side, equally eliminates action and results in idealistic emanationism. Thus conditions may be conceived at one pole, ends and normative rules at the other, means and effort as the connecting links between them.

Third, there is inherently a temporal reference. Action is a process in time. The correlate of the teleological character is a time coordinate in the relation of normative and non-normative elements. The concept end always implies a future reference, to an anticipated state of affairs, but which will not necessarily exist without intervention by the actor. The end must in the mind of the actor be contemporaneous with the situation and precede the "employment of means." And the latter must, in turn, precede the outcome. It is only in temporal terms that the relations of these elements to each other can be stated. Finally, the schema is inherently subjective, in the sense of the above discussion. This is most clearly indicated by the fact that the normative elements can be conceived of as "existing" only in the mind of the actor. They can become accessible to an observer in any other form only through realization, which precludes any analysis of their causal relation to action. From the objective point of view alone all action is, it will be remembered, "logical."

These underlying features of the action schema which are here called the "frame of reference" do not constitute "data" of any empirical problem; they are not "components" of any concrete system of action. They are in this respect analogous to the space-time framework of physics. Every physical phenomenon must involve processes in time, which happen to particles which can be located in space. It is impossible to talk about physical processes in any other terms, at least so long as the conceptual scheme of the classical physics is employed. Similarly, it is impossible even to talk about action in terms that do not involve a means-end relationship with all the implications just discussed. This is the common conceptual framework in which all change and process in the action field is grasped.

4

HOBBES AND THE PROBLEM OF ORDER

For present purposes the basis of Hobbes' social thinking lies in his famous concept of the state of nature as the war of all against all. Hobbes is almost entirely devoid of normative thinking. He sets up no ideal of what conduct should be, but merely investigates the ultimate conditions of social life. Man, he says, is guided by a plurality of passions. The good is simply that which any man desires.[1] But unfortunately there are very severe limitations on the extent to which these desires can be realized, limitations which according to Hobbes lie primarily in the nature of the relations of man to man.

Man is not devoid of reason. But reason is essentially a servant of the passions—it is the faculty of devising ways and means to secure what one desires. Desires are random, there is "no common rule of good and evil to be taken from the nature of the objects themselves."[2] Hence since the passions, the ultimate ends of action, are diverse there is nothing to prevent their pursuit resulting in conflict.

In Hobbes' thinking, the reason for this danger of conflict is to be found in the part played by power. Since all men are seeking to realize their desires they must necessarily seek command over means to this realization. The power a man has is in Hobbes' own words[3] simply "his present means to obtain some future apparent good." One very large element of power is the ability to command the recognition and services of other men. To Hobbes this is the most important among those means which, in the nature of things, are limited. The consequence is that what means to his ends one man commands another is necessarily shut off from. Hence power as a proximate end is inherently a source of division between men.

> Nature hath made men so equal in the faculties of body and mind, that though there be found one man sometimes manifestly stronger in body or of quicker mind than another, yet when all is reckoned together the difference between man and man is not so considerable as that one man can thereupon claim to himself any benefit, to which another may not pretend as well as he . . . . From this equality of ability ariseth equality of hope in the attaining of our ends. And therefore if any two men desire the same thing which nevertheless they cannot both enjoy, they become enemies; and in the way to their end endeavor to destroy or subdue one another.[4]

In the absence of any restraining control men will adopt to this immediate end the most efficient available means. These means are found in the last analysis to be force and fraud.[5] Hence a situation where every man is the enemy of every other, endeavoring to destroy or subdue him by force or fraud or both. This is nothing but a state of war.

But such a state is even less in conformity with human desires than what most of us know. It is in Hobbes' famous words a state where the life of man is "solitary, poor, nasty, brutish and short."[6] The fear of such a state of things calls into action, as a servant of the most fundamental of all the passions, that of self-preservation, at least a modicum of reason which finds a solution of the difficulty in the social contract. By its terms men agreed to give up their natural liberty to a sovereign authority which in turn guarantees them security, that is immunity from aggression by the force or fraud of others. It is only through the authority of this sovereign that the war of all against all is held in check and order and security maintained.

Hobbes' system of social theory is almost a pure case of utilitarianism. The basis of human action lies in the "passions." These are discrete, randomly variant ends of action, "There is no common rule of good and evil to be taken from the nature of the objects themselves." In the pursuit of these ends men act rationally, choosing, within the limitations of the situation, the most efficient means. But this rationality is strictly limited, reason is the "servant of the passions," it is concerned only with questions of ways and means.

But Hobbes went much farther than merely defining with extraordinary precision the basic units of a utilitarian system of action. He went on to deduce the character of the concrete system which would result if its units were in fact as defined. And in so doing he became involved in an empirical problem which has not yet been encountered, as the present discussion so far has been confined to defining units and noting merely their logical relations in utilitarian thought—the problem of *order*. This problem, in the sense in which Hobbes posed it, constitutes the most fundamental empirical difficulty of utilitarian thought. It will form the main thread of the historical discussion of the utilitarian system and its outcome.

Before taking up his experience with it, two meanings of the term which may easily become confused should be distinguished. They may be called normative order and factual order respectively. The antithesis of the latter is randomness or chance in the strict sense of phenomena conforming to the statistical laws of probability. Factual order, then, connotes essentially accessibility to understanding in terms of logical theory, especially of science. Chance variations are in these terms impossible to understand or to reduce to law. Chance or randomness is the name for that which is incomprehensible, not capable of intelligible analysis.

Normative order, on the other hand, is always relative to a given system of norms or normative elements, whether ends, rules or other norms. Order in this sense means that process takes place in conformity with the paths laid down in the normative system. Two further points should, however, be noted in this connection. One is that the breakdown of any given normative order, that is a state of chaos from a normative point of view, may well result in an order in the factual sense, that is a state of affairs susceptible of scientific analysis. Thus the "struggle for existence" is chaotic from the point of view of Christian ethics, but that does not in the least mean that it is not subject to law in the scientific sense, that is to uniformities of process in the phenomena. Secondly, in spite of the logically inherent possibility that any normative order may break down into a "chaos" under certain conditions, it may still be true that the normative elements are essential to the maintenance of the *particular* factual order which exists when processes are to a degree in conformity with them. Thus a social order is always a factual order in so far as it is susceptible of scientific analysis but, as will be later maintained, it is one which cannot have stability without the effective functioning of certain normative elements.

As has been shown, two normative features play an essential role in the utilitarian scheme, ends and rationality. Thus, for Hobbes, given the fact that men have passions and seek to pursue them rationally, the problem arises of whether, or under what conditions, this is possible in a social situation where there is a plurality of men acting in relation to one another. Given one other fact, which Hobbes refers to as the "equality of hope," the problem of order in the normative sense of a degree of attainability of ends, of satisfaction of the passions, becomes crucial. For under the assumption of rationality men will seek to attain their ends by the most efficient means available. Among their ends is empirically found to be attainment of the recognition of others. And to them under social conditions the services of others are always and necessarily to be found among the potential means to their ends. To securing both these, recognition and service, whether as ultimate or as proximate ends, the most immediately efficient means, in the last analysis, are force and fraud. In the utilitarian postulate of rationality there is nothing whatever to exclude the employment of these means. But the effect of their unlimited employment is that men will "endeavor to destroy or subdue one another." That is, according to the strictest utilitarian assumptions, under social conditions, a complete system of action will turn out to be a "state of war" as Hobbes says, that is, from the normative point of view of the attainment of human ends, which is itself the utilitarian starting point, not an order at all, but chaos. It is the state where any appreciable degree of such attainment becomes impossible, where the life of man is "solitary, poor, nasty, brutish and short."

The point under discussion here is not Hobbes' own solution of this crucial problem, by means of the idea of a social contract. This solution really involves stretching, at a critical point, the conception of rationality beyond its scope in the rest of the theory, to a point where the actors come to realize the situation as a whole instead of pursuing their own ends in terms of their immediate situation, and then take the action necessary to eliminate force and fraud, and, purchasing security at the sacrifice of the advantages to be gained by their future employment. This is not the solution in which the present study will be interested. But Hobbes saw the problem with a clarity which has never been surpassed, and his statement of it remains valid today. It is so fundamental that a genuine solution of it has never been attained on a strictly utilitarian basis, but has entailed either recourse to a radical positivistic expedient, or the breakdown of the whole positivistic framework.

Before leaving Hobbes it is important to elaborate a little further the reasons for the precariousness of order so far as the utilitarian elements actually dominate action. This precariousness rests, in the last analysis, on the existence of classes of things which are scarce, relative to the demand for them, which, as Hobbes says, "two [or more] men desire" but "which nevertheless they cannot both enjoy." Reflection will show that there are many such things desired by men either as ends in themselves or as means to other ends. But Hobbes, with his characteristic penetration, saw that it was not necessary to enumerate and catalogue them and to rest the argument on such a detailed consideration, but that their crucial importance was inherent in the very existence of social relations themselves. For it is inherent in the latter that the actions of men should be potential means to each other's ends. Hence as a proximate end it is a direct corollary of the postulate of rationality that all men should desire and seek power over one another. Thus the concept of power comes to occupy a central position in the analysis of the problem of order. A purely utilitarian society is chaotic and unstable, because in the absence of limitations on the use of means, particularly force and fraud, it must, in the nature of the case, resolve itself into an unlimited struggle for power; and in the struggle for the immediate end, power, all prospect of attainment of the ultimate, of what Hobbes called the diverse passions, is irreparably lost.

If the above analysis is correct one might suppose that Hobbes' early experiments with logical thinking on a utilitarian basis would have brought that type of social thought to a rapid and deserved demise. But such was very far from being the case, indeed in the eighteenth and nineteenth centuries it enjoyed a period of such vogue as to be considered almost among the eternal verities themselves. But this was not because the Hobbesian problem was satisfactorily solved. On the contrary, as so often happens in the history of thought, it was blithely ignored and covered up by implicit assumptions. How did this happen?

It is significant that the immediate practical animus of Hobbes' social thought lay in the defense of political authority on a secular basis. A strong government, justified by the social contract, was a necessary bulwark of the security of the commonwealth, threatened as it was by the imminent danger of the resurgence of force and fraud. It has already been remarked that in the argument over political obligation those who defend individual liberty tend to make use of normative rather than factual arguments. It is largely in this context that what later came to be the dominant stream of utilitarian thought developed, so that Hobbes was virtually forgotten. In the process of development there took place a subtle change. What started as normative arguments about what ought to be, became embodied in the assumptions of what was predominantly considered a factual, scientific theory of human action as it was. By some this theory was looked upon as literally descriptive of the existing social order; by others, more skeptically as, though not the whole truth, at least justified for heuristic purposes; and above all in either case as constituting the working conceptual tools of a great tradition of thought. Hence for present purposes it matters little which of the two positions was taken since the empirical qualifications of utilitarian theory were embodied in residual categories which played no positive part in the theoretical system itself, at least until the time of its incipient breakdown.

5

RATIONALITY AND UTILITARIANISM

The starting point, both historical and logical, is the conception of intrinsic rationality of action. This involves the fundamental elements of "ends," "means" and "conditions" of rational action and the norm of the intrinsic means-end relationship. The rationality of action in terms of the latter is measured by the conformity of choice of means, within the conditions of the situation, with the expectations derived from a scientific theory applied to the data in question and stated, as Pareto puts it, in the "virtual" form. Action in these terms is rational in so far as there is a scientifically demonstrable probability that the means employed will, within the conditions of the actual situation, bring about or maintain the future state of affairs that the actor anticipates as his end.

Historically, this concept of rationality of action, not always clearly and unambiguously stated, has played the central role in what has been called the utilitarian branch of the positivistic tradition. In spite of differences due to varying assumptions about the environment in which rational action operates, it has been, in its essential structure, a constant structural element of the systems of thought considered here. The two radically positivistic polar positions do, however, alter its status in essential respects. The rationalistic position does so by erasing the distinctions between ends, means and conditions of rational action, making action a process only of adaptation to given conditions and predictions of their future state. The anti-intellectualistic position in its really radical form alters the status of rationality still more fundamentally; at the pole, indeed, eliminating it altogether. Both radical positivist positions, however, involve insuperable difficulties—methodological and empirical.

The utilitarian type of theory concentrated on the means-end relationship and left the character of ends on the whole uninvestigated. This was sound. But in so far as it tended to become a closed system on a positivistic basis it was forced to the assumption that ends were random relative to the positivistically determinate elements of action. On this basis any attempt to bring order into this random variation led in the direction of radical positivistic determinism. In the cases of hedonism, the theory of natural selection, etc. several of these attempts have been reviewed and their consequences worked out. The utilitarian assumption, explicit or implicit, of random ends is the only possible way to uphold on a positivistic basis the voluntaristic character of action, the independence of ends and the other normative elements of the structure of action from determinism in terms of heredity and environment.

Within the range of the utilitarian tradition and variations from it in the direction of the radical positivistic pole, there have appeared all the main relations of the norm of intrinsic rationality to the elements formulated in the radical positivistic theories, that is, to heredity and environment. These may be seen in two main contexts. In so far as action is conceived as a process of rational adaptation of means to ends, they appear in the role of ultimate means and conditions of action. The qualification "ultimate" is made necessary by the fact that what are means and conditions to any given concrete actor may be in large part results of the other action elements of other individuals. To avoid reasoning in a circle it is necessary to think in terms of what are ultimate analytical conditions of action in general, abstracting from the concrete conditions of a particular concrete act. Failure clearly to make this distinction has been shown to be a prolific source of confusion. Another warning of the same order may be repeated. The same elements of heredity and environment play a part in determining the concrete ends of action. Such a concrete end is an anticipated concrete state of affairs, involving elements of the external environment and of heredity. Hedonism clearly illustrates this situation. Pleasure as an end of action was plausible because the psychological mechanisms that produce pleasurable feelings in certain circumstances are, in fact, expected to operate in the process leading to the desired state of affairs. But this has nothing to do with the analytical concept of end as part of a generalized system. It is a feature of the organism which we know by experience we can count on to operate in certain ways, and which hence belongs analytically to the conditions of action. To speak of ends as determined by the mechanism of pleasure is to that extent to eliminate ends from the generalized theoretical system.

Secondly, the same elements of heredity and environment appear in relation to failure to attain the rational norm. From the objective point of view they appear mainly as reasons why action either falls short of or deviates from the norm, what have been called the resistant and the deviating factors, respectively. Subjectively the same factors in the same role appear as the sources of ignorance and error. Error in this sense is not random, but rather the existence of a bias of error in a particular direction is *ipso facto* evidence that a nonrational deviating factor is at work. Above all, within the positivistic framework, departures from the norm of rationality must be reducible, from the subjective point of view, to terms of ignorance or error or both.

Finally, it is not to be forgotten that there may well be hereditary elements which "drive" behavior in conformity with a rational norm but without the independent agency of the actor which is basic to the voluntaristic conception of action. In so far as this is true, whatever subjective aspect there is to action will turn out, on thorough investigation, to be reducible to terms of nonsubjective systems. The test is always whether an adequate explanation of the concrete behavior in question can be attained without reference to the elements formulated in concepts with an inherent subjective reference.

Thus it is seen that both the norm of intrinsic rationality itself, and its main relations to heredity and environment in all three of the modes just outlined, could on the whole be adequately formulated within the general framework of the positivistic theoretical system, so long as it does not go over to the radical positivistic pole. It has, however, been shown that the utilitarian position is inherently unstable, and that in order to maintain it within a positivistic framework it is necessary to employ an extra-positivistic, metaphysical prop, which in the cases analyzed here has taken the form of the postulate of the natural identity of interests. Hence the more rigorously and systematically the implications of the positivistic position have been carried through, the more precarious has become the status of the normative elements of action which could find adequate formulation within a positivistic framework.

Indeed it may be held that the growing pressure of this increasingly rigorous systematization of the remoter implications of the positivistic approach to the study of human action has played an important part in the movement of thought which has occupied this study. The form of primary interest here is an increasingly sharp presentation of the "utilitarian dilemma": either a really radical positivistic position or the strictly utilitarian. The former course involved abandoning completely the means-end schema as analytically indispensable, the latter meant increasing dependence on extrascientific metaphysical assumptions. In the generally positivistic state of opinion all the weight of "hard-boiled" scientific prestige seemed to lie on the radically positivistic side. But at the same time the utilitarian tenets rested on sound empirical insight which could not readily be explained away. Hence the stage was set for a radical theoretical reconstruction that would transcend the dilemma altogether.

6

THE PATTERN VARIABLES

The role-partner in a social relationship is a social object. To
develop a systematic scheme of points of reference for the
analysis of orientations in roles it is then essential first to analyze
those basic alternatives of selection which are particularly
significant in defining the character of relations to such a social
object, and which are constitutive of the character of the relationship pattern itself rather than of its "content" in interest
terms, its cultural or motivational aspects in any sense other than
as constitutive of relational patterns. The following discussion is
posited on the view that there is on a given level of generality a
strictly limited and defined set of such alternatives, and that the
relative primacies given to choices between them can be treated
as constitutive of the patterning of relational institutions.

We will bring out a limited number of polar alternatives of
possible orientation-selection. These alternatives will be defined
in terms of relative primacies among the types of orientation possibilities which have been discussed in previous sections.

The first problem then is that of primary relations as between
instrumental, expressive and moral orientations (including the
sub-types of the latter). In motivational terms it may be presumed
that the "ultimate" interest of any actor is in the optimization of
gratification. The most *direct* path to gratification in an organized
action system is through expressive orientations; hence relative
to the expressive, both the instrumental and the moral modes of

orientation impose renunciations or discipline. The social object is always actually and potentially to some degree an object of cathexis.

Hence in patterning the orientation to that object it is always a problem whether in certain relevant respects, expressive orientation in terms of relatively immediate gratification interests is permissible, or is to be renounced in favor of instrumental or moral, that is certain types of evaluative interests. The first alternative may be defined as that of "affectivity," the second of "affective neutrality." This basic alternative is grounded in the nature of action systems. No actor can subsist without gratifications, while at the same time no action system can be organized or integrated without the renunciation of *some* gratifications which are available in the given situation. The polarity of affectivity-neutrality formulates the patterning out of action with respect to this basic alternative, in direct orientations to the social objects with whom an actor interacts in a role, and in its relevance to the structure of the expectations of his action in that role.

This first alternative-pair focuses on the permissibility or nonpermissibility of gratifying the actor's *immediate* adjustive interests by expressive activity. The second concerns the same intrinsic problem approached from the other end, as it were, namely the permissibility of his pursuing *any* interests "private" to himself as distinguished from those shared with the other members of the collectivity in which he plays a role. Thus not only his expressive, but his instrumental and ego-integrative orientations and the corresponding interests are defined as "private" in so far as they do not coincide with those recognized as collective by the collectivity. A role, then, may define certain areas of pursuit of private interests as legitimate, and in other areas obligate the actor to pursuit of the common interests of the collectivity. The primacy of the former alternative may be called "self-orientation," that of the latter, "collectivity-orientation."

Both these alternative-pairs raise an important problem of interpretation. It may rightly be said that just as every actor must both have immediate gratifications and accept discipline, so must every role both provide for pursuit of private interests and ensure

the interests of the collectivity. This circumstance is not a
paradox, because, defined as a matter of orientation-primary in
role-expectations these alternatives apply to specifically relevant
selection-contexts, not necessarily to every specific act within the
role. Thus where effective instrumental pursuit of a certain class
of goals is institutionalized as part of the role, *only* the gratification of expressive interests which might interfere with the attainment of these goals must be subordinated; the role is defined in
affectively neutral terms in *this* context but not necessarily in all
others. In the relevant choice-dilemma one alternative is prescribed. But this prescription is always relative to a specified
context in which the dilemma arises. Similarly we would only
speak of a role as collectivity-oriented if the pursuit of *certain*
private interests which were relevant possibilities in the *given*
type of situation was subordinated to the collective interest. Thus
the public official has an interest in his own financial well-being,
which for example he may take into account in deciding between
jobs, but he is expected not to take this into consideration in his
specific decisions respecting public policy where the two potentially conflict. This is the subordination of an instrumental (or
ego-integrative) personal value.

The first two alternative pairs have been concerned with the
expression-discipline problem which confronts all action systems
on two levels: first, the obligation to acceptance of discipline by
the individual actor vis-à-vis his expressive interests, the
gratification of which would, in *this* role context, be felt to be
disruptive; second the same dilemma reappears in relation to the
pursuit of *any* sort of private interests, no matter how highly
disciplined in a personality sense vis-à-vis the definition of obligations to the collectivity. Indeed, in this context often the most
highly disciplined pursuit of private interests may be the most
dysfunctional in collectivity terms. The third alternative pair concerns not subordination to vs. freedom from certain value standards whatever their content, but the *type* of value-standard
which is defined as relevant to the role-expectation. Here recourse must be had to primacy relations among the modes of
value-orientation themselves, since these define types of standard
by which action-orientations are evaluated. Hence the basic

alternative is between the primacy of cognitive and appreciative standards. What does this mean in the present context?

Cognitive orientation is, it may be said, essentially orientation to the element of generalization in the object-world. Cathectic orientation on the other hand, is inherently particularized, to particular objects and ordered combinations of them. If generalization is paramount in cognitive orientation, then the standards characterized by cognitive primacy cannot be particular to the specific relational system (with non-social as well as social objects) in which the actor is involved. It transcends this relational context. Normatively its orientation is to universal canons of validity.

In the case of cathectic orientation and the cognate modes of action- and value-orientation, there is an inherently "subjective" reference to gratification-significance. But the gratificational significance of an orientation can never transcend the particular relational system of which it is a part. The standard must be couched in terms of significance *for this particular actor in these particular relations with these particular objects*. The primacy of cognitive values then may be said to imply a *universalistic* standard of role-expectation, while that of appreciative values implies a *particularistic* standard. In the former case the standard is derived from the validity of a set of existential ideas, or the generality of a normative rule, in the latter from the particularity of the cathectic significance of an object or of the status of the object in a relational system. Thus definitions of role-expectations in terms of a universally valid moral precept, e.g., the obligation to fulfill contractual agreements, an empirical cognitive generalization, or a selection for a role in terms of the belief that technical competence in the relevant respects will increase the effectiveness of achievement in the role, are universalistic definitions of roles. On the other hand definitions in such terms as "I must try to help him because he is my friend," or of obligations to a kinsman, a neighbor, or the fellow-member of any solidary group *because of this membership as such* are particularistic.

There is one common source of confusion in this field which must be cleared up at once. It derives from the fact that a particularistic role-obligation may be formulated in terms of a general rule in the sense that it states *in general terms* the particularistic obligations of all those in the relevant class of roles. Thus "honor thy father and thy mother" is stated as a general rule of morality. But it is its form that is general. The *content* of the obligation is particularistic, namely for each child, toward *his particular* parents. If the rule were, on the other hand, "pay honor to parents because of their quality of parenthood as such, regardless of whose parents they are," it would be a universalistic norm. *All* norms are capable of generality of statement and application (though varying greatly in degree of generality). The question is whether or not a *discrimination* is made between those objects with which ego stands in a particularistic relationship and *other objects possessing the same attributes.* Such a discrimination is incompatible with the conception of a universalistic norm. If parenthood is the relevant attribute, then the norm, if it is universalistic, applies equally to all objects possessing that attribute.

The first three alternative-pairs have been defined in terms of relative primacy relations of the orientational components of action, that is, with reference to ego as actor. In terms of primary functional significance for the patterning of role-orientations these three are exhaustive of the major possibilities, *on the same level of generality.* But they have not taken account of the total frame of reference. There remain alternatives with respect to the *characteristics* of social objects themselves, that is, from ego's point of view of the *alter* in the complementary role-orientation structure or to ego himself as an object, and with reference to the *scope* of relevance of alter as an object. These contexts produce two further alternative-pairs.

In both cases it is essential to strike just the right level of generality which is coordinate with that of the relevance of the first three pairs. Applying this criterion it seems that there is one dilemma which is of the most generalized significance in each context. With respect to characteristics of the object it is that of the focus on its qualities or attributes as distinguished from focus on its performances. "Performance" in this sense is a characteristic which, by definition, we have confined to the category of social objects. But the "alter" who is the complementary member of a reciprocal role-orientation system is also by definition a social object, and therefore is characterized by performance.

Orientation to the actor's performance (which may be either ego's or alter's or both) means that the focus is on his achievement. The expectation is that the actor is committed to the achievement of certain goals or expressive performances and that expectations are oriented to his "effectiveness" or "success" in achieving them, hence that positive sanctions will reward such success and negative sanctions will ensue in case of failure to achieve. There are of course all manner of complications such as the definition of what constitute "extenuating circumstances," but this is the major axis of the expectation structure.

On the other hand, even though actors can and do perform in the above sense, the major focus of a particular role-expectation need not be on this performance. All objects have attributes, they not only *do* this or that, but they *are* such and such. They have attributes of sex, age, intelligence, physical characteristics, statuses in relational systems, e.g., collectivity memberships. The focus of orientation then may be what the object *is* in this sense, e.g., *that* he is ego's father, that he is a physician, or that he is over six feet tall. Such attributes or quality-complexes may be conditions of a variety of performances, for physical or social reasons, but even so the orientation focus may still be the quality as such. This may be the criterion for differentiation of treatment and of expectations of his behavior.

This distinction has become current in the sociological literature in Linton's terms of achieved and ascribed status and hence it seems advisable to adopt those terms here. Achievement-oriented roles are those which place the accent on the performances of the incumbent, ascribed roles, on his qualities or attributes independently of specific expected performances.

The incidence of the alternative as between qualities and performances involves a further set of ramifications beyond the ascription-achievement distinction with reference to role-expectations, which because of their general importance in the theory of action may be brought to attention here. These concern its application to the definition of ideal states of affairs where they differ from a given initial state. Where performances are the focus of value-orientation the emphasis may be on the goal as the "expression," as it were, of the valued achievement-process. On the other hand the valuation of the goal-state as such may emphasize its qualities independently of the processes of its achievement. We shall see that this distinction is of considerable significance in defining different patterns of orientation to "ideal" states of affairs.

The achievement-ascription alternative-pair concerns characteristics of the object which may be selected as the focus of orientation. There remains the question of the scope of ego's "interest" in the object. It has been noted above how crucially important is the differentiation of modes of orientation of action and the corresponding differentiation of types of orientations in terms of primacies. But this differentiation has been treated in terms of the orientation of an actor taken as a point of reference without regard to the question of whether the different modes of orientation were segregated out in relation to different objects, or combined in orientation to the same object. This question of the relative incidence of "fusions" and "segregations" of action-orientation types will be seen to be of the greatest importance for the analysis of social structure.

When many empirical differences are taken into account it will prove to be possible to derive very complex permutations and combinations in this respect. But on the present level of generality the starting point should again be the evaluative types of action-orientation as such. Here a particular instrumental or expressive orientation or interest has a certain specificity such that is capable of clear analytical segregation from the other or from moral orientations. Hence one horn of the dilemma will be the definition of the role as orienting to the social object in *specific* terms, that is in terms of a specific instrumental or expressive interest. This is, it will be noted, a definition of the scope of the object's (alter's) significance to ego. Since it is defined in terms of a moral value-pattern it means that he is held to be *entitled* or even obligated to confine the relevance of this particular object or class of them within these limits. Hence the burden of proof rests on him who would suggest that ego has obligations vis-à-vis the object in question which transcend this specificity of relevance.

The alternative is to treat the object as significant in an indefinite plurality of specific orientation contexts. This always implies a moral element because the problem of evaluative integration of the different components of the total orientation to the object is by definition involved. Conversely the binding together of such a plurality of such specific interests in a single object-relation always implies a moral component in the orientation (note, this may be only ego-integrative, not relational. It does not imply consideration for the welfare of the object—a range of variation which is conceptualized in terms of self- vs. collectivity-orientation). Hence the clear antithesis of the specific, interest-segregated type of orientation is a *diffuse* mode, where the burden of proof is on the side of the exclusion of an interest or mode of orientation as outside the range of obligations defined by the role-expectation. This proof can be furnished by invoking an obligation higher in a scale of evaluative priority.

As in the cases of the other alternative-pairs it is essential here to keep in mind the relativity of this conceptualization. Like the others it applies at the choice-point to *directions* of orientation. It is a question at such a point of confining relevance and hence obligation to a specific interest (definable on various levels of generality) or of admitting the *possible* relevance in terms of integrative evaluation and subject to a priority scale, of any contingency which might arise.

If the derivation of these five alternative pairs from possibilities of the combination of the basic components of the action system has been correct, if they are in fact all on the same level of generality and are exhaustive of the relevant logical possibilities on that level, they may be held to constitute a system. Then, on the relevant level which, as we shall see is *only one* which needs to be considered, their permutations and combinations should yield a system of types of possible role-expectation pattern, on the relational level, namely defining the pattern of orientation to the actors in the role relationship. This system [consists of] thirty-two types, which may in turn be grouped into a smaller number of more fundamental ones.

For the convenience of the reader these five concept-pairs, called the *pattern variables* of role-definition, may be schematically outlined as follows:

   I. The Gratification-Discipline Dilemma
      Affectivity vs. Affective Neutrality
  II. The Private vs. Collective Interest Dilemma
      Self-Orientation vs. Collectivity-Orientation
 III. The Choice Between Types of Value-Orientation Standard
      Universalism vs. Particularism
  IV. The Choice between "Modalities" of the Social Object
      Achievement vs. Ascription
   V. The Definition of Scope of Interest in the Object
      Specificity vs. Diffuseness.

That these five pattern variables are focused on the relational aspect of the role structure of the social system does not mean that they are irrelevant to the definition of the patterns of regulative and of cultural institutions. They cannot be, if only because of the element of consistency of pattern which must run throughout a system of value-orientations in a cultural tradition. But for us the system of relational institutions is the core of the social structure and it will facilitate development of the analysis to start from this core and work out from there.

II. INSTITUTIONALIZATION

"Integration and Institutionalization in the Social System" is a brief but key passage from *Toward a General Theory of Action* (1951). This selection enunciates the key theorem of the theory of action: The integration of social systems is a consequence of the institutionalization of normative culture. That is, social interaction can be coordinated because norms and values come to be stably defined and routinely supported by the fixed interests of actors. The next two selections, "The Superego and the Theory of Social Systems" (1952) and "Illness and the Role of the Physician" (1951), illustrate the importance of Freudian approaches to institutionalization in Parsons's work of the early fifties. As long as the internalization of norms was viewed as the principal mechanism of institutionalization, Freud's account of socialization provided a compelling starting point.

In "The Hierarchy of Control," a brief selection from the "Outline of the Social System" (*Theories of Society,* 1961), we see a new macrosociological account of institutionalization: institutionalization involves not just the socialization of individual actors but the accommodation of cultural values to the full range of the exigencies of organized social life. There follow two selections illustrating analyses of the opposite ends of the hierarchy of control. "Specification," another portion of the

"Outline of the Social System," describes the highest
level of the hierarchy of control, the interpretation of
the meaning of high-order social values and norms.
"Jurisdiction," a selection from "The Principal
Structures of Community" (1961), describes the lowest
level of social condition within the hierarchy of control:
control ultimately implies physical access to concrete
persons in concrete territorial locations.

7

INTEGRATION AND INSTITUTIONALIZATION IN THE SOCIAL SYSTEM

Institutionalization

In a social system, roles vary in the degree of their institutionalization. By institutionalization we mean the integration of the complementary role-expectation and sanction patterns with a generalized value system *common* to the members of the more inclusive collectivity, of which the system of complementary role-actions may be a part. Insofar as ego's set of role-expectations is institutionalized, the sanctions which express the role-expectations of the other actors will tend to reinforce his own need-dispositions to conform with these expectations by rewarding it and by punishing deviance.

Solidarity is characterized by the institutionalization of shared value-orientations; the values being, of course, oriented toward collective gratifications. Acceptance of common value patterns permits the more differentiated institutionalization of the action of the members of the collectivity in a wide range of specific situations. The range may be broad or narrow, but in each specific situation institutionalization exists when each actor in the situation does, and believes he should do, what the other actors whom he confronts believe he should do. Thus institutionalization is an articulation or integration of the actions of a plurality of actors in a specific type of situation in which the various actors accept

Reprinted by permission with deletions from *Toward a General Theory of Action* by Talcott Parsons (Cambridge: Harvard University Press, 1951). Copyright 1951 by The President and Fellows of Harvard College.

jointly a set of harmonious rules regarding goals and procedures. The concrete content of these rules will differ, in the same situation, from actor to actor and from role to role. But the rules, if followed in such a situation of full institutionalization, will lead to perfectly articulated, conflictless action on the part of the several actors. These rules possess their harmonious character by virtue of their derivation, by deliberation and less conscious processes, from common value-orientations which are the same for all members of the institution or the set of institutions in the collectivity. These value-orientations contain general standards in accordance with which objects of various classes are judged, evaluated, and classified as worthy of various types of response of rewards and punishments.

Institutionalizing Roles

A social system is a system of the actions of individuals, the principal units of which are roles and constellations of roles. It is a system of differentiated actions, organized into a system of differentiated roles. Internal differentiation, which is a fundamental property of all systems, requires integration. It is a condition of the existence of the system that the differentiated roles must be coördinated either negatively, in the sense of the avoidance of disruptive interference with each other, or positively, in the sense of contributing to the realization of certain shared collective goals through collaborated activity.

When a plurality of individual actors are each oriented in a situation to gratify sets of need-dispositions, certain resultant phenomena are inevitable. By virtue of the primordial fact that the objects—social and nonsocial—which are instrumentally useful or intrinsically valuable are scarce in relation to the amount required for the full gratification of the need-dispositions of every actor, there arises a problem of allocation: the problem of who is to get what, who is to do what, and the manner and conditions under which it is to be done. This is the fundamental problem which arises from the interaction of two or more actors.

As a result of the scarcity of the social and nonsocial objects of need-dispositions, the mutual incompatibility of claims might extend theoretically in the extreme case to the "state of nature." It would be the war of "each against all" in its Hobbesian formulation. The function of allocation of roles, facilities, and rewards does not, however, have to contend with this extreme possibility. The process of socialization in the family, school, and play groups, and in the community focuses need-dispositions in such a way that the degree of incompatibility of the active aspirations and claims for social and nonsocial objects is reduced, in "normal conditions," to the usually executable task of making allocations among sectors of the population, most of whose claims will not too greatly exceed what they are receiving. Without a solution of this problem, there can be no social system. It is indeed one of the functions which makes the social system. It arises in every social system, and though the solutions can vary within limits which from the standpoint of ethical values might be very wide apart, yet every allocative process must have certain properties which are common to all of them. Where the allocative process is not carried out successfully—where the allocative process either interferes with effective collaboration or is not regarded as sufficiently legitimate—the social system in question will tend to disintegrate and to give way to another social system.

The term *allocation* should not be interpreted anthropomorphically. Allocation is a resultant that is only in part a product of deliberate decision; the total allocation in a social system especially may be the product of many processes that culminate in a distribution which no individual or collective actor in the system has sought.

A social system must possess a minimum degree of integration; there must be, that is, a sufficient complementarity of roles and clusters of roles for collective and private goals to be effectively pursued. Although conflict can exist within a social system and, in fact, always does, there are limits beyond which it cannot go and still permit a social system to exist. By definition the complementarity of expectations which is associated with the complementarity of roles is destroyed by conflict. Consequently, when conflict becomes so far reaching as to negate the complementarity of expectations, there the social system has ceased to exist. Hence, for conflict among individuals and groups to be kept within bounds, the roles and role clusters must be brought into appropriately complementary relations with one another.

It is highly important to what follows to distinguish here two functional problems of social systems: (1) *What* roles are to be institutionalized in the social system? (2) *Who* is to perform these roles? Every social system has certain tasks imposed on it by the fact that its members are mortal physiological organisms, with physiological and social needs, existing in a physical environment together with other like organisms. Some variability is possible regarding the tasks which are considered as worthy of being undertaken (in the light of the prevailing value-orientations and the external situation of the social system). This selection of tasks or functions may be phrased as an answer to the question "what should be done with the existing resources of the society?" in the sense of what *jobs* are to be done.

The first allocative function of a social system, therefore, is the allocation of human capacities and human resources among tasks. In addition to a distribution of resources among tasks or functions which can be performed only by a complex of roles, each social system, inasmuch as its members are not born genetically destined to particular functional roles, must allocate its members among those roles. Also, since tasks change, and with them the roles by which they can be met, reallocation is a necessity quite in addition to that imposed by man's birth, plasticity and mortality. One of the ways in which this is done in some social systems is by definition of the criteria of eligibility for incumbency of the role by membership in solidary groups, thus regulating the flow of persons into such roles. In all social systems access to roles is regulated by the possession of qualifications which might be, but are not always necessarily, memberships or qualities.

A closely related allocative problem in the social system concerns the allocation of *facilities* for the performance of roles. The concept of role has been defined as a complementary set of expectations and the actions to be performed in accordance with these expectations. It includes as part of the expectations the rights to certain types of reaction which the actor is entitled to expect from others and the obligations to perform certain types of action which the actor believes others are entitled to expect from him. It is convenient to distinguish *facilities* from the other components in the definition of role. The term refers to those features of the situation, outside the actual actions entailed in the performance of role itself, which are instrumentally important to the actor in the fulfillment of the expectations concerning his role. Thus one cannot be a scholar without the use of books or a farmer without the use of the land for cultivation.

Facilities thus are objects of orientation which are actually or potentially of instrumental significance in the fulfillment of role-expectations. They *may* consist of physical objects, but not necessarily. The physical objects may, to varying degrees, be "natural" objects or manmade objects, such as buildings or tools. They may be the physical embodiments of cultural objects, such as books. The cultural objects may be accessible not through a physical but through a human agent; we may cite as an illustration of such a facility the type of knowledge which must be secured orally from another human being.

In the same sense that we speak of the *rights* to the *action of others* and the *obligations* to perform the *actions expected by others*, the facilities which are necessary roles are likewise the objects of rights and obligations. When the facility is a social object—that is, the action of another person—it becomes identical with the action to which one has a right and concerning which one has certain obligations. It should, however, be stressed that not all the complementary responses of alter are classifiable as facilities. Only those which ego has the right to use in an instrumental manner, without *specific* regulation by a shared and collective value-orientation, are to be designated as facilities. When a social object, either an individual or a collective action system, is a facility, it may be called an opportunity; privileges are unequally distributed opportunities.

The regulation of the relationship between the incumbent of a role or the "possessor" of a facility and actual or potential claimants to displace that possessor is part of the allocation problem. This is of course a major aspect of the institution of "property." The allocation of facilities, as of roles, is made on the basis of the actor's possession of qualities or his manifestation of performances. Rights of access to facilities may, for example, be contingent on the possession of a membership "quality" or on certain performances. The peasant may own his own land by virtue of his membership in a family; the factory worker does not himself own his machine, and his access to it is dependent on his fulfillment of certain performances specified in the "contract of employment" with the company in which ownership is vested, and whose claims are protected by the power of the state and the general value-orientation prevailing in the culture.

The allocation of facilities in a social system may be viewed as an aspect of the allocation of power. There are two senses in which this is so. First is the fact that, while the particular facilities appropriate to the attainment of particular goals may have many singular characteristics, the widespread competition for facilities (which are used to reward collaborators) gives an especially high value to those facilities which have the generalized property of enabling more specific facilities to be acquired. A facility is often such that it can be used to pursue quite a wide variety of goals that might themselves be facilities or substantive goals. This generalized potency is enormously enhanced by the development of money, which is a general medium of exchange, so that "having the price" becomes in effect equivalent to having the concrete facility on the more general level. To have the power to command by virtue of the possession of money or any other qualification is equivalent to having the concrete facility, since the latter can be purchased with the former.

Second, the achievement of goals is often possible in a social system only through collaboration in complementary role situations. One of the means of ensuring collaboration in the pursuit of goals is to control the actions of others in the relevant respects—positively by commanding their services or negatively by at least being in a position to prevent their interference. Therefore the degrees to which and the ways in which an actor (individual or collective) is enabled to control the action of others in the same social system is dependent on the facilities which have been allocated to it (or him). Facilities are powers over objects, social and nonsocial. Power, by its very nature, is a relatively scarce object; its possession by one actor in a relationship is a restriction of the other actor's power. Its intrinsic scarcity and its generalized instrumental status make it into one of the most avidly and vigorously competed for of all objects—we pass over here its very great importance as a direct cathectic object for the immediate gratification of a variety of derivative need-dispositions. It is therefore of the greatest urgency for the determinate allocation of power and the derivative allocations of other facilities to be established and generally accepted in a society. Unless this allocation is well integrated internally and with the value system so that its legitimacy is widely acknowledged, the amount of conflict within the social system may very well rise to the point of disintegration.

The allocation of rewards is the systematic outcome of the gratification-orientation of action. It is in the nature of action for gratifications to be sought. Here as much as in the preceding categories of allocation, the objects which gratify need-dispositions are scarcer than would be necessary to satisfy the demand—indeed, in the allocation of rewards, it is sometimes its very scarcity which gives an object its function of gratifying a need-disposition, that is, makes it into a reward. In a system of interaction each of the actors will strive for rewards, the attainment of which might not only be reciprocally contingent, but they might indeed actually come from the same source. The amount one actor gets will affect the amounts other actors get. The resultant, in most societies, is a distribution of rewards that is deliberately controlled only to a restricted extent. It is a resultant of the prior distribution of facilities and is effected by allocative mechanisms which work within the framework of a system of value-orientation.

In the social system the allocation of rewards has the dual function of maintaining or modifying motivation and of affecting the allocation of facilities. Where allocations of rewards diverge too widely from what is thought by the aspirant to be his right in the light of his qualifications, his motivation for the performance of his role will be affected. The effects might range from the inhibition of the need-disposition underlying the previous action to fixation and intensification of the attachment to the gratification object, to the point of disregarding the obligations usually associated with the rights to the object. The maintenance or change of object-attachment is influenced not only by the degree of congruity or discrepancy between expected (entitled) and received rewards but also by the actor's beliefs about the prevailing congruities and discrepancies between entitled and received rewards in the social system at large. Hence, as a cognitive and cathectic-evaluative object, the distribution of rewards plays a large independent part in the motivation of action and particularly in the motivation of conformity and alienation vis-à-vis general value-orientations and specific role-expectations.

The distinction between rewards and facilities is by and large not one between the "intrinsic" properties of the relevant objects, but concerns rather their functional relation in systems of action. A facility has instrumental significance; it is desired for uses to which it can be put. A reward, on the other hand, is an object desired for its own sake. The same concrete object may be, and indeed often is, *both* facility and reward to an actor. Not only may an object which is useful as a facility be accepted as a reward, but objects which have a high significance as rewards might also be facilities leading to further rewards. Also, in the motivational system of the actor, there is a tendency for particular facilities to acquire reward value. Hence an object which is useful as a facility comes to be cathected directly so that its possession is also interpreted by the actor and by others as a reward. Nevertheless, it is proper to distinguish these two phases of the allocative problem of the social system.

Just as the problem of allocation of facilities raises the problem of the allocation of power, so the allocation of rewards raises the problem of the allocation of *prestige,* and for similar reasons. Specific rewards, like specific facilities, may have highly specific relations with certain actions which they reward. But the very fact that they become the objects of competing claims—which is, of course, the fact from which the "problem" of allocation derives—is in part evidence of their generalizability to cover the claims of different individuals and to reward the different types of performance. This generalizability intensifies the concentrations of reward value on certain classes of valued objects: especially income, power, and prestige. To possess this generalized quality, each class of rewards must, in some sense, constitute a single

scale rendering equivalent different qualifications for the reward.
There will also tend to be a common evaluative scale cutting
across the different classes of rewards; for example, a scale which
enables income to be roughly equated to prestige. This evaluative
scale, of course, is seldom explicitly invoked.

It should be made somewhat clearer in just what senses income
and power are to be treated as rewards and not as facilities. Their
generalized character is of significance to *both* functions. But the
way in which income and power are integrated into systems of
instrumental orientation makes it inevitable that they should be
valued; the possession of *anything* valued—the more so if comparison with others is, as it must be, involved—is a source of
prestige. Their acquisition, then, can become a goal of action and
success in acquisition a *measure* of achievement. Finally, the
man with money or power is valued not only for what he has done
but for what he *can do,* because possession of generalized
facilities widens the range of capacity for achievement. Thus the
status of money and power as rewards goes back fundamentally
to the valuation of achievement and to their acceptance as *symbols* of achievement, whether actual or potential.

The allocation of power in a society is the allocation of access
to or control over the means of attaining goals, whatever they
may be. The allocation of prestige, correspondingly, is the
allocation of one of the most generalized gratifications which is, at
the same time, a very generalized qualification for access to
facilities and thus to further and other rewards.

The Integration of the Social System

This brings us to the consideration of the integrative problems
of the social system. From the present point of view, the primary
integration of the social system is based on an integrated system
of generalized patterns of value-orientation. These patterns of
value-orientation are to be described in the categories of the pattern variables. The pattern variables and the derivative patterns
of value-orientation can, however, never by themselves
adequately define the specific role-expectations which govern behavior in particular situations. Orientation to specific features of

the situation in particular ways must be developed in any social system. These will be elaborations and concrete specifications of the values derived from the pattern variables. .

A system or a subsystem of concerted action which (1) is governed by a *common* value-orientation and in which (2) the common values are motivationally integrated in action is, as we have said, a collectivity. It is this integration by common values, manifested in the action of solidary groups or collectivities, which characterizes the partial or total integrations of social systems.

Social integration, however much it depends on internalized norms, cannot be achieved by these alone. It requires also some supplementary coördination provided by explicit prescriptive or prohibitory role-expectations (e.g., laws) enunciated by actors in specially differentiated roles to which is attached "responsibility" in collective terms. *Responsibility* in this sense may be subdivided into two types: first, responsibility for the allocative functions in the social systems themselves, the definition and enforcement of the norms governing the allocative processes; second, responsibility for the conduct of communal affairs, for the performance of positive functions on behalf of the collectivity, especially vis-à-vis "foreign" social systems or subsystems. Insofar as such roles of responsibility are institutionally defined, they always involve a collective orientation on the part of their incumbents as one of their fundamental components.

The word institutionalization means both the internalization of common values by the members of a collectivity, and also the enunciation of prescriptive or prohibitory role expectations by occupants of responsible roles.

The institutionalization of value-orientation patterns thus constitutes, in the most general sense, the mechanisms of integration for social systems. However, social integration does not require a single uniform set of value-orientations equally and universally distributed throughout the social system. Social integration may well include a whole series of subsystems of common value-orientations varying around a basic pattern. Institutionally, this brings us before the integrative problem of partial integrations or collectivities within the larger social system, on the one hand, and the total collectivity as an integrated entity, on the other.

The role-expectations in all these situations are focused by the pattern variable of self- and collective-orientation. Every social system will have institutionalized definitions of the spheres within which a collective subunit or an individual is legitimately permitted to go its own way without specific reference to the interests of a larger collectivity, or to specific obligations toward it. On the other hand, there will be institutionalized spheres of direct obligation to the larger collectivity. This usually will be latent and will be active only discontinuously when situations arise in which the objects are threatened or in which conflict occurs. In the first case, negative sanctions apply only when the limits of permission are exceeded; in the second, they apply whenever the positive obligations fail to be fulfilled. Social systems, of course, will vary greatly with respect to the points at which this line is drawn. Only the solidary group in which there are positive collective obligations would, in a specific sense, be called an integrated social system.

There is a final point to be made in connection with social integration and nonintegration. No social system can be completely integrated; there will, for many reasons, always be some discrepancies between role-expectations and performances of roles. Similarly, at the other extreme, there is never likely to be a completely disintegrated society. The mere fact that the human beings who live in a social system are socialized to some extent gives them many need-dispositions which can be gratified only by conformity with the expectations of others and which make them responsive to the expectations of others. Even societies ridden with *anomie* (for example, extreme class conflict to the point of civil war) still possess within themselves considerable zones of solidarity. No society ever "disintegrates completely"; the "state of nature" depicted by Hobbes is never reached by any real society. Complete disintegration is a limiting case toward which social systems might sometimes move, especially in certain sectors of the structure, but they never arrive there. A particular social system might, of course, lose its identity, or it might be transformed into one which is drastically different and can become absorbed into another social system. It might split into several social systems where the main cleavages follow territorial lines. But dissolution into the "state of nature" is impossible.

A basic hypothesis in this type of analysis asserts the imperfect integration of all actual social systems. No one system of value-orientation with perfect consistency in its patterns can be fully institutionalized in a concrete society. There will be uneven distributions among the different parts of the society. There will be value conflicts and role conflicts. The consequence of such imperfect integration is in the nature of the case a certain instability, and hence a susceptibility to change if the balance of these forces, which is often extremely delicate, is shifted at some strategic point. Thus, change might result not only from open deviation from unequivocally institutionalized patterns but also from a shift in the balance between two or more positively institutionalized patterns, with an invasion of part of the sphere of one by another. The loopholes in the institutionalized system are one of the main channels through which such shifts often take place. Hence, in the combination of the inherent tendencies to deviation and the imperfections of the integration of value-orientations, there are in every social system inherent possibilities of change.

8

THE SUPEREGO AND THE THEORY OF SOCIAL SYSTEMS

In the broadest sense, perhaps, the contribution of psycho-analysis to the social sciences has consisted of an enormous deepening and enrichment of our understanding of human motivation. This enrichment has been such a pervasive influence that it would be almost impossible to trace its many ramifications. In the present paper I have chosen to say something about one particular aspect of this influence, that exerted through the psychoanalytic concept of the superego, because of its peculiarly direct relevance to the central theoretical interests of my own social-science discipline, sociological theory. This concept, indeed, forms one of the most important points at which it is possible to establish direct relations between psychoanalysis and sociology, and it is in this connection that I wish to discuss it.

Psychoanalysis, in common with other traditions of psychological thought, has naturally concentrated on the study of the personality of the individual as the focus of its frame of reference. Sociology, on the other hand, has equally naturally been primarily concerned with the patterning of the behavior of a plurality of individuals as constituting what, increasingly, we tend to call a social system. Because of historical differences of perspective and points of departure, the conceptual schemes arrived at from these two starting points have in general not been fully congruent

Reprinted with deletions by special permission of The William Alanson White Psychiatric Foundation, Inc., from "The Superego and the Theory of Social Systems." *Psychiatry* 15 (1952):15–24. Copyright © 1952 by The William Alanson White Psychiatric Foundation, Inc.

with each other, and this fact has occasioned a good deal of misunderstanding. However, recent theoretical work[1] shows that, in accord with convergent trends of thought, it is possible to bring the main theoretical trends of these disciplines together under a common frame of reference, that which some sociologists have called the "theory of action." It is in the perspective of this attempt at theoretical unification that I wish to approach the analysis of the concept of the superego.

One of the principal reasons for the selection of this concept lies in the fact that it has been, historically, at the center of an actual process of convergence. In part at least, it is precisely because of this fact that Freud's discovery of the internalization of moral values as an essential part of the structure of the personality itself constituted such a crucial landmark in the development of the sciences of human behavior. Though there are several other somewhat similar formulations to be found in the literature of roughly the same period, the formulation most dramatically convergent with Freud's theory of the superego was that of the social role of moral norms made by the French sociologist Emile Durkheim—a theory which has constituted one of the cornerstones of the subsequent development of sociological theory.

Durkheim's insights into this subject slightly antedated those of Freud.[2] Durkheim started from the insight that the individual, as a member of society, is not wholly free to make his own moral decisions but is in some sense "constrained" to accept the orientations common to the society of which he is a member. He went through a series of attempts at interpretation of the nature of this constraint, coming in the end to concentrate on two primary features of the phenomenon: first, that moral rules "constrain" behavior most fundamentally by moral authority rather than by any external coercion; and, secondly, that the effectiveness of moral authority could not be explained without assuming that, as we would now say, the value patterns were internalized as part of personality. Durkheim, as a result of certain terminological peculiarities which need not be gone into here, tended to identify "society" as such with the system of moral norms. In this very special sense of the term society, it is significant that he set forth the explicit formula that "society exists only in the minds of individuals."

In Durkheim's work there are only suggestions relative to the psychological mechanisms of internalization and the place of internalized moral values in the structure of personality itself. But this does not detract from the massive phenomenon of the convergence of the fundamental insights of Freud and Durkheim, insights not only as to the fundamental importance of moral values in human behavior, but of the internalization of these values. This convergence, from two quite distinct and independent starting points, deserves to be ranked as one of the truly fundamental landmarks of the development of modern social science. It may be likened to the convergence between the results of the experimental study of plant breeding by Mendel and of the microscopic study of cell division—a convergence which resulted in the discovery of the chromosomes as bearers of the genes. Only when the two quite distinct bodies of scientific knowledge could be put together did the modern science of genetics emerge.

The convergence of Freud's and Durkheim's thinking may serve to set the problem of this paper, which is: How can the fundamental phenomenon of the internalization of moral norms be analyzed in such a way as to maximize the generality of implications of the formulation, both for the theory of personality and for the theory of the social system? For if it is possible to state the essentials of the problem in a sufficiently generalized way, the analysis should prove to be equally relevant in both directions. It should thereby contribute to the integration of the psychoanalytic theory of personality and of the sociological theory of the social system, and thus to the further development of a conceptual scheme which is essentially common to both.

The essential starting point of an attempt to link these two bodies of theory is the analysis of certain fundamental features of the *inter*action of two or more persons, the process of interaction itself being conceived as a system. Once the essentials of such an interactive system have been made clear, the implications of the analysis can be followed out in *both* directions; the study of the structure and functioning of the personality as a system, in relation to other personalities; and the study of the functioning of the social system as a system. It may be surmised that the difficulty of bringing the two strands of thought together in the past has stemmed from the fact that this analysis has not been carried through; and this has not been done because it has "fallen between two stools," On the one hand, Freud and his followers, by concentrating on the single personality, have failed to consider adequately the implications of the individual's interaction with other personalities *to form a system*. On the other hand, Durkheim and the other sociologists have failed, in their concentration on the social system as a system to consider systematically the implications of the fact that it is the *interaction of personalities* which constitutes the social system with which they have been dealing, and that, therefore, adequate analysis of motivational process in such a system must reckon with the problems of personality. This circumstance would seem to account for the fact that this subject has been so seriously neglected.

It may first be pointed out that two interacting persons must be conceived to be objects to each other in two *primary* respects, and in a third respect which is in a sense derived from the first two. These are (1) cognitive perception and conceptualization, the answer to the question of *what the object is,* and (2) cathexis—attachment or aversion—the answer to the question of *what the object means* in an emotional sense. The third mode by which a person orients himself to an object is by evaluation—the integration of cognitive and cathectic meanings of the object to form a system, including the stability of such a system over time. It may be maintained that no stable relation between two or more objects is possible without all three of these modes of orientation being present for *both* parties to the relationship.

Consideration of the conditions on which such a stable, mutually oriented system of interaction depends leads to the conclusion that on the human level this mutuality of interaction must be mediated and stabilized by a *common culture*—that is, by a commonly shared system of symbols, the meanings of which are understood on both sides with an approximation to agreement. The existence of such symbol systems, especially though not exclusively as involved in language, is common to every known society. However the going symbol systems of the society may have developed in the first place, they are involved in the socialization of every child. It may be presumed that the prominence of common symbol systems is both a consequence and a condition of the extreme plasticity and sensitivity of the human organism, which in turn are essential conditions of its capacity to learn and, concomitantly, to mislearn. These features of the human organism introduce an element of extreme potential instability into the process of human interaction, which requires stabilizing mechanisms if the interactive system, as a system, is to function.

The elements of the common culture have significance with reference to all three of the modes of orientation of action. Some of them are primarily of cognitive significance; others are primarily of cathectic significance, expressive of emotional meanings or affect; and still others are primarily of evaluative significance. Normative regulation for the establishing of standards is characteristic of all of culture; thus there is a right way of symbolizing any orientation of action in any given culture. This is indeed essential to communication itself: the conventions of the language must be observed if there is to be effective communication.

That a person's cathexis of a human object—that is, what the object means to the person emotionally—is contingent on the responsiveness of that object is a fact familiar to psychoanalytic theory. It may be regarded as almost a truism that it is difficult if not impossible in the long run to love without being loved in return. It is more difficult to see that there is an almost direct parallelism in this respect between cathexis and cognition. After all, a person's cathexis of an inanimate object, such as a food object, is not directly dependent on the responsiveness of the object; it is surely anthropomorphism to suggest that a steak likes to be eaten in the same sense in which a hungry man likes to eat the steak. Similarly the cognition of the inanimate object by a person is not directly dependent on the object's reciprocal cognition of the person. But where the object is another person, the two, as ego and alter, constitute an *inter*active system. The question is what, in a cognitive sense, *is* alter from the point of view of ego, and vice versa. Clearly the answer to this question must involve the place—or "status," as sociologists call it—of ego and alter in the structure of the interactive system. Thus when I say a person is my mother, or my friend, or my student, I am characterizing that person as a participant in a system of social interaction in which I also am involved.

Thus not only the cathectic attitudes, but also the cognitive images, of persons relative to each other are functions of their interaction in the system of social relations.

Thus a social system is a function of the common culture, which not only forms the basis of the intercommunication of its members, but which defines, and so in one sense determines, the relative statuses of its members. There is, within surprisingly broad limits, no intrinsic significance of persons to each other independent of their actual interaction. In so far as these relative statuses are defined and regulated in terms of a common culture, the following apparently paradoxical statement holds true: what persons *are* can only be understood in terms of a set of beliefs and sentiments which define what they *ought to be*. This proposition is true only in a very broad way, but is none the less crucial to the understanding of social systems.

It is in this context that the central significance of moral standards in the common culture of systems of social interaction must be understood. Moral standards constitute, as the focus of the evaluative aspect of the common culture, the core of the stabilizing mechanisms of the system of social interaction. These mechanisms function, moreover, to stabilize not only attitudes—that is, the emotional meanings of persons to each other—but also categorizations—the cognitive definitions of what persons are in a socially significant sense.

If the approach taken above is correct, the place of the superego as part of the structure of the personality must be understood in terms of the relation between personality and the total common culture, by virtue of which a stable system of social interaction on the human levels becomes possible. Freud's insight was profoundly correct when he focused on the element of moral standards. This is, indeed, central and crucial, but it does seem that Freud's view was too narrow. The inescapable conclusion is that not only moral standards, but *all the components of the common culture* are internalized as part of the personality structure. Moral standards, indeed, cannot in this respect be dissociated from the *content* of the orientation patterns which they regulate; as I have pointed out, the content of both cathectic-attitudes and cognitive-status definitions have cultural, hence normative significance. This content is cultural and learned.

Neither what the human object *is,* in the most significant respects, nor what it *means* emotionally, can be understood as given independently of the nature of the interactive process itself; and the significance of moral norms themselves very largely relates to this fact.

It would seem that Freud's insight in this field was seriously impeded by the extent to which he thought in terms of a frame of reference relating a personality to its situation or environment without specific reference to the analysis of the social interaction of persons as a system. This perspective, which was overwhelmingly dominant in his day, accounts for two features of his theory. In the first place, the cognitive definition of the object world does not seem to have been problematical to Freud. He subsumed it all under "external reality," in relation to which "ego-functions" constitute a process of adaptation. He failed to take explicitly into account the fact that the frame of reference in terms of which objects are cognized, and therefore adapted to, is cultural and thus cannot be taken for granted as given, but must be internalized as a condition of the development of mature ego-functioning. In this respect it seems to be correct to say that Freud introduced an unreal separation between the superego and the ego—the lines between them are in fact difficult to define in his theory. In the light of the foregoing considerations, the distinction which Freud makes between the superego and the ego—that the former is internalized, by identification, and that the latter seems to consist of responses to external reality rather than of internalized culture—is not tenable. These responses are, to be sure, *learned* responses; but internalization is a very special kind of learning which Freud seemed to confine to the superego.

If this argument raises questions about cognitive function and therefore about the theory of the ego, there are implications, *ipso facto,* for the superego. The essential point seems to be that Freud's view seems to imply that the object, as cognitively significant, is given independently of the actor's internalized culture, and that superego standards are then applied to it. This fails to take account of the extent to which the constitution of the object and its moral appraisal are part and parcel of the *same* fundamental cultural patterns; it gives the superego an appearance of arbitrariness and dissociation from the rest of the personality—particularly from the ego—which is not wholly in accord with the facts.

The second problem of Freud's theory concerns the relation of cathexis or affect to the superego. In a sense, this is the obverse of its relation to cognition. The question here is perhaps analogous to that of the transmission of light in physics: how can the object's cathectic significance be mediated in the absence of direct biological contact? Indeed, embarrassment over this problem may be one source of the stressing of sexuality in Freudian theory, since sexuality generally involves such direct contact.

To Freud, the object tends, even if human, to be an inert something on which a "charge" of cathectic significance has been placed. The process is regarded as expressive of the actor's instincts or libido, but the element of mutuality tends to be treated as accessory and almost arbitrary. This is associated with the fact that, while Freud, especially in his *Interpretation of Dreams*, made an enormous contribution to the theory of expressive or cathectic symbolism, there is a very striking limitation of the extension of this theory. The basis of this may be said to be that Freud tended to confine his consideration of symbolism in the emotional context to its directly expressive functions and failed to go on to develop the analysis of its communicative functions. The dream symbol remained for him the prototype of affective symbolism. It is perhaps largely because of this fact that Freud did not emphasize the common culture aspect of such symbolism, but tended to attempt to trace its origins back to intrinsic meanings which were independent of the interactive process and its common culture. More generally the tenor of the analysis of affect was to emphasize a fundamental isolation of the individual in his lonely struggle with his id.[3]

This whole way of looking at the problem of cathexis seems to have a set of consequences parallel to these outlined above concerning cognition; it tends to dissociate the superego from the sources of affect. This derives from the fact that Freud apparently did not appreciate the presence and significance of a common culture of expressive-affective symbolism and the consequent necessity for thinking of the emotional component of interaction as mediated by this aspect of the common culture. Thus, the aspect of the superego which is concerned with the regulation of emotional reactions must be considered as defining the regulative principles of this interactive system. It is an integral *part* of the symbolism of emotional expression, not something over, above, and apart from it.

The general purport of this criticism is that Freud, with his formulation of the concept of the superego, made only a beginning at an analysis of the role of the common culture in personality. The structure of his theoretical scheme prevented him from seeing the possibilities for extending the same fundamental analysis from the internalization of moral standards—which he applied to the superego—to the internalization of the cognitive frame of reference for interpersonal relations and for the common system of expressive symbolism; and similarly it prevented him from seeing the extent to which these three elements of the common culture are integrated with each other.

This very abstract analysis may become somewhat more understandable if examples are given of what is meant by the cognitive reference or categorization system, and by the system of expressive symbolism, considering both as parts of the internalized common culture.

One of the most striking cases of the first is that of sex categorization—that is, the learning of sex role. Freud speaks of the original "bi-sexuality" of the child. The presumption is that he postulated a constitutionally given duality of orientation. In terms of the present approach, there is at least an alternative hypothesis possible which should be explored.[4] This hypothesis is that some of the principal facts which Freud interpreted as manifestations of constitutional bisexuality can be explained by the fact that the categorization of human persons—including the actor's categorization of himself taken as a point of reference— into two sexes is not, except in its somatic points of reference, biologically given but, in psychological significance, must be learned by the child. It is fundamental that children of both sexes start life with essentially the same relation to the mother, a fact on which Freud himself rightly laid great stress. It may then be suggested that the process by which the boy learns to differentiate himself in terms of sex from the mother and in this sense "identify" with the father, while the girl learns to identify with the mother, is a learning process. One major part of the process of growing up is the internalization of one's own sex role as a critical part of the self-image. It may well be that this way of looking at the process will have the advantage of making the assumption of constitutional bisexuality at least partly superfluous as an explanation of the individual's sex identification. In any case it has the great advantage of linking the determination of sex categorization directly with the role structure of the social system in a theoretical as well as an empirical sense. Every sociologist will appreciate this since he is familiar with the crucial significance of sex role differentiation and constitution for social structure.

An example of the second role, that of common expressive symbolism, may be found in terms of the process by which a reciprocal love attitude between mother and child is built up. Freud quite rightly, it seems, points to the origin of the child's love attitude as found in his dependency on the mother for the most elementary sources of gratification, such as food, elementary comforts, and safety. Gradually, in the process of interaction, a system of expectations of the continuation and repetition of these gratifications comes to be built up in the child; and these expectations are bound together as a result of the fact that a variety of such gratifications comes from the single source, the mother.

In this process, one may assume that well before the development of language there begins to occur a process of generalization, so that certain acts of the mother are interpreted as *signs* that gratifying performances can be expected—for example, the child becomes able to interpret her approaching footsteps or the tone of her voice. It is suggested that one of the main reasons why the erotic component of the child's relation to the mother is so important lies in the fact that, since bodily contact is an essential aspect of child care, erotic gratifications readily take on a symbolic significance. The erotic element has the extremely important property that it is relatively diffuse, being awakened by any sort of affectionate bodily contact. This diffuseness makes it particularly suitable as a vehicle of symbolic meanings. By this process, then, gradually, there is a transition from the child's focus on erotic stimulation as such, to his focus on the mother's *attitude* which is expressed by the erotically pleasurable stimulation. Only when this transition has taken place can one correctly speak of the child's having become dependent on the *love* of the mother and not merely on the specific pleasures the mother dispenses to him. Only when this level is reached, can the love attitude serve as a motivation to the acceptance of disciplines, since it can then remain stable—even though many specific gratifications which have previously been involved in the relationship are eliminated from it.

The essential point for present purposes is that, in its affective aspect, the child's interaction with the mother is not *only* a process of mutual gratification of needs, but is on the child's part a process of learning of the symbolic significance of a complicated system of acts on the part of the mother—of what they signify about what she feels and of how they are interdependent with and thus in part consequences of his own acts. That is to say, there is developed a complex language of emotional communication between them. Only when the child has learned this language on a relatively complex level, can he be said to have learned to love his mother or to be dependent on her love for him. There is, thus, a transition from "pleasure dependence" to "love dependence." One primary aspect of learning to love and be loved is the internalization of a common culture of expressive symbolism which makes it possible for the child to express *and communicate* his feelings and to understand the mother's feelings toward him.

It would seem that only when a sufficiently developed cognitive reference system and a system of expressive symbolism have been internalized is the foundation laid for the development of a superego; for only then can the child be said to be capable of understanding, in both the cognitive and the emotional senses, the meaning of the prescriptions and prohibitions which are laid upon him. The child must mature to the point where he can begin to play a *responsible* role in a system of social interaction, where he can understand that what people feel is a function of his and their conformity with mutually held standards of conduct. Only when he has become dependent on his mother's love, can he develop meaningful anxiety in that then he might jeopardize his security in that love by not living up to her expectations of being a good boy.

The above considerations have important implications for the nature of the process of identification in so far as that is the principal mechanism by which the superego is acquired. If this analysis is correct, the crucial problem concerns the process of internalization of the common culture, including all three of its major components—the cognitive reference system, the system of expressive symbolism, and the system of moral standards.

In the first place, it would seem to be clear that *only* cultural symbol systems can be internalized. An object can be cathected, cognized, and appraised, but it cannot as such be taken into the personality; the only sense in which the latter terminology is appropriate is in calling attention to the fact that the common culture is indeed part of the personality of the object but it is only an aspect, not the whole of it. Two persons can be said to be identified with each other in so far as they *share* important components of common culture. But since roles in the social system are differentiated, it should be noted that it is always important to specify *what* elements of culture are common.

Secondly, it is important to point out that the learning of the common culture may lead to the assumption either of a role identical with that of the object of identification or of a role differentiated from that object's role. Thus in the case of the boy vis-à-vis his mother, the learning of his sex categorization enables him to understand and accept the fact that with respect to sex he is different from her. The standards of proper behavior for both sexes are shared by the members of both, but their *application* is differentiated. The usage of the term identification has often been ambiguous, since it has been used to imply a likeness both of standards and of application. From the present point of view it is quite correct to speak of a boy learning his sex role by identification with the mother—in that he learns the sex categorization partly from her—and by the fact that he and she belong to different sex categories, which has important implications for *his* behavior. This is different from identification with his father in the sense that he learns that, with respect to sex, he is classed with his father and not with his mother.

Thirdly, there seems to be excellent evidence that while identification cannot mean coming *to be the object*, it is, as internalization of common culture, dependent on *positive cathexis of the object*. The considerations reviewed above give some suggestions as to why this should be true. Internalization of a culture pattern is not merely knowing it as an object of the external world; it is incorporating it into the actual structure of the personality as such. This means that the culture pattern must be integrated with the affective system of the personality.

Culture, however, is a system of generalized symbols and their meanings. In order for the integration with affect, which constitutes internalization, to take place, the individual's own affective organization must achieve levels of generalization of a high order. The principal mechanism by which this is accomplished appears to be through the building up of attachments to other persons—that is, by emotional communication with others so that the individual is sensitized to the *attitudes* of the others, not merely to their specific acts with their intrinsic gratification-deprivation significance. In other words, the process of forming attachments is *in itself* inherently a process of the generalization of affect. But this generalization in turn actually is in one major aspect the process of symbolization of emotional meanings—that is, it is a process of the acquisition of a culture. The intrinsic difficulty of creation of cultural patterns is so great that the child can only acquire complex cultural generalization through interaction with others who already possess it. Cathexis of an object as a focal aspect of identification is then another name for the development of *motivation* for the internalization of cultural patterns, at least for one crucially important phase of this process.

The conditions of socialization of a person are such that the gratifications which derive from his cathexis of objects cannot be secured unless, along with generalization of emotional meanings and their communication, he also develops a cognitive categorization of objects, including himself, and a system of moral norms which regulate the relations between himself and the object (a superego). This way of looking at the process of identification serves perhaps to help clear up a confusing feature of Freud's method of treatment. Freud, it will be remembered, denies that the very young child is capable of object cathexis, and speaks of identification, in contrast with object cathexis, as "the earliest form of emotional tie with an object." He then speaks o identification with the father in the oedipus situation as a rever sion to the more "primitive" form of relation to an object.

I would agree that the child's early attachment to the mothei and his later cathexis of her are not the same thing. It seems prob able that the earliest attachment is, as it were, precultural, while true object cathexis involves the internalization of a cultural sym bol system. But it seems extremely doubtful whether the relatior to the father in the oedipus situation can be correctly described a: a reversion to a presymbolic level. It is impossible to go into thi: problem fully here; but it may be suggested that the oedipus situ ation might be better interpreted as the strain imposed on the child by forcing him to take a major further step in growing up, ir the process of which the father becomes the focus of his ambiva lent feelings precisely because the child dare not jeopardize hi: love relation to the mother. Although regressive patterns of reac tion would be expected under such a strain, these are not the core of the process of identification; however important, they are only secondary phenomena.

If the foregoing account of the internalized content of person ality and of the processes of identification points in the right di rection, it would seem to imply the necessity for certair modifications of Freud's structural theory of personality. The first point is that it is not only the superego which is internalized—that is, taken over by identification from cathected social objects—bui that there are involved other important components which pre sumably must be included in the ego—namely, the system of cognitive categorizations of the object world and the system of expressive symbolism.

If this is correct, it would seem to necessitate, secondly, an important modification of Freud's conception of the ego. The element of *organization,* which is the essential property of the ego, would then not be derived from the "reality-principle"—that is, from adaptative responses to the external world alone. Instead it would be derived from *two* fundamental sources: the external world as an environment; and the common culture which is ac quired from objects of identification. Both are, to be sure, ac quired from outside, but the latter component of the ego is, in origin and character, more like the superego than it is like the lessons of experience.

Third, there are similar problems concerning the borderline between the ego and the id. A clue to what may be needed here is given in Freud's own frequent references to what have here been called "expressive symbols," as representatives to the ego of the impulses of the id. It seems to be a necessary implication of the above analysis that these symbolized and symbolically organized emotions are not only representatives *to* the ego; they should also be considered as integral *parts* of the ego. This may be felt to be a relatively radical conclusion—namely, that emotions, or affect on the normal human adult level, should be regarded as a *symbolically generalized* system, that it is never "id-impulse" as such. Affect is not a direct expression of drive-motivation, but involves it only as it is organized and integrated with both the reality experience of the individual and the cultural patterns which he has learned through the processes of identification.

More generally, the view of personality developed in this paper seems to be broadly in line with the recent increasing emphasis in psychoanalytic theory on the psychology of the ego, and the problems of its integration and functioning as a system. Freud's structural theory was certainly fundamentally on the right track in that it clearly formulated the three major points of reference of personality theory—the needs of the organism, the external situation, and the patterns of the culture. In view of the intellectual traditions within which Freud's own theoretical development took place, it was in the nature of the case that the cultural element, as he formulated it in the concept of the superego, should have been the last of the three to be developed and the most difficult to fit in.

In the light of the development of the more general theory of action, however, the cultural element must, as I have attempted to show, certainly occupy a very central place. For if the ego and the id in Freud's formulations are taken alone, there is no adequate bridge from the theory of personality to the theoretical analysis of culture and of the social system. The superego provides exactly such a bridge because it is not explicable on any other basis than that of acquisition from other human beings, and through the process of social interaction.

Essentially what this paper has done has been to examine the concept of the superego in the light of the maturing bodies of theory in the fields of culture and of the social system; and it has attempted to follow through the implications of the appearance of the superego in Freud's thinking for the theory of personality itself. The result has been the suggestion of certain modifications in Freud's own theory of personality.

In this sense the paper has contained a good deal of criticism of Freud, which may appear to be out of place in a paper dealing with the contributions of psychoanalysis to social science. It is, however, emphatically not the intent of the author to have this appear as primarily a critical paper. It has been necessary to emphasize the critical aspect at certain points since the psychiatric or psychoanalytic reader is not likely to be adequately familiar with the developments in sociological theory which are so importantly related to the concept of the superego. The essential intent, however, is to contribute to the development of a common foundation for the theoretical analysis of human behavior which can serve to unify all of the sciences which take this as their subject matter. The massive and fundamental fact is that Freud formulated the concept of the superego and fitted it into his general analysis of human motivation. This and the parallel formulations in the field of sociology are the solid foundations on which we must build. I believe it can truthfully be said that we are now in a position to bring the theory of personality and the theory of the social system within essentially the same general conceptual scheme. Freud's contribution of the concept of the superego has been one of the important factors making this possible.

9

LLNESS AND THE ROLE
)F THE PHYSICIAN:
\ SOCIOLOGICAL PERSPECTIVE

WITH RENE FOX

The present paper will attempt to discuss certain features of the
)henomena of illness, and of the processes of therapy and the role
•f the therapist, as aspects of the general social equilibrium of
nodern Western society. This is what is meant by the use of the
erm "a sociological perspective" in the title. It is naturally a
,omewhat different perspective from that usually taken for
;ranted by physicians and others, like clinical psychologists and
ocial workers, who are directly concerned with the care of sick
•eople. They are naturally more likely to think in terms of the
imple application of technical knowledge of the etiological fac-
ors in ill health and of their own manipulation of the situation in
he attempt to control these factors. What the present paper can
lo is to add something with reference to the social setting in
vhich this more "technological" point of view fits.

Undoubtedly the biological processes of the organism con-
titute one crucial aspect of the determinants of ill health, and
heir manipulation one primary focus of the therapeutic process.
With this aspect of "organic medicine" we are here only in-
lirectly concerned. However, as the development of psycho-
.omatic medicine has so clearly shown, even where most of the
ymptomatology is organic, very frequently a critically important
)sychogenic component is involved. In addition, there are the
ieuroses and psychoses where the condition itself is defined
)rimarily in "psychological" terms, that is, in terms of the moti-

Reprinted by permission from "Illness and the Role of the Physician: A Socio-
ogical Perspective," *American Journal of Orthopsychiatry* 21 (1951):452–60.

vated adjustment of the individual in terms of his own personality, and of his relations to others in the social world. It is with this motivated aspect of illness, whether its symptoms be organic or behavioral, that we are concerned. Our fundamental thesis will be that illness to this degree must be considered to be an integral part of what may be called the "motivational economy" of the social system and that, correspondingly, the therapeutic process must also be treated as part of that same motivational balance.

Seen in this perspective illness is to be treated as a special type of what sociologists call "deviant" behavior. By this is meant behavior which is defined in sociological terms as failing in some way to fulfill the institutionally defined expectations of one or more of the roles in which the individual is implicated in the society. Whatever the complexities of the motivational factors which may be involved, the dimension of conformity with, versus deviance or alienation from, the fulfillment of role expectations is always one crucial dimension of the process. The sick person is, by definition, in some respect disabled from fulfilling normal social obligations, and the motivation of the sick person in being or staying sick has some reference to this fact. Conversely, since being a normally satisfactory member of social groups is always one aspect of health, mental or physical, the therapeutic process must always have as one dimension the restoration of capacity to play social roles in a normal way.

We will deal with these problems under four headings. First, something will have to be said about the processes of genesis of illness insofar as it is motivated and thus can be classed as deviant behavior. Secondly, we will say something about the role of the sick person precisely as a social role, and not only a "condition"; third, we will analyze briefly certain aspects of the role of the physician and show their relation to the therapeutic process, and finally, fourth, we will say something about the way in which both roles fit into the general equilibrium of the social system.

Insofar as illness is a motivated phenomenon, the sociologist is particularly concerned with the ways in which certain features of the individual's relations to others have played a part in the process of its genesis. These factors are never isolated; there are, of course, the constitutional and organically significant environ mental factors (e.g., bacterial agents), and undoubtedly also psychological factors internal to the individual personality. But evidence is overwhelming as to the enormous importance of relations to others in the development and functioning of personality. The sociologist's emphasis, then, is on the factors responsible for "something's going wrong" in a person's relationships to others during the processes of social interaction. Probably the most significant of these processes are those of childhood, and centering in relations to family members, especially, of course, the parents. But the essential phenomena are involved throughout the life cycle.

Something going wrong in this sense may be said in general to consist in the imposition of a strain on the individual, a strain with which, given his resources, he is unable successfully to cope. A combination of contributions from psychopathology, learning theory, and sociology makes it possible for us to say a good deal, both about what kinds of circumstances in interpersonal relations are most likely to impose potentially pathogenic strains, and about what the nature of the reactions to such strains is likely to be.

Very briefly we may say that the pathogenic strains center at two main points. The first concerns what psychiatrists often call the "support" a person receives from those surrounding him. Essentially this may be defined as his acceptance as a full-fledged member of the group, in the appropriate role. For the child this means, first of all, acceptance by the family. The individual is emotionally "wanted" and within considerable limits this attitude is not conditional on the details of his behavior. The second aspect concerns the upholding of the value patterns which are constitutive of the group, which may be only a dyadic relationship of two persons, but is usually a more extensive group. Thus rejection, the seducibility of the other, particularly the more responsible, members of the group in contravention of the group norms, the evasion by these members of responsibility for enforcement of norms, and, finally, the compulsive "legalistic" enforcement of them are the primary sources of strain in social relationships. It is unfortunately not possible to take space here to elaborate further on these very important problems.

Reactions to such strains are, in their main outline, relativel familiar to students of mental pathology. The most important ma be enumerated as anxiety, production of fantasies, hostile im pulses, and the resort to special mechanisms of defense. In gei eral we may say that the most serious problem with reference t social relationships concerns the handling of hostile impulses. the strain is not adequately coped with in such ways as to reduc anxiety to manageable levels, the result will, we believe, be th generating of ambivalent motivational structures. Here, becaus intrinsically incompatible motivations are involved, there must b resort to special mechanisms of defense and adjustment. A titudes toward others thereby acquire the special property c compulsiveness because of the need to defend against the re pressed element of the motivational structure. The ambivale structure may work out in either of two main directions: first, b the repression of the hostile side, there develops a compulsiv need to conform with expectations and retain the favorable a titudes of the object; second, by dominance of the hostile side compulsive alienation from expectations of conformity and froi the object results.

The presence of such compulsive motivation inevitably distort the attitudes of an individual in his social relationships. Thi means that it imposes strains upon those with whom he interact: In general it may be suggested that most pathological motivatio arises out of vicious circles of deepening ambivalence. An ind vidual, say a child, is subjected to such strain by the compulsiv motivation of adults. As a defense against this he himself deve ops a complementary pattern of compulsive motivation, and th two continue, unless the process is checked, to "work on eac other." In this connection, it may be especially noted that som patterns of what has been called compulsive conformity are nc readily defined as deviant in the larger social group. Such peopl may in a sense be often regarded as "carriers" of mental patho ogy in that, though themselves not explicitly deviant, either in th form of illness or otherwise, by their effects on others they cor tribute to the genesis of the kinds of personality structure whic are likely to break down into illness or other forms of deviance

Two important conclusions seem to be justified from these cor siderations. The first is that the types of strain on persons which we have discussed are disorganizing both to personalities and to social relationships. Personal disorganization and social disorganization are, in a considerable part, two sides of the same concrete process. This obviously has very important implications both for psychiatry and for social science. Secondly, illness as a form of deviant behavior is not a unique phenomenon, but one type in a wider category. It is one of a set of alternatives which are open to the individual. There are, of course, reasons why some persons will have a psychological make-up which is more predisposed toward illness, and others toward one or another of the alternatives; but there is a considerable element of fluidity, and the selection among such alternatives may be a function of a number of variables. This fact is of the greatest importance when it is seen that the role of the sick person is a socially structured and in a sense institutionalized role.

The alternatives to illness may be such as to be open only to the isolated individual, as in the case of the individual criminal or the hobo. They may also involve the formation of deviant groups as in the case of the delinquent gang. Or, finally, they may involve a group formation which includes asserting a claim to legitimacy in terms of the value system of the society, as in joining an exotic religious sect. Thus to be a criminal is in general to be a social outcast, but in general we define religious devoutness as "a good thing" so that the same order of conflict with society that is involved in the criminal case may not be involved in the religious case. There are many complex and important problems concerning the genesis and significance of these various deviant patterns, and their relations to each other, which cannot be gone into here. The most essential point is to see that illness is one pattern among a family of such alternatives, and that the fundamental motivational ingredients of illness are not peculiar to it, but are of more general significance.

We may now turn to our second main topic, that of the sense in which illness is not merely a "condition" but also a social role. The essential criteria of a social role concern the attitudes both of the incumbent and of others with whom he interacts, in relation to a set of social norms defining expectations of appropriate or

proper behavior for persons in that role. In this respect we ma·
distinguish four main features of the "sick role" in our society.

The first of these is the exemption of the sick person from th·
performance of certain of his normal social obligations. Thus, t·
take a very simple case, "Johnny has a fever, he ought not to g·
to school today." This exemption and the decision as to when ·
does and does not apply should not be taken for granted. Psychi·
atrists are sufficiently familiar with the motivational significanc·
of the "secondary gain" of the mentally ill to realize that con·
scious malingering is not the only problem of the abuse of th·
privileges of being sick. In short, the sick person's claim t·
exemption must be socially defined and validated. Not every cas·
of "just not feeling like working" can be accepted as such a vali·
claim.

Secondly, the sick person is, in a very specific sense, als·
exempted from a certain type of responsibility for his own state
This is what is ordinarily meant by saying that he is in a "condi·
tion." He will either have to get well spontaneously or to "b·
cured" by having something done to him. He cannot reasonabl·
be expected to "pull himself together" by a mere act of will, an·
thus decide to be all right. He may have been responsible fo·
getting himself into such a state, as by careless exposure to acci·
dent or infection, but even then he is not responsible for th·
process of getting well, except in a peripheral sense.

This exemption from obligations and from a certain kind o·
responsibility, however, is given at a price. The third aspect o·
the sick role is the partial character of its legitimation, hence th·
deprivation of a claim to full legitimacy. To be sick, that is, is t·
be in a state which is socially defined as undesirable, to be gotte·
out of as expeditiously as possible. No one is given the privilege·
of being sick any longer than necessary but only so long as h·
"can't help it." The sick person is thereby isolated, and by hi·
deviant pattern is deprived of a claim to appeal to others.

Finally, fourth, being sick is also defined, except for the mildes·
cases, as being "in need of help." Moreover, the type of hel·
which is needed is presumptively defined; it is that of person·
specially qualified to care for illness, above all, of physicians
Thus from being defined as the incumbent of a role relative t·

people who are not sick, the sick person makes the transition to the additional role of patient. He thereby, as in all social roles, incurs certain obligations, especially that of "co-operating" with his physician—or other therapist—in the process of trying to get well. This obviously constitutes an affirmation of the admission of being sick, and therefore in an undesirable state, and also exposes the individual to specific reintegrative influences.

It is important to realize that in all these four respects, the phenomena of mental pathology have been assimilated to a role pattern which was already well established in our society before the development of modern psychopathology. In some respects it is peculiar to modern Western society, particularly perhaps with respect to the kinds of help which a patient is felt to need; in many societies magical manipulations have been the most prominent elements in treatment.

In our society, with reference to the severer cases at any rate, the definition of the mental "case" as sick has had to compete with a somewhat different role definition, namely, that as "insane." The primary difference would seem to center on the concept of responsibility and the mode and extent of its application. The insane person is, we may say, defined as being in a state where not only can he not be held responsible for getting out of his condition by an act of will, but where he is held not responsible in his usual dealings with others and therefore not responsible for recognition of his own condition, its disabilities, and his need for help. This conception of lack of responsibility leads to the justification of coercion of the insane, as by commitment to a hospital. The relations between the two role definitions raise important problems which cannot be gone into here.

It may be worth while just to mention another complication which is of special interest to members of the Orthopsychiatric Association, namely, the situation involved when the sick person is a child. Here, because of the role of child, certain features of the role of sick adult must be altered, particularly with respect to the levels of responsibility which can be imputed to the child. This brings the role of the mentally sick child in certain respects closer to that of the insane than, particularly, of the neurotic adult. Above all it means that third parties, notably parents, must play a particularly important part in the situation. It is common for pediatricians, when they refer to "my patient," often to mean the mother rather than the sick child. There is a very real sense in which the child psychiatrist must actively treat the parents and not merely the child himself.

We may now turn to our third major problem area, that of the social role of the therapist and its relation to the motivational processes involved in reversing the pathogenic processes. These processes are, it is widely recognized, in a certain sense definable as the obverse of those involved in pathogenesis, with due allowance for certain complicating factors. There seem to be four main conditions of successful psychotherapy which can be briefly discussed.

The first of these is what psychiatrists generally refer to as "support." By this is here meant essentially that acceptance as a member of a social group the lack of which we argued above played a crucial part in pathogenesis. In this instance it is, above all, the solidary group formed by the therapist and his patient, in which the therapist assumes the obligation to do everything he can within reason to "help" his patient. The strong emphasis in the "ideology" of the medical profession on the "welfare of the patient" as the first obligation of the physician is closely related to this factor. The insistence that the professional role must be immune from "commercialism," with its suggestion that maximizing profits is a legitimate goal, symbolizes the attitude. Support in this sense is, so long as the relationship subsists, to be interpreted as essentially unconditional, in that within wide limits it will not be shaken by what the patient does. As we shall see, this does not, however, mean that it is unlimited, in the sense that the therapist is obligated to "do anything the patient wants."

The second element is a special permissiveness to express wishes and fantasies which would ordinarily not be permitted expression in normal social relationships, as within the family. This permissiveness must mean that the normal sanctions for such expression in the form of disapproval and the like are suspended. There are of course definite limits on "acting out." In general the permissiveness is confined to verbal and gestural levels, but this is nonetheless an essential feature of the therapeutic process.

The obverse of permissiveness, however, is a very important restriction on the therapist's reaction to it. In general, that is, the therapist does not reciprocate the expectations which are expressed, explicitly or implicitly, in the patient's deviant wishes and fantasies. The most fundamental wishes, we may presume, involve reciprocal interaction between the individual and others. The expression of a wish is in fact an invitation to the other to reciprocate in the complementary role, if it is a deviant wish, an attempt to "seduce" him into reciprocation. This is true of negative as well as positive attitudes. The expression of hostility to the therapist in transference is only a partial gratification of the wish; full gratification would require reciprocation by the therapist's becoming angry in return. Sometimes this occurs; it is what is called "countertransference"; but it is quite clear that the therapist is expected to control his countertransference impulses and that such control is in general a condition of successful therapy. By showing the patient the projective character of this transference reaction, this refusal to reciprocate plays an essential part in facilitating the attainment of insight by the patient.

Finally, fourth, over against the unconditional element of support, there is the conditional manipulation of sanctions by the therapist. The therapist's giving and withholding of approval is of critical importance to the patient. This seems to be an essential condition of the effectiveness of interpretations. The acceptance of an interpretation by the patient demonstrates his capacity, to the relevant extent, to discuss matters on a mature plane with the therapist, who shows his approval of this performance. It is probably significant that overt disapproval is seldom used in therapy, but certainly the withholding of positive approval is very significant.

The above four conditions of successful psychotherapy, it is important to observe, are all to some degree "built into" the role which the therapist in our society typically assumes, that of the physician, and all to some degree are aspects of behavior in that role which are at least partially independent of any conscious or explicit theory or technique of psychotherapy.

The relation of support to the definition of the physician's role as primarily oriented to the welfare of the patient has already been noted. The element of permissiveness has its roots in the general social acceptance that "allowances" should be made for sick people, not only in that they may have physical disabilities, but that they are in various ways "emotionally" disturbed. The physician, by virtue of his special responsibility for the care of the sick, has a special obligation to make such allowances. Third, the physician is, however, by the definition of his role, positively enjoined not to enter into certain reciprocities with his patients, or he is protected against the pressures which they exert upon him. Thus giving of confidential information is, in ordinary relationships, a symbol of reciprocal intimacy, but the physician does not tell about his own private affairs. Many features of the physician-patient relationship, such as the physician's access to the body, might arouse erotic reactions, but the role is defined so as to inhibit such developments even if they are initiated by the patient. In general the definition of the physician's role as specifically limited to concern with matters of health, and the injunction to observe an "impersonal," matter-of-fact attitude without personal involvement, serve to justify and legitimize his refusal to reciprocate his patient's deviant expectations. Finally, the prestige of the physician's scientific training, his reputation for technical competence, gives authority to his approval, a basis for the acceptance of his interpretations.

All of these fundamental features of the role of the physician are given independently of the technical operations of psychotherapy; indeed they were institutionalized long before the days of Freud or of psychiatry as an important branch of the medical profession. This fact is of the very first importance.

First, it strongly suggests that in fact deliberate, conscious psychotherapy is only part of the process. Indeed, the effective utilization of these aspects of the physician's role is a prominent part of what has long been called the "art of medicine." It is highly probable that, whether or not the physician knows it or wishes it, in practicing medicine skillfully he is always in fact exerting a psychotherapeutic effect on his patients. Furthermore, there is every reason to believe that, even though the cases are not explicitly "mental" cases, this is necessary. This is, first, because a "psychic factor" is present in a very large proportion of ostensibly somatic cases and, secondly, apart from any psychic factor in the etiology, because illness is always to some degree a situation of strain to the patient, and mechanisms for coping with his reactions to the strain are hence necessary, if the strain is not to have psychopathological consequences. The essential continuity between the art of medicine and deliberate psychotherapy is, therefore, deeply rooted in the nature of the physician's function generally. Modern psychotherapy has been built upon the role of the physician as this was already established in the social structure of Western society. It has utilized the existing role pattern and extended and refined certain of its features, but the roles of the physician and of the sick person were not created as an application of the theories of psychiatrists.

The second major implication is that, if these features of the role of the physician and of illness are built into the structure of society independent of the application of theories of psychopathology, it would be very strange indeed if they turned out to be isolated phenomena, confined in their significance to this one context. This is particularly true if, as we have given reason to believe, illness is not an isolated phenomenon, but one of a set of alternative modes of expression for a common fund of motivational reaction to strain in the social system. But with proper allowances for very important differences we can show that certain of these features can also be found in other roles in the social system. Thus to take an example of special interest to you, there are many resemblances between the psychotherapeutic process and that of the normal socialization of the child. The differences are, however, great. They are partly related to the fact that a child apparently needs two parents while a neurotic person can get along with only one psychiatrist. But also in the institutions of leadership, of the settlement of conflicts in society and of many others, many of the same factors are operative.

We therefore suggest that the processes which are visible in the actual technical work of psychotherapy resemble, in their relation to the total balance of forces operating within and upon the individual, the part of the iceberg which protrudes above the surface of the water; what is below the surface is the larger, and, in certain respects, probably still the more important part.

It also shows that the phenomena of physical and mental illness and the counteraction are more intimately connected with the general equilibrium of the social system than is generally supposed. We may close with one rather general inference from this generalization. It is rather generally supposed that there has been a considerable increase in the incidence of mental illness within the last generation or so. This is difficult to prove since statistics are notably fragmentary and fashions of diagnosis and treatment have greatly changed. But granting the fact, what would be its meaning? It could be that it was simply an index of generally increasing social disorganization. But this is not necessarily the case. There are certain positive functions in the role of illness from the social point of view. The sick person is isolated from influence upon others. His condition is declared to be undesirable and he is placed in the way of re-equilibrating influences. It is altogether possible that an increase in mental illness may constitute a diversion of tendencies to deviance from other channels of expression into the role of illness, with consequences less dangerous to the stability of society than certain alternatives might be. In any case the physician is not merely the person responsible for the care of a special class of "problem cases." He stands at a strategic point in the general balance of forces in the society of which he is a part.

10

THE HIERARCHY OF CONTROL

I. The Hierarchy of Relations of Control

The development of theory in the past generation in both the biological and the behavioral sciences has revealed the primary source of the difficulty underlying the prominent reductionism of so much earlier thought. This was the reductionist tendency to ignore the importance of the ways in which the organization of living systems involved structures and mechanisms that operated as agencies of control—in the cybernetic sense of control—of their metabolic and behavioral processes. The concept of the "behavioral organism" put forward above is that of a cybernetic system located mainly in the central nervous system, which operates through several intermediary mechanisms to control the metabolic processes of the organism and the behavioral use of its physical facilities, such as the motions of limbs.

The basic subsystems of the general system of action constitute a hierarchical series of such agencies of control of the behavior of individuals or organisms. The behavioral organism is the point of articulation of the system of action with the anatomical-physiological features of the physical organism and is its point of contact with the physical environment. The personality system is, in turn, a system of control over the behavioral organism; the social system, over the personalities of its participating members;

Reprinted with deletions with permission of Macmillan Publishing Co., Inc., from *Theories of Society* by Talcott Parsons. © 1961 by The Free Press.

and the cultural system, a system of control relative to social systems.

It may help if we illustrate the nature of this type of hierarchical relationship by discussing the sense in which the social system "controls" the personality. There are two main empirical points at which this control operates, though the principles involved are the same in both cases. First, the situation in which any given individual acts is, far more than any other set of factors, composed of *other* individuals, not discretely but in ordered sets of relationship to the individual in point. Hence, as the source of his principal facilities of action and of his principal rewards and deprivations, the concrete social system exercises a powerful control over the action of any concrete, adult individual. However, the *patterning* of the motivational system in terms of which he faces this situation also depends upon the social system, because his own personality *structure* has been shaped through the internalization of systems of social objects and of the patterns of institutionalized culture. This point, it should be made clear, is independent of the sense in which individuals are concretely autonomous or creative rather than "passive" or "conforming," for individuality and creativity are, to a considerable extent, phenomena of the institutionalization of expectations. The social system which controls the personality is here conceived analytically, not concretely.

Control Relations within the Social System. The same basic principle of cybernetic hierarchy that applies to the relations between general subsystems of action applies again *within* each of them, notably to social systems, which is of primary concern here. The principle of the order of cybernetic priority, combined with primacy of relevance to the different boundary-interchange exigencies of the system, will be used as the fundamental basis for classifying the components of social systems.

The more strategic starting point for explaining this basic set of classifications is the category of functions, the link between the structural and the dynamic aspects of the system. I have suggested that it is possible to reduce the essential functional imperatives of any system of action, and hence of any social system, to four, which I have called pattern-maintenance, integration, goal-attainment, and adaptation. These are listed in order of significance from the point of view of cybernetic control of action processes in the system type under consideration.

The Function of Pattern-Maintenance. The function of pattern-maintenance refers to the imperative of maintaining the stability of the patterns of institutionalized culture defining the structure of the system. There are two distinct aspects of this functional imperative. The first concerns the character of the normative pattern itself; the second concerns its state of "institutionalization." From the point of view of the individual participant in a social system, this may be called his motivational *commitment* to act in accordance with certain normative patterns; this, as we shall see, involves their "internalization" in the structure of his personality.

Accordingly, the focus of pattern-maintenance lies in the structural category of *values,* which will be discussed presently. In this connection, the essential function is maintenance, at the cultural level, of the stability of institutionalized values through the processes which articulate values with the belief system, namely, religious beliefs, ideology, and the like. Values, of course, are subject to change, but whether the empirical tendency be toward stability or not, the potentialities of disruption from this source are very great, and it is essential to look for mechanisms that tend to protect such order—even if it is orderliness in the process of change.

The second aspect of this control function concerns the motivational commitment of the individual—elsewhere called "tension-management." A very central problem is that of the mechanisms of socialization of the individual, i.e., of the processes by which the values of the society are internalized in his personality. But even when values have become internalized, the commitments involved are subject to different kinds of strain. Much insight has recently been gained about the ways in which such mechanisms as ritual, various types of expressive symbolism, the arts, and indeed recreation, operate in this connection. Durkheim's analysis of the functions of religious ritual may be said to constitute the main point of departure here.

Pattern-maintenance in this sense plays a part in the theory of social systems, as of other systems of action, comparable to that of the concept of inertia in mechanics. It serves as the most fundamental reference point to which the analysis of other, more variable factors can be related. Properly conceived and used, it does not imply the empirical predominance of stability over change. However, when we say that, because of this set of functional exigencies, social systems show a *tendency* to maintain their structural patterns, we say essentially two things. First, we provide a reference point for the orderly analysis of a whole range of problems of variation which can be treated as arising from sources *other* than processes of structural change in the system, including, in the latter concept, its dissolution. Second, we make it clear that when we do analyze structural change we are dealing with a different kind of theoretical problem than that involved in equilibration. Hence, there is a direct relation between the function of pattern-maintenance—as distinguished from the other three functional imperatives—and the distinction between problems of equilibrium analysis, on the one hand, and the analysis of structural change on the other. The distinction between these two types of problems comes to focus at this point in the paradigm.

The Function of Goal-Attainment. For purposes of exposition it seems best to abandon the order of control set forth above and to concentrate next upon the function of goal-attainment and its relation to adaptation. In contrast to the constancy of institutionalized cultural patterns, we have emphasized the variability of a system's relation to its situation. The functions of goal-attainment and adaptation concern the structures, mechanisms, and processes involved in this relation.

We have compared pattern-maintenance with inertia as used in the theory of mechanics. Goal-attainment then becomes a "problem" in so far as there arises some discrepancy between the inertial tendencies of the system and its "needs" resulting from interchange with the situation. Such needs necessarily arise because the internal system and the environing ones cannot be expected to follow immediately the changing patterns of process. A goal is therefore defined in terms of equilibrium. It is a directional change that tends to reduce the discrepancy between the needs of the system, with respect to input-output interchange, and the conditions in the environing systems that bear upon the "fulfilment" of such needs. Goal-attainment or goal-orientation is thus, by contrast with pattern-maintenance, essentially tied to a specific situation.

A social system with only one goal, defined in relation to a generically crucial situational problem, is conceivable. Most often, however, the situation is complex, with many goals and problems. In such a case two further considerations must be taken into account. First, to protect the integrity of the system, the several goals must be arranged in some scale of relative urgency, a scale sufficiently flexible to allow for variations in the situation. For any complex system, therefore, it is necessary to speak of a system of goals rather than of a single unitary goal, a system, however, which must have some balance between integration as a system and flexible adjustment to changing pressures.

For the social system as such, the focus of its goal-orientation lies in its relation as a system to the personalities of the participating individuals. It concerns, therefore, not commitment to the values of the society, but motivation to contribute what is necessary for the functioning of the system; these "contributions" vary according to particular exigencies. For example, considering American society, one may suggest that, given the main system of values, there has been in the cold-war period a major problem of motivating large sectors of the population to the level of national effort required to sustain a position of world leadership in a very unstable and rapidly changing situation. I would interpret much of the sense of frustration expressed in isolationism and McCarthyism as manifestations of the strains resulting from this problem.

The Function of Adaptation. The second consequence of plurality of goals, however, concerns the difference between the functions of goal-attainment and adaptation. When there is only one goal, the problem of evaluating the usefulness of facilities is narrowed down to their relevance to attaining this particular goal. With a plurality of goals, however, the problem of "cost" arises. That is, the same scarce facilities will have *alternative* uses within the system of goals, and hence their use for one purpose means sacrificing the gains that would have been derived from their use for another. It is on this basis that an analytical distinction must be made between the function of effective goal-attainment and that of providing disposable facilities independent of their relevance to any particular goal. The adaptive function is defined as the provision of such facilities.

Just as there is a pluralism of lower-order, more concrete goals, there is also a pluralism of relatively concrete facilities. Hence there is a parallel problem of the organization of such facilities in a system. The primary criterion is the provision of flexibility, so far as this is compatible with effectiveness; for the system, this means a maximum of generalized disposability in the processes of allocation between alternative uses. Within the complex type of social system, this disposability of facilities crystallizes about the institutionalization of money and markets. More generally, at the macroscopic social-system level, the function of goal-attainment is the focus of the political organization of societies, while that of adaptation is the focus of economic organization.

The most important kinds of facilities involve control of physical objects, access to the services of human agents and certain cultural elements. For their mechanisms of control to be at all highly generalized, particular units of such resources must be "alienable," i.e., not bound to specific uses through ascription. The market system is thus a primary focus of the society's organization for adaptation. Comparable features operate in less differentiated societies, and in more differentiated subsystems where markets do not penetrate, such as the family.

Within a given system, goal-attainment is a more important control than adaptation. Facilities subserve the attainment of goals, not vice versa—though of course the provision or "production" of facilities may itself be a goal, with a place within the more general system of goals.

The Function of Integration. The last of the four functional imperatives of a system of action—in our case, a social system—is that of integration. In the control hierarchy, this stands between the functions of pattern-maintenance and goal-attainment. Our recognition of the significance of integration implies that all systems, except for a limiting case, are differentiated and segmented into relatively independent units, i.e., must be treated as boundary-maintaining systems within an environment of other systems, which in this case are other subsystems of the same, more inclusive system. The functional problem of integration concerns the mutual adjustments of these "units" or subsystems from the point of view of their "contributions" to the effective functioning of the system as a whole. This, in turn, concerns their relation to the pattern-maintenance problem, as well as to the external situation through processes of goal-attainment and adaptation.

In a highly differentiated society, the primary focus of the integrative function is found in its system of legal norms and the agencies associated with its management, notably the courts and the legal profession. Legal norms at this level, rather than that of a supreme constitution, govern the *allocation* of rights and obligations, of facilities and rewards, between different units of the complex system; such norms facilitate internal adjustments compatible with the stability of the value system or its orderly change, as well as with adaptation to the shifting demands of the external situation. The institutionalization of money and power are primarily integrative phenomena, like other mechanisms of social control in the narrower sense. These problems will be further discussed in later sections of this essay.

For any given type of system—here, the social—the integrative function is the focus of its most distinctive properties and processes. We contend, therefore, that the problems focusing about the integrative functions of social systems constitute the central core of the concerns of sociological theory.

II. Categories of Social Structure

Historically, the theoretical preoccupations of sociological theory have emerged from two main points of reference. One concerns the relations of social systems and culture and focuses on the problem of values and norms in the social system. The second concerns the individual as organism and personality and focuses on the individual's participation in social interaction. Generally, neither of these reference points may be considered more important than the other. However, since the foregoing discussion of functional imperatives has started with pattern-maintenance, which chiefly concerns the institutionalization of normative culture, it may help to balance the picture if we begin our detailed discussion of structure at the other end, with the problem of the interaction of individuals.

Social Interaction and Roles

For sociology, the essential concept here is that of *role*. I should like to treat this concept as the "bottom" term of a series of structural categories, of which the other terms, in ascending order, are *collectivity, norm,* and *value*. (It is interesting, and I think significant, that systematic introduction of the concept of role has been, perhaps, the most distinctively American contribution to the structural aspects of sociological theory.)

The essential starting point is the conception of two (or more) individuals interacting in such a way as to constitute an interdependent system. As personalities, each individual may be considered a system with its own values, goals, etc., facing the others as part of an "environment" that provides certain opportunities for goal-attainment as well as certain limitations and sources of frustration. Though interdependence can be taken into account at this level, this is not equivalent to treating the process of interaction as a social system. True, the action of alter is an essential part of the conditions bearing on the attainment of ego's goals, but the vital sociological question concerns the nature and degree of the integration of the *system* of interaction as a social system. Here the question arises of the conditions under which the interaction process can be treated as stable—in the sense, at least, that it does not prove to be so mutually frustrating that dissolution of the system (i.e., for the individual, "leaving the field") seems more likely than its continuation.

The problem of stability introduces considerations of temporal continuity, which immediately brings us to the relevance of normative orientation. It can be shown that, within the action frame of reference, stable interaction implies that acts acquire "meanings" which are interpreted with reference to a common set of normative conceptions. The particularity of specific acts is transcended in terms of the generalization of the normative common culture as well as in the normative component of the expectations that get built into the guiding mechanisms of the process. This means that the response of Alter to an act of Ego may be interpreted as a sanction expressing an evaluation of the past act and serving as a guide to desirable future behavior.

The essentials of the interaction situation can be illustrated by any two-player game, such as chess. Each player is presumed to have some motivation to participate in the game, including a "desire to win." Hence, he has a goal, and, relative to this, some conception of effective "strategies." He may plan an opening gambit but he cannot carry advance planning too far, because the situation is not stable: it is contingent on the moves made both by himself and by his opponent as the game proceeds. The basic facilities at his command consist of his knowledge of the opportunities implicit in the changing situation; his command of these opportunities means performance of the adaptive function. Hence, at the goal-attainment and adaptive levels, goals are defined and facilities are provided, but *specific acts are not prescribed*. The facilities are generalized, and their allocation between the players depends upon each player's capacities to take advantage of opportunities.

In turn, the meaningfulness of the goals and the stability of the generalized pattern of facilities depend on the existence of a well defined set of rules, which forms the center of the integration of the system. The roles, in this case, are not differentiated on a permanent basis; rather, the rules define the consequences of any given move by one player for the situation in which the other must make his next choice. Without such rules the interactive process could not be stable, and the system of adaptive facilities would break down; neither player would know what was expected of him or what the consequences of a given set of moves would be. Finally, the differentiated and contingent rules must be grounded in a set of values which define the nature of a "good game" of this sort, including the value of equality of opportunity for both contestants and the meaningfulness of the goal of "winning."

A stable system of interaction, therefore, orients its partici-

pants in terms of mutual expectations, which have the dua
significance of expressing normative evaluations and stating con
tingent predictions of overt behavior. This mutuality of expecta
tions implies that the *evaluative* meanings of acts are shared b
the interacting units in two ways: what a member does can b
categorized in terms meaningful to both; also, they share criteri
of behavior, so that there are common standards of evaluation fo
particular acts.

We can say that even such an elementary two-member systen
of social interaction has most of the structural essentials of a
social system. The essential property is mutuality of orientation
defined in terms of shared patterns of normative culture. Such
normative patterns are *values;* the normatively regulated comple:
of behavior of one of the participants is a *role;* and the systen
composed by the interaction of the two participants, so far as i
shares a common normative culture and is distinguishable from
others by the participation of these two and not others, is a *col
lectivity*.

One further condition, not present in our chess game example
is necessary in order to complete the roster of structural compo
nents, namely, differentiation between the roles of the partici
pants. This is to say that, in most social systems, participants de
not *do* the same things; their performances may be conceived a:
complementary contributions to the "functioning" of the inter
action system. When there are two or more structurally distinc
units which perform essentially *the same* function in the systen
(e.g., nuclear families in a community) we will speak of segmen
tation as distinguished from differentiation. When differentiation
of roles is present, it becomes necessary to distinguish between
two components of the normative culture of the system: that o
values, which are shared by the members over and above thei
particular roles, and that of role-expectations, which are dif
ferentiated by role and therefore define rights and obligation:
applicable to one role but not to the other. I propose to use the
term *values* for the shared normative component, and the tern
(differentiated) *norm* for the component that is specific to a give
role or, in more complex systems, to other empirical units of the
system, i.e., various collectivities such as families, churches
business firms, governmental agencies, universities.

Where roles are differentiated, the sharing of values becomes an essential condition of integration of the system. Only on this assumption can the reactions of Alter to Ego's performances have the character of sanctions regulating Ego's action in the interests of the system. However, it should be clear that for Alter to be in a position to evaluate Ego's acts, the acts need not be such that Alter is, by virtue of his role, expected to perform. Thus, in marriage, one of the most important diadic relationships in all societies, the roles of the partners are differentiated by sex. The mutual evaluation of performance is an essential regulatory mechanism, but to be in a position to evaluate the partner's performance is not to assume his role.

The Concepts of Role and Collectivity. A role may now be defined as the structured, i.e., normatively regulated, participation of a person in a concrete process of social interaction with specified, concrete role-partners. The system of such interaction of a plurality of role-performers is, so far as it is normatively regulated in terms of common values and of norms sanctioned by these common values, a collectivity. Performing a role within a collectivity defines the category of *membership,* i.e., the assumption of obligations of performance in that concrete interaction system. Obligations correlatively imply rights.

Since the normal individual participates in many collectivities, it is a commonplace, though a crucial one, that only in a limiting case does a single role constitute the entire interactive behavior of a concrete individual. The role is rather a *sector* in his behavioral system, and hence of his personality. For most purposes, therefore, it is not the individual, or the person as such, that is a unit of social systems, but rather his role-participation at the boundary directly affecting his personality. It is largely when interpreted as this particular boundary-concept that the concept of role has an important theoretical significance for sociology.

So long as we restrict our illustrations to the diadic interaction system it may seem that the distinction of four analytical structural components—role, collectivity, norm, and value—is overelaborate. At this level it is still possible to identify values and the collectivity, norms and the role. In more complex social systems, however, there is not just one collectivity but many; and a differentiated norm does not define expectations for just one role but for a class of roles (and also for classes of collectivities). The social systems with which the sociologist normally deals are complex networks of many different types or categories of roles and collectivities on many different levels of organization. It therefore becomes essential to conceptualize values and norms independently of any particular collectivity or role.

The Structure of Complex Systems

Having outlined these essential structural components of a social system and their rank in the general hierarchy of control, we can now outline their main pattern of organization so as to constitute a relatively complex system. What is here presented is necessarily a schematic "ideal type," one that pretends merely to define and distinguish rather broad structural categories; we cannot take into account the immense richness of various concrete social structures.

The main guiding line of the analysis is the concept that a complex social system consists of a network of interdependent and interpenetrating subsystems, each of which, seen at the appropriate level of reference, is a social system in its own right, subject to all the functional exigencies of any such system relative to *its* institutionalized culture and situation and possessing all the essential structural components, organized on the appropriate levels of differentiation and specification.

The Concept of a Society. The starting point must be the concept of a *society,* defined as a collectivity, i.e., a system of concrete interacting human individuals, which is the primary bearer of a distinctive institutionalized culture and which cannot be said to be a differentiated subsystem of a higher-order collectivity oriented to most of the functional exigencies of a social system. It will be noted that this conception is stated in terms that leave the question of the "openness" of a society in various directions to be treated empirically. At the social-system level, however, rather than the cultural, the main criterion is *relative* self-sufficiency.

To approach the structural analysis of the subsystem organization of a society, we must refer to the appropriate functional exigencies of both the societal system itself and its various subsystems. The primary, over-all principle is that of differentiation in relation to functional exigency; this is the master concept for the analysis of social structure. By itself, however, it is not adequate; it must be supplemented by the two principles of specification and segmentation. The first refers primarily to the institutionalized culture components of the structure, the second to the exigencies confronting the concrete behaving units, i.e., to collectivities and roles. It seems preferable to discuss the latter first.

We have noted that, in *one* (but only one) of its aspects, a society is a *single* collectivity with a specifiable, though naturally changing, membership of individuals. This fact is related to three fundamental imperatives. First, there must be, to some degree and on some level, a unitary system of institutionalized values, in this aspect a common culture. In so far as maintenance of a common value system requires the kinds of functions collectivities must perform, the society will have to constitute a single collectivity—what Durkheim called a "moral community." Second, however, since the system is differentiated, the implementation of these values for different units requires a relatively *consistent* system of norms that receive a unitary formulation and interpretation. In highly differentiated societies this system of norms takes the form of an integrated legal system administered by courts. The need for co-ordinated dealing with the external situation is also relevant, as will be brought out presently.

The Segmentation of Social Units. But if, for one set of reasons, a society must be a single collectivity, other reasons prevent its being only that. These reasons can be summed up in the generalized principles economists refer to as determining the "economies of scale." Beyond certain points, that is to say, "costs" increase as the size of the unit of organization increases, though what the points are varies greatly according to the specific factors involved. Thus, under modern industrial conditions the manufacture of such commodities as automobiles takes place in very large units indeed, whereas there seem to be important reasons which inhibit entrusting the early socialization of children primarily to units with membership much larger than the nuclear family.

Perhaps the most fundamental determinant underlying t
segmentation of social systems is the indispensability of t
human individual as an agency of performance. But there a
essential limits, not only to what a given individual can do, but
the effectiveness with which individuals can co-operate. T
problems of communication and other aspects of integration m
thus multiply as a result of an increasing scale of organization;
certain respects, therefore, subcollectivities may acquire a d
tinctive organization, including a special integration or solidari
relative to the larger systems of which they are parts.

By the concept *segmentation* I refer, in discussing the form
tion of collectivities, to the development of subcollectivitie
within a larger collectivity system, in which some of the membe
of the larger system participate more intimately than in others.
this sense, segmentation is a factor independent of the differenti
tion of function between the subcollectivities. Thus a large-sca
society may comprise millions of nuclear families, all of whi
perform essentially similar functions in the socialization of ch
dren; here the structure is highly segmented but not highly diffe
entiated.

The necessity of segmentation derives largely from the pro
lems of integration resulting from the other exigencies to whi
units of the system are subject. At the same time, however,
gives rise to new problems of integration: the more units the
are, the less likely they will be just "naturally" to co-ordina
their activities in ways compatible with the smooth functioning
the system as a whole. This tends, in more complex systems,
give rise to special mechanisms of integration, which will have
be discussed in due course.

The Specification of Normative Culture. As already note
there is an important relation between the hierarchy of contr
and the levels of generality of the components of normative cu
ture. Thus, values were defined as standing at the highest level
generality of "conceptions of the desirable," i.e., witho
specification of function or situation. In comparison to value
therefore, norms are differentiated on the basis of specification
function of the units or subunits to which they apply. Su
collectivities, in turn, involve further specification on the basis

situation. This is to say that, given its function(s), a collectivity is identified in terms of specified memberships of concrete individuals acting in concrete situations. When the collectivity is treated as a differentiated system, there must be further specifications applicable to the roles of the participating members.

There is, therefore, a hierarchy of generality of the patterns of normative culture institutionalized in a social system, one that corresponds to the general hierarchical relations of its structural components. Each subunit of the society, as collectivity, will have its own institutionalized values, which should be conceived as specifications, at the appropriate level, of the more general values of the society. To cope with its own internal differentiation of function, then, each subunit will have a set of differentiated norms, which should be regarded as specifications both of the subcollectivity values and of the more general norms applicable both to it and to other types of subcollectivity. The principle of specification restricts the generality of the pattern of culture by introducing qualifications arising from specialization of function, on the one hand, and from specificity of situation, on the other.

The last of the three principles of organization of complex systems, functional differentiation, has already been discussed in general terms. In accord with this principle, structured units acquire specialized significance in the functioning of the system. The general scheme of functional categories that we have presented is very simple, being limited to four categories. In using it, however, one must do justice to the empirical complexity of the situation by taking account of the many steps in segmentation and specification, and hence of the compounding of the patterns of differentiation by their repetition for subsystems at each level of segmentation.

Since our general approach has been in terms of the hierarchy of control observed in descending order, a brief account should now be given of the "anchorage" of social systems as the base. This anchorage is in the personalities and behavioral organisms of the individual members and, *through* these, in the lower-order subsystems of the organism and in the physical environment. Concretely, all social interaction is bound to the physical task performance of individuals in a physical environment; it is bound to spatial location in the physical sense. Following the usage of ecologically oriented theory, I have elsewhere referred to this spatial location as the "community" aspect of social structure. It can be broken down most conveniently into four complexes: (1) residential location and the crystallization of social structure around that focus; (2) functional task-performance through occupation, and the attendant locational problems; (3) jurisdictional application of normative order through the specification of categories of persons, and the relevance of this to the spatial locations of their interests and activities; and (4) the physical exigencies of communication and of the movements of persons and commodities. More generally, the category of technology—not only what is usually called "physical production," but all task-performance involving the physical organism in relation to its physical environment—belongs in this area of borderline problems. Technology relates to physical exigencies, but it is also based on *cultural* resources in their significance as facilities for social action. Empirical knowledge of the physical world is an instance of such a cultural resource.

11

SPECIFICATION

We now turn from the analysis of interaction to that of the more explicitly normative content of the structure of social systems, within which values and norms have been distinguished. We have already suggested that such values and norms must be involved in any stable process of interaction, however simple. In the attempt to analyze the structure of complex societies, however, the analytically distinct significance of these components becomes much more salient. The following sections will therefore be devoted to a more explicit analysis of them and of their relations to the segmentation of social structure, to the various levels of values and norms, and to the patterns of differentiation of structure, always taking account both of the problems of function and of the system's relation to its situation.

Throughout this analysis, our major concern will be to make clear the basic functional paradigm we have presented for the intricate relations involved in a complex society segmented and differentiated into many subsystems. A paramount underlying question will be, how is the integration of a system with a large population and high differentiation possible? Or, more theoretically, what kinds of statements have to be made, what concepts formulated, and what discriminations worked out in order to do justice to these empirical intricacies?

The concepts of universalism and particularism will be helpful in this connection. In any given system, the concepts of role and

Reprinted with deletions with permission of Macmillan Publishing Co., Inc., from *Theories of Society* by Talcott Parsons. © 1961 by The Free Press.

collectivity are particularistic. Though, of course, we must ta▐ about classes and types of roles, a role is always the role of▐ particular concrete individual. Similarly, a collectivity always h▐ a concrete membership of specific interacting role-incumbents.▐ norm, however, is always universalistically defined within t▐ universe of its relevance, whether it be a universe of acts, ▐ roles, or of collectivities. To be sure, the definition of a releva▐ universe involves a particularistic reference of a higher orde▐ thus, a norm may apply only to citizens or residents of the Unit▐ States, but it may cut across all concrete collectivity-membersh▐ differences within that universe. Values are also universalistica▐ defined in terms of relevance. When a particular *type* of society▐ evaluated as good, the judgment is inherently applicable to mo▐ than one specific society.

The universalistic aspect of values implies that, at the releva▐ level of reference, they are neither situation-specific n▐ function-specific. In this connection, it should be remembere▐ that the most crucial aspects of the situation of a social syste▐ consist in the personalities and the patterns of culture with whic▐ the system is in contact. When values are said not to ▐ situation-specific, it is implied that their normative validity is n▐ a function of the particular categories of personalities availab▐ for membership, nor, for example, of the particular levels ▐ technological knowledge available for implementing these value▐ When situation-specificity is introduced, we speak analytical▐ not of values, but of goals.

Similarly, values are independent of the internal differentiatio▐ of the systems in which they are institutionalized; they are rel▐ vant on a level of generality which "transcends" functional di▐ ferentiation. The keynote of differentiation, however, is func▐ tional. Hence, norms, which by the above definition are diffe▐ entiated with reference to function, must be function-specifi▐ They are "legitimized" by values, but operate at a lower level ▐ generality with respect to expected concrete collective and rol▐ performance. With respect to concrete roles in concrete colle▐ tivities, however, most norms are still not situation-specific–▐ especially since they do not specify the particular roles but a▐

generally formulated in classes and types of roles, and hence of persons and collectivities.

The relativity of the universalistic-particularistic distinction must again be emphasized. In general, the principle is that the universe relevant to the universalistic elements of normative culture is defined by the role and collectivity structure at the next higher level of system organization. It thus refers to a hierarchy of system-subsystem organization. The top of this hierarchy is the concept of society, which is the highest-order concrete system of interaction treated as theoretically relevant for the analytical purposes of sociology (including the possibility of an emergent "world society").

In line with the conception of the structure of social systems as consisting in the normative culture institutionalized in the system, we have so far presented a classification of its components organized with reference to the hierarchical order of the organization of the system. Structurally speaking, then, the role component is the normative component which governs the participation of individual persons in given collectivities. The collectivity component is the normative culture which defines the values, norms, goal-orientations, and ordering of roles for a concrete system of interaction of specifiable persons; the component of norms is the set of universalistic rules or norms which define expectations for the performance of classes of differentiated units within the system—collectivities, or roles, as the case may be; and values are the normative patterns defining, in universalistic terms, the pattern of desirable orientation for the system as a whole, independent of the specification of situation or of differentiated function within the system.

It should be made clear that roles are governed or controlled by the normative exigencies of the functioning of the collectivities within which they operate, if the collectivity itself is to be defined as a system. Therefore, in so far as a more inclusive social system comprises many collectivities as subsystems, the behavior of these collectivities is controlled by the institutionalized norms that specify how each type of collectivity must and may behave according to its place within the system. Finally, norms themselves are legitimized, and therefore, in a normative sense, con trolled, by the values institutionalized in the society. Subject t exigencies of situation and function, values define the direction c orientation that is desirable for the system as a whole.

Structures with Integrative Primacy. It has been suggested tha the focus of the integrative subsystem is the legal system; in modern Western type of society, particularly in the functioning c the appellate courts, and their relation to the more generalize aspects of legislation (much actual legislation is, considered func tionally, more concerned with policy decisions than wit establishing generalized norms). The establishment of a norm i not alone functionally adequate. The courts are concerned wit fundamental problems: interpretation; determination of jurisdic tional problems, i.e., in what circumstances a norm applies and t whom; and problems of sanctions or enforcement, i.e., de termining the consequences to the actor of compliance or non compliance. The central judicial function is interpretation, c which these other two are subcategories.

Norms, however, must be defined and interpreted, and also implemented. (We are not here concerned primarily with th executive function of enforcement, which is goal-attainmen rather than integration.)

The first imperative of a system of norms is its internal con sistency. This is a primary focus of the function of interpretatio and, in highly differentiated systems, is primarily a judicial func tion, though sometimes codes are prepared and legislativel enacted. Second, however, there is the specification of the appli cation of higher-order norms to levels where they can guide th action of the society's lower-level structural units by defining th situation for them. This particularly involves the collectivity an role levels of structure, and hence the institutionalization of th basic patterns governing these in political and economic respects

Another major functional problem of a normative system con cerns the adjustments occurring because a social system is alway involved in processes of interchange with a changin environment—indeed, always is subject to endogenous sources o change as well. These naturally have repercussions on units interrelationships, whose significance for the integration of th system is focussed in the bearing of these relations on the content of the system of norms, and on the degrees and motivation of conformity with norms.

There seem to be three basic types of processes of adjustment. One concerns keeping the regulatory norms at a sufficiently high level of generality so that much of the adjustment can be left to the spontaneous, i.e., unprescribed, action of the units themselves. A system of norms is analogous to a language, in that its rules as such do not "say" anything concrete, but provide a framework within which very many different things can be said and understood according to the occasion for saying them. In certain respects—not exclusively the economic sense—it is legitimate to refer to this as the area within which self-interest is permitted to operate. This "unit-individualism"—*unit* rather than *personal,* for much of it concerns collectivities—is not emancipation from all control through institutionalized norms. Rather, as Durkheim so clearly brought out, high levels of "responsible freedom" can be attained only through positive institutionalization, through systems of norms and sanctions imposing the *obligation* of accepting responsibility and utilizing freedom over wide areas. It may thus be referred to as "institutionalized individualism."

The second basic process of integrative adjustment is altering the content of normative patterns. The great integrative problem is to make such adjustments meet the varying functional needs without threatening the stability of the higher-level system of norms. The dangers of a system of norms are rigidity, or such flexibility that either adequate definition of the situation is lost or that what there is is functionally inappropriate. This operates at the higher levels through legislative, judicial, and administrative rulings and decisions, and, at lower and private collectivities, through functionally cognate mechanisms.

The third type of process operates, short of major structural change itself, in the areas where the other two are inadequate. The essential common feature of the first two is the expectation that the acting unit whose activities are to be controlled will, properly situated through definition of norms and sanctions, act as desired—operating through the situation, without attempting to change the internal structure of the unit, be it person-in-role collectivity. The processes of social control, in the narrow sociological sense, operate upon the "internal" system of tl unit; in the case of the individual-in-role, on his motivations sentiments. They not only facilitate or hinder his getting what l wants, but they redefine what he wants. Behavior subject to co trol can be technically termed deviant only when seen this wa

12

JURISDICTION

The main problems for analysis in this paper are the questions of what role-categories of social structure are most directly relevant to the relations of persons to territorial locations; what in turn are the principal categories of *meaning* of territorial location to persons in roles, and how are all these related to each other? From this point of view a territorial location is always significant as a "place where" something socially significant has happened or may be expected to happen. As points of reference always *both* the place where the person of reference is or is to be located, *and* the place where the significant object to which his action is oriented is located, must be considered.

[One] element of community structure I call *jurisdiction*. By this I mean obligations which are imposed on categories of persons by some process of decision-making where the ultimately relevant agency is held to have "legitimate authority" under a system of normative order. The most important point about obligations, however, is that at some level they imply a conditional procedure of "enforcement." This is to say that in attempting to control the fulfilment of the obligation, it is regarded as legitimate or even mandatory to apply "sanctions." The promise or threat of such sanctions, explicit or implicit, may also, of course, serve as a means of controlling compliance with, or infraction of, obligations.

Reprinted with deletions from "Principal Structures of Community: A Sociological View," in *Community*, ed. C. J. Friedrich (Liberal Arts Press, 1959), by permission of The American Society for Political and Legal Philosophy.

Sanctions, in the nature of the case, are specific to persons an categories of persons. The effectiveness of sanctions, again pos tive as well as negative, further depends on their *reaching* th object to whom they are directed. And to reach him, it has to be i a territorial location where he is, or may be expected to be at th relevant time. In its community reference, then, I would like t define an area of jurisdiction as the *area* in which an agency wit legitimate authority, which is attempting to control the behavic of persons or categories of persons, has the right to apply sanc tions to them.

So far I have referred to sanctions both positive and negative There is, however, an essential asymmetry between them. Th rests on the fact that, in the case of positive sanctions, there little inducement for the object of the sanctions to question th right of the agent to apply them in the place where he does. In th case of negative sanctions, on the other hand, since there is i centive to avoid them if possible, obvious strategies for suc avoidance are to question the right of the agent to apply th sanctions at all, or in the *place* in question, or to escape to a plac outside the range of jurisdiction.

For present purposes the difference between right and power i not important. The point is that a social system must be struc tured not only with respect to the *persons* and categories of the upon which obligations may be imposed, but also with respect t the *places* at which sanctions may be imposed.

The basic reason for the importance of place is, of course, tha if there is no physical organism in a specific place there is n action, and hence no effect of the sanction component of *inter* action. This means that control of the physical movements c people, in the sense of change of location, becomes an aspect c controlling their performance in social relationships. Th strategic role of physical force rests on two main consideration first, that in a "regression scale" of punishment the infliction c pain or injury on the organism is an ultimate recourse when othe fail, second, that while there are critical limits on the effective ness of force or the threat of force in motivation of positive ac tion, in the *prevention* of feared or disapproved action, force i the ultimate sanction. If the magnitude of the force is sufficier *any* person may be prevented from leaving a place or communicating from it, and hence significant action can be blocked. And in the very last analysis, in the human social sense of action, a dead man does not act.

The above statements should not in the least be taken to imply that "in the last analysis human action is controlled by force, or motivated by fear of force." It implies only that certain relatively *specific* conditions which affect systems of action, with special reference to its discouragement or prevention, can be controlled by force. But to imply that because a factor can prevent something or stop it, the whole process is determined by that factor is to argue as if, by equipping a vehicle with sufficiently powerful brakes alone you could make it run and steer it anywhere you wanted it to go.

One further proposition about force is essential, namely that *socially organized* force is inherently superior to what any unaided individual can ever muster. Hence, insofar as force is a *factor* in power, it is the control of organized force which matters, not the strength, or skill of the individual.

It should also be clearly understood that I am not limiting the concept of jurisdiction to contexts where the use of force is institutionalized, or a serious possibility. Thus, it is common for churches to claim jurisdiction over all persons of their faith resident within a territorial area; the parish or the diocese is in one aspect a jurisdictional area. But the church may be forbidden both by its own code and by the law to attempt or threaten to enforce this jurisdiction by force. It is fundamentally for jurisdictional reasons that an organization oriented to the implementation of codes always has a prominent element of territorial structuring. Thus there are usually a "central" office, and perhaps regional and local offices.

If, now, it is clear that jurisdiction in my sense does not as such imply the use of force, it is possible to proceed to develop a few implications of the strategic significance of force which nevertheless remains. The most important of these is that the *combination* of territorial jurisdiction and the attempted monopoly of the legitimate use of organized force is *one* of the primary features of political organization.

There have, in the history of political theory, been many controversies over the delineation of the category "political." I shall not try to review the alternatives but only to state my own view which derives from the attempt to place political aspects of organization in the context of a general analysis of the social system as a whole. Here I would give primary emphasis to the organization of the social system relative to the attainment of goals accepted as *binding* on the system as a whole.

For collective action in pursuit of such goals to be effective there naturally has to be integration of the system with reference to their acceptance and with reference to the distribution of responsibilities and burdens which it entails; this is the "consent" aspect of political organization. But jurisdiction relates to the use of force because if the political authority does not control the use of force, force controlled by other agencies, inside or outside the jurisdictional area, may serve to *prevent* the attainment of any goal politically accepted in the system. Hence the special criterion that attainment of a goal should be treated as *binding* would be directly jeopardized if force were not controlled. And because the sanctions of force must be applied to concrete physical persons in concrete physical locations, control of force without territorial jurisdiction is impossible.

Effectiveness in the control of force is, however, obviously central consideration. This depends on the effectiveness with which a population can be integrated in political terms. Hence, so far political jurisdiction has existed only for limited territorial areas, and many of the wider extensions have proved unstable and broken down rather rapidly.

It seems to be for reasons such as this that the *primary* framework of jurisdiction is found to be in the political reference and that the boundaries of integrated societal systems have strong tendency to coincide with the territorial jurisdictions of their political systems.

I have spoken of *tendency* because of the extent to which in fact countervailing tendencies also operate. The mixed "nationalities" problems of central and eastern Europe provide sufficient example that political jurisdiction and ethnic identity very often do not coincide.

The same general considerations which are relevant to the "state" as the widest area of firm political jurisdiction also apply with qualifications to the subdivisions of it. Here, of course, I mean subdivisions in a sense which does not beg the question of the relations between narrower and wider units of government or political jurisdiction. In the United States, we have both a federal system and a system of considerable local autonomy and "home rule" within the state in the sense of one of the fifty. Other systems are much more centralized and "provinces" are nearer to being branches of the central government, even towns and cities are branches. The central point is not this, but that *whatever* the pattern of centralization or decentralization, the *main* framework of subdivision of political organization is territorial. Government, like all organized subsystems of a society, has to have *functional* subdivisions, but these must in turn be brought together in terms of territorial organization at every level. You cannot *operate* a bureau of internal revenue without access to the taxpayers *where they are*, and they cannot be "got at" without the backing of *general* governmental authority in the specific local area.

A general point about social structures is relevant here. This is the distinction between differentiation and segmentation. Two differentiated subsystems of a larger system have different functions in the system so that their "contributions" are complementary; but they do not *do* the same things. The roles of husband and wife in the family are differentiated in this sense. Two subsystems are segments when they are structurally distinct units both performing essentially *the same* functions. Thus two infantry companies in a regiment, or two Ford assembly plants in different parts of the country are segments. Segmentation develops essentially from what economists would call limitations on the economies of scale, if this concept can be generalized so that it is not confined to economically relevant factors. Thus families are very small segments of the social structure. The fact that child rearing is not, in the usual familial respects, carried on in large organizations has something to do with the importance of very great "individualizing" which, in turn, one may suspect has something to do with the extreme "diffuseness" of the relevant communication, as that conception will be noted below.

Any exigency which influences the functioning of a social unit may be a factor in segmentation, but those linked with territoriality and physical processes are certainly prominent among them. The division of governmental units just mentioned is certainly a case in point, and all large organizations which operate in relation to a widely dispersed "public" tend to have segmentary administrative units arranged by territorial jurisdiction.

Another particularly important aspect of this problem is the relation of political jurisdiction to law. In the most general sociological sense, law may be said to be any relatively formalized and integrated body of rules which imposes obligations on persons playing particular roles in particular collectivities. Such a conception implies, I think further, that there is a machinery of authoritative interpretation, i.e., something analogous to a system of courts, and a machinery of the definition and implementation of sanctions, and a relatively clear focus of legitimation. It is quite clear that the concept of obligation from which I embarked on this discussion of jurisdiction, in any at all highly differentiated social system implies law.

Why then does the *highest* level of binding law in a highly differentiated society tend to be, as Dean Pound put it, the law of "*politically* organized society"? The answer, I think, is to be found in the relation of law to jurisdiction. It is because the highest *jurisdictional* authority is political. This, in turn, is true because, first, a system of law must eventually apply to defined categories of territorially located persons in roles. But secondly, to apply sanctions there must, for the reasons discussed above, be a jurisdictional reference. Though part of government, the "legal" system in modern societies (legal system in the sense not of the body of rules itself, but of the courts) is a very special part of it, enjoying a special kind of independence from the rest. The main reason why it is in government at all is that the reference to jurisdiction and to sanctions is essential if law is to be *binding*.

I have referred to the political as the "highest" jurisdictional authority. This certainly should not be interpreted to mean, for example, that political obligations are the "highest" human obligations, for instance, in a "moral" sense. I am speaking here of the jurisdictional aspect of the organization of the *society* as a system, and am saying that no society can be effectively integrated which permits other jurisdictional claims to take precedence over those of its governmentally sanctioned legal system. However, human responsibility is not defined only in terms of responsibility in the society. But when the reference *is* to the society, an obligation not "in principle" directly incorporated in the law of the state must fall in one or more of three categories. First, it may fall within the range of freedom allowed and defined by the law of the state. This is the case with the whole range of *socially* sanctioned "private" interests, be they personal, economic, religious or what not. Second, it may be felt to be an obligation *in conflict* with those imposed by the law. In this case the only recourses are to change the law, or to resort to the various tactics of deviant behavior, e.g., evasion or rebellion. Third, it may fall in an extra-social realm. Thus a person may feel for himself an obligation to "think straight" about a certain personal problem. So long as the consequence is not identifiably expressed in his interactive behavior, the law has nothing to say about it nor any sanctions to impose. In principle, the same is true of "the state of his immortal soul" which, being a nonempirical state of affairs, cannot be reached by empirical sanctions in any earthly jurisdiction.

Some would argue that historically the role of the church did not fit this view of political primacy in the field of jurisdiction. I do not think this is the case if we stick strictly to the treatment of jurisdiction as a structural aspect of a social system. It would certainly be correct to say that the Medieval Church (and churches today as well) claimed to define the highest *moral* obligations of its members, and to impose the ultimate *religious* sanctions in relation to this obligation; but moral obligations are not *ipso facto* social obligations and religious sanctions are not *ipso facto* social sanctions. Only when the moral-religious jurisdiction of the church had been *translated into* political jurisdiction could it be said to be *socially* paramount. This means that, though in the Middle Ages the "state" was organizationally differentiated from the church, it was only in a highly qualified sense *independent* of the church. On the societal level orthodoxy of belief could only become a *sine qua non* of membership in the society in good standing if, as was in fact the case, heresy was a *civil* crime. The church, to be sure, did not "itself" burn heretics at the stake. But if the political authority had not lent *its* jurisdictional backing to the service of the obligations insisted upon by the church, the medieval system of religious unity on the *social* level could not have been maintained.

For the society as a whole, I have argued that political jurisdiction is paramount, and no society can be effectively "politically organized" if a claim of other jurisdictions to supersede that of the law is successfully put through. But this does not mean that the concept of jurisdiction does not apply to *all* subsystems of the society so far as they are governed by a normative order defining obligations, which will be enforced by sanctions. They will of course differ in territorial area, but also in the nature of the obligations and of the sanctions. The cases of "delegation" of the legitimate use of force are on the whole minor, such as parents' rights to spank children. For this reason the ultimate negative sanction of non-governmental collectivities is usually expulsion from membership.

III. INSTITUTIONALIZED EXCHANGE

As Parsons moved to a more macrosociological approach to the study of institutional order, his concept of normative structure came to stress norms as a general framework for stabilizing exchange rather than as rules directly regulating conduct. In this respect he was influenced by Emile Durkheim, whose notion of "noncontractual elements of contract" provided a model for the analysis of institutionally regulated systems of exchange. The first selection in this section is from Parsons's article of homage to Durkheim: "Durkheim's Contribution to the Theory of Integration of Social Systems" (1959). "Double Exchanges," a selection from *Economy and Society* (1956), provides a systematic account of the idea that social processes may be described and explained as exchanges between the subsystems of a larger system—the economy, the polity, and the integrative and pattern-maintenance systems. Parsons spent most of the second half of his intellectual career extending and elaborating the ideas introduced in *Economy and Society*.

The exchanges between subsystems are facilitated by symbolic media, of which money is the prototypical example. "On the Concept of Influence" (1963), is an illustrative example of Parsons's extensive use of the analogy to money. Influence, like money, mediates exchanges of resources between subsystems of the social system; like money, it can be created, and its value is subject to inflation and deflation. The rise and fall of confidence in symbolic media are among the more potent forces in modern society.

13

DURKHEIM ON ORGANIC SOLIDARITY

It is appropriate at this time, just a little over one hundred years after the birth of Emile Durkheim, to take stock of his contributions to what was perhaps the central area of his theoretical interest. The development of theoretical thinking that has taken place in the intervening years enables us to achieve greater clarity in the identification and evaluation of these contributions.

It can be said, I think, that it was the problem of the integration of the social system, of what holds societies together, which was the most persistent preoccupation of Durkheim's career. In the situation of the time, one could not have chosen a more strategic focus for contributing to sociological theory. Moreover, the work Durkheim did in this field can be said to have been nothing short of epoch-making; he did not stand entirely alone, but his work was far more sharply focused and deeply penetrating than that of any other author of his time. Because of this profundity, the full implications of his work have not yet been entirely assimilated by the relevant professional groups. Furthermore, in addition to the intrinsic complexity of the subject, the rather special frame of reference of French Positivism in which he couched his analysis has made it difficult to interpret him.

There are two essential reference points in Durkheim's initial orientation: one is positive and the other negative. The positive is the Comtean conception of "consensus" as the focus of unity in

Reprinted by permission with deletions from "Durkheim's Contribution to the Theory of Social Systems," in *Emile Durkheim, 1858–1917*, ed. Kurt H. Wolff (Columbus: Ohio State University Press, 1960).

societies. This was the primary origin of the famous concept of the *conscience collective;* this rather than any German conception of *Geist* is clearly what Durkheim had in mind. It was a sound starting point, but it was much too simple and undifferentiated to serve his purposes; primarily, perhaps, becuase it could not account for the fundamental phenomenon of unity in diversity, the phenomenon of the integration of a highly differentiated system.

The negative reference point is the utilitarian conception of the interplay of discrete individual interest, as first put forward by Herbert Spencer who conceived of an industrial society as a network of "contractual relations."[1] The importance of relations of contract, that is, relations in which terms are settled by some type of *ad hoc* agreement, was an immediate consequence of the division of labor which had been emphasized in the long tradition of utilitarian economics deriving from Locke and from Adam Smith's famous chapter. Durkheim made this tradition the focal point of his criticism, tackling it in one of its main citadels; and, in so doing, he raised the problem of the differentiated system which Comte had not really dealt with.

In this critique, Durkheim shows, with characteristic thoroughness and penetration, that Spencer's assumptions—which were those common to the whole liberal branch of the utilitarian tradition—failed to account for even the most elementary component of order in a system of social relations that was allegedly based on the pursuit of individual self-interest. To put it a little differently, no on had been able to answer Hobbes's fundamental question *from within the tradition,*[2] since Hobbes's own solution was palpably unacceptable. As is well known, Durkheim's emphasis is on the *institution* of contract, which at one point he characterizes as consisting in the "noncontractual elements" of contract. These are not items agreed upon by contracting parties in the particular situation, but are norms established in the society, norms which underlie and are independent of any particular contract. They are partly embodied in formal law, though not necessarily only in what in a strict technical sense is called the law of contract by jurists, and partly in more informal "understandings" and practice. The content of these norms may be summed up as follows: They consist, first of all, in definitions of what content is permitted and what content is prohibited in contractual agreement—in Western society of recent times, for instance, contracts that infringe on the personal liberty of either party or of any third party in his private capacity are prohibited; second, in definitions of the means of securing the assent of the other party that are legitimate and of those that are illegitimate—in general, coercion and fraud are considered illegitimate, however difficult it may be to draw exact borderlines; third, in definitions of the scope and limits of responsibility which may be reasonably (or legally) imputed to one or another party to a contractual relation, either originally on the basis of his "capacity" to enter binding agreements—as agent for a collectivity, for example—or subsequently on the basis of the consequences to himself and others of the agreements made; and, fourth, in definitions of the degree to which the interest of the society is involved in any particular private agreement, the degree to which private contracts bear on the interests of third parties or on those of the collectivity as a whole.[3]

Durkheim postulated the existence of what he called organic solidarity as a functional necessity underlying the institutionalization of contract. This may be characterized as the integration of units, units which, in the last analysis, are individual persons in roles, who are performing qualitatively differentiated functions in the social system. The implication of such differentiation is that the needs of the unit cannot be met solely by his own activities. By virtue of the specialization of his function, the unit becomes dependent on the activities of others who must meet the needs which are not covered by this specialized function. There is, therefore, a special type of interdependence that is generated by this functional differentiation. The prototype is the kind of division of labor described by the economists. Clearly, Durkheim's conception is broader than this. For example, he describes the differentiation of function between the sexes, in social as well as biological terms, as a case of the division of labor in his sense.

What, then, is indicated by "organic solidarity"? The most important problem in interpreting the meaning of the concept is to determine its relation to the conception of the *conscience collec-*

tive. Durkheim's primary interest is in the fact that units agree on norms because they are backed by values held in common, although the interests of the differentiated units must necessarily diverge. Durkheim's original definition of the *conscience collective* is as follows: "L'ensemble des croyances et des sentiments communs à la moyenne des membres d'une même société forme un système déterminé qui a sa vie propre; on peut l'appeler la conscience collective ou commune."[4] The keynote of this definition is, clearly, beliefs and sentiments that are held in common. This formula is essential, for it indicates that the problem of solidarity is located in the area of what may very broadly be called the motivational aspects of commitment to the society, and to conformity with the expectations institutionalized within it. Taken alone, however, it is too general to serve as more than a point of departure for an analysis of the problems of solidarity and hence of societal integration. Furthermore, Durkheim himself was seriously embarrassed by the problem of how to connect the *conscience collective* with the differentiation resulting from the division of labor.

It seems to me that Durkheim's formula needs to be further elaborated by two sets of distinctions. He himself made essential contributions to one of these, the distinction between mechanical and organic solidarity; but one of the main sources of difficulty in understanding his work is his relative neglect of the second set of distinctions, and his tendency to confuse it with the first. This second set concerns the levels of generality achieved by the cultural patterns—values, differentiated norms, collectivities, and roles—that have been institutionalized in a society. It also concerns the controls that articulate these levels and that determine the direction in which the controls operate. A discussion of the levels of generality of these four cultural patterns will provide a setting for a consideration of mechanical and organic solidarity and of the relations between them.

Values are the "normative patterns" that are descriptive of a positively evaluated social system. Norms are generalized patterns of expectation which define differentiated patterns of expectation for the differentiated kinds of units within a system. In a particular system, norms always stand at a lower level of cultural generality than do values. Put a little differently, norms can be legitimized by values, but not vice versa.

A collectivity stands at a still lower level in the hierarchy of the normative control of behavior. Subject both to the more general values of the system and to the norms regulating the behavior of the relevant differentiated types of units within the system, the normative culture of a collectivity defines and regulates a concrete system of coordinated activity that can at any given time be characterized by the commitments of specifically designated persons, and which can be understood as a specific system of collective goals in a specific situation. The functional reference of norms at the level of the collectivity is, then, no longer general, but is made specific in the particular goals, situations, and resources of the collectivity, including its "share" in the goals and resources of society.

All social systems arise out of the interaction of human individuals as units. Hence the most important exigencies of the situation in which collectivities as units perform social functions are the conditions for effective performance by the constituent human individuals (including their command of physical facilities). But since the typical individual participates in more than one collectivity, the relevant structural unit is not the "total" individual or personality, but the individual in a role. In its normative aspect, then, a role may be thought of as the system of normative expectations for the performance of a participating individual in his capacity as a member of a collectivity. The role is the primary point of direct articulation between the personality of the individual and the structure of the social system.

Values, norms, and collective goals—all in some sense control, "govern," and "regulate" the behavior of individuals in roles. But only at the level of the role is the normative content of expectations specifically oriented to the exigencies presented by the personalities or "motives" of individuals (and categories of them differentiated by sex, age, level of education, place of residence, and the like) and by the organic and physical environment.

Values, norms, collectivities, and roles are categories that are descriptive of the structural aspect of a social system only. In addition to such categories, it is necessary to analyze the system in functional terms in order to analyze processes of differentiation and the operation of these processes within a structure. Furthermore, process utilizes resources, carrying them through a series of stages of genesis, and either "consuming" them or incorporating and combining them into types of output or product, such as cultural change. The structure of institutionalized norms is the main point of articulation between these societal structures and the functional exigencies of the system. These exigencies, in turn, determine the mechanisms and categories of input and output relative to integration. Let us try to relate these considerations to the categories of mechanical and organic solidarity.

Durkheim's conception of mechanical solidarity is rooted in what I have called the system of common societal values. This is evident from the strong emphasis which he places on the relation of mechanical solidarity to the *conscience collective*. As a system of "beliefs and sentiments" that are held in common, Durkheim's *conscience collective* is more broadly defined than the system of societal values which I have given above. But it is certain that such a system is included in Durkheim's definition, and it can be argued that a system of values is the structural core of the system of beliefs and sentiments to which he refers. It should be clear, however, that Durkheim did not attempt systematically to distinguish and classify the components of the *conscience collective*, and this would seem to be essential if a satisfactory analysis of its relation to the problem of solidarity is to be made.

Such an analysis must do at least two things. In the first place, the value component must be distinguished from the others, that is, from cognitive (existential) beliefs, patterns of motivational commitment (these are close to Durkheim's "sentiments"), and patterns of legitimation of collective action (these will figure in the discussion presently). The second task involves the determination of the variations in the levels of generality and degrees of specificity of the components—of values, in particular—which eventuates in a scale corresponding to the differentiation of a society into numerous subsystems. Because of his failure to perform these two tasks, Durkheim was not able to be very exact about the relation of the *conscience collective* to mechanical solidarity, and was forced to resort to contrasting this relation with that of the *conscience collective* to organic solidarity—and this relation gave him considerable difficulty.

Mechanical solidarity is rooted in the common value component of the *conscience collective* and is an "expression" of it. Its relation to the other components is problematical. There is, however, another major aspect of mechanical solidarity, namely, its relation to the structure of the society as a collectivity. Every society is organized in terms of a paramount structure of the total system as a collectivity. In the highly differentiated modern society, this structure takes the form of governmental organization. In addition, there is, of course, an immensely complex network of lower-level collectivities, some of which are subdivisions of the governmental structure, while others are independent of it in various ways and degrees. The problem of mechanical solidarity arises wherever a collectivity is organized, but it is essential to understand what system is under consideration.

The focus of Durkheim's analysis of mechanical solidarity, in so far as it concerns the structure of the social system, lies, I suggest, in the relation between the paramount values of the society and its organization as a collectivity at the requisite level; that is, the governmental organization of the society where the system of reference is, as it is for Durkheim, the society as a whole. Mechanical solidarity is the integration of the common values of the society with the commitments of units within it to contribute to the attainment of collective goals—either negatively by refraining from action which would be felt to be disruptive of this function, or positively by taking responsibility for it.

This duality of reference is brought out with particular clarity in Durkheim's discussion of criminal law as an index or expression of mechanical solidarity. On the one hand, he makes reference to common "sentiments"; on the other, to obligations to the organized collectivity as such.[5] Also, since in all advanced societies government is the paramount agent for the application of coercion, Durkheim strongly emphasizes the role of the element of sanction in the repressive type of law. Two of the four primary functional references of a legal system noted above, legitimation and enforcement through sanctions, figure importantly in what Durkheim calls repressive law.

The preceding considerations account for the location of the phenomenon of mechanical solidarity with reference to the structure of the social system. This solidarity or integration of the system is brought about by the interplay of the system of common values, which legitimizes organization in the interest of collective goals with the commitments of units of the system (which are, in the last analysis, individual persons in roles) to loyalty and responsibility. This loyalty and responsibility are not only to the values themselves, but to the collectivity whose functioning is guided by those values and which institutionalizes them. This location in the social structure does not, however, tell us anything about the mechanisms by which the integration is generated.

Before approaching the question of the mechanisms that produce integration, it will be well to raise the corresponding question of structural location with respect to "organic solidarity." My suggestion is that, by contrast with the question of mechanical solidarity, this one does not concern the value system directly, but rather the system of institutionalized norms in relation to the structure of roles in the society. This is not putting it in Durkheim's own terms, for he did not use the concept of role that has become so important to sociological theory in the last generation. The importance of the reference to norms in his analysis is, however, entirely clear.

Furthermore, Durkheim's discussion is fully in accord with the distinction made previously between values and differentiated norms as structural components of the social system, since he so strongly emphasized the relation of organic solidarity to the differentiation of functions among units in the system, and specifically to the differentiation of expectations of behavior.[6]

Though he enumerated a number of other fields, it is also clear that there is, for Durkheim, a special relation between organic solidarity, contract, and the economic aspects of the organization of societies. This relation can, I think, provide the principal clue to the way in which roles are involved. Collectivities, it has been suggested previously, constitute the primary operative agencies for the performance of social function. The resources necessary for that performance consist, in turn, besides solidarity itself and the related patterns of "organization," in cultural resources, physical facilities, and human services. "Solidarity" cannot be treated as a component for Durkheim's purposes because it is his dependent variable; he is concerned with the conditions on which it depends. He does not treat cultural resources—knowledge, for example. He is careful, nevertheless, to take account of the role of physical facilities in discussing the institutionalization of property rights. His main concern, however, is with human services and the ways in which they can be integrated for the performance of social function.

The central problem involved here may be looked at, in the first instance, in a developmental setting. It is a general characteristic of "primitive" societies that the allocation of resources among their structurally significant units is overwhelmingly ascribed. This is most obvious in the economic sphere itself. The factors of production are controlled by units that do not have specialized economic primacy of function, and they are typically not transferable from one unit to another. Indeed, even products are seldom exchanged, and when they are, the transfer is likely to take place as a ceremonial exchange of gifts rather than in barter, as we understand it—to say nothing of market exchange. This is particularly true of labor, often thought to be the central factor of economic production.

The division of labor brings freedom from ascriptive ties regarding the utilization of consumable goods and services and the factors of production themselves. The structural location of organic solidarity thus concerns the dual problem of how the processes by which the potentially conflicting interests that have been generated can be reconciled without disruptive conflict (this leads, of course, into the Hobbesian problem), and of how the societal interest in efficient production can be protected and promoted.

Every society must, as a prerequisite of its functioning, presume some integration of the interest of units with those of the society—elsewhere I have called this the "institutional integration of motivation."[7] But by itself this is not enough. One path to further development is to use the organs of the collective attainment of goals as the agencies for defining and enforcing integration or solidarity of this type. This involves a near fusion of mechanical and organic bases of solidarity of the sort that is most conspicuous in socialistic economies. An independent basis of integration can develop, however, from the institutionalization of systems of norms and mechanisms that without centralized direction permit the allocation of fluid resources to proceed in a positively integrated manner.

This set of norms and mechanisms is organized in terms of two complementary reference points. One of these is the sociological reference to economic analysis and interests, the process by which generalized disposability of resources builds up. This concerns above all the institutionalization of contract, of property and of the disposability of labor service through employment in occupational roles. Property and labor then become generalized resources. They can be allocated and controlled through processes which establish functionally specific claims, rather than through prior (and, therefore, in all likelihood, functionally irrelevant) bases of ascriptive claim, such as membership in a common kinship unit. This, of course, involves some sort of process of exchange among functionally differentiated units in the system.

It is an essential aspect of Durkheim's argument that this generalizability and fluid disposability of resources requires more than a freeing from irrelevant, usually ascriptive constraints. It also requires a positive institutionalization of correlative obligations and rights which are defined in terms of a normative structure. From the point of view of the definition of resources, this type of normative regulation becomes the more imperative the further removed the ultimate utilization of the resource is from what may be thought of as a "natural" to-be-taken-for-granted set of rights to this utilization. From the point of view of the resource, then, a dual process is necessary: First, the resource must be "generalized"—this involves freeing it from ascriptive controls; and, second, the positive obligation to enter into the generalized allocative system must be established. Thus in a primary ascriptive society, the equivalent of what are occupational oles in our own were filled on the basis of kinship obligations, as n the case of a son who follows his father as the proprietor and cultivator of the land held by the continuing kinship unit. In our own society, to train for an occupation in which one can compete n the labor market, and to be willing to take one's chances on inding satisfactory employment constitute a positively institutionalized obligation of the normal adult male, and of a considerable number of the members of the other sex. Therefore, here is, in a sense, a "speculative" production of labor power which precedes any specification of its channels of use. This is, of course, even more true of the control of physical facilities.

At the same time, there must also be a series of mechanisms which can determine the patterns in which such a generalized esource is utilized. As the division of labor becomes more highly leveloped, the proportion of such resources which are utilized in collectivities that have specific functions becomes greater. These collectivities command monetary resources which can in turn be used to contract for labor services and to provide necessary physical facilities. The institutionalization of contract is the normative system which offers access to such resources—whatever he function of the organization itself may be. The institution of property, then, regulates monetary resources and physical facilities; the institution of occupation controls human services.

It is important to note here the complex relation which exists between the economic and non-economic aspects of the constellation of factors that I am outlining. Economic production as such is only one of the primary societal functions served by the processes of production and mobilization of fluid resources through the institutionalization of contract, markets, money, property, and occupational roles. Indeed, any major function may be promoted in that way—education, health care, scientific research, and governmental administration. There are only certain special limiting cases, like the family and certain aspects of the political process, which cannot be "bureaucratized" in this sense.

At the same time, it is correct to say that the mechanisms involved here—regardless of the ultimate function that they subserve in any particular case—are primarily economic; namely, contract, markets, money, and the like. We must exercise great care, therefore, when using such a term as economic in this kind of analysis.

The generalized disposability of resources, then, is one major aspect of the functional complex which is institutionalized through organic solidarity. The other aspect concerns the standards and mechanisms by which their allocation among alternative claimant units of the social structure is worked out. Here it is clear that, within the institutional framework of contract, property, and occupation, the primary direct mechanisms concern the structuring of markets and the institutionalization of money.

This brings us back to the subtle ways in which conventional economic and non-economic elements are involved. The market may be regarded as the structural framework for the allocation of disposable resources in so far as the mechanism of this allocation is primarily freely contractual at the level of the operative organization or collectivity. Two other types of mechanism must be distinguished from this one, however. The first is administrative allotment, which is a "free" disposal of resources by those who supposedly enjoy nearly full control of them. Theoretically, this would be the case if the economy were fully socialized, for a central planning body would simply make decisions and assign budgetary quotas—indeed it might also directly distribute labor and physical facilities. The second mechanism involves negotiation between the higher agencies which hold the resources and their prospective users in such a way that political power plays a prominent part in determining the outcome whether or not governmental structures are prominently involved. An example of this would be the distribution through legislative action of public works benefits on the basis of regional and local interests, a procedure which often involves a good deal of "log-rolling."

Empirically, there is shading-off between these types. Typologically, however, in the market the bargaining powers of the contracting partners are approximately equal; neither the holders nor the utilizers of resources are simply "told" where they are to go or what they are to get; and the degree of power held by the higher level of the goal-directed organization of the relevant collectivity structure is not the decisive mechanism in the process of allocation. The market is an institutionalized mechanism which neutralizes both these potential mechanisms of allocation in a number of areas, preventing them from being the primary determinants of more detailed allocations. This means essentially that there is a hierarchy of allocative mechanisms, whose relations to each other are ordered by institutionalized norms. Among these norms are those which define the areas within which, and the occasions on which, the more "drastic" controls may and may not be allowed to supersede the "freer" mechanism of the market. Thus the taxing power of government determines a compulsory allocation of monetary resources; and certain allocations are subject to legislative control in that limitations are placed on the freedom of individual units to contract for them at will.

However, it is clearly in accord with Durkheim's views of organic solidarity to point out that within the market sphere freedom is balanced and controlled by complex sets of institutionalized norms, so that the freedoms themselves and the rights and obligations associated with them are defined in terms of such institutionalized norms. There are, in this area, two main categories of such institutionalized structures. One concerns the institutionalization of the monetary mechanism itself, the definition of the sphere of its legitimate use, and, of course, the limits of this sphere. The other concerns the institutionalization of conditions under which market transactions involving different subcategories of resources may be entered into. Let us take up the latter class of norms first.

In general terms, norms of the highest order in a modern society clearly have the status of formal legal rules and principles. They are subject to the legislative power, and the task of interpreting and administering them is the responsibility of the courts of law. For organic solidarity, as noted above, the complex of contract, property, and occupation is central; whereas leadership, authority, and what I have elsewhere called regulation are central to mechanical solidarity.

Freedom of contract, then, includes the freedom to define the conditions and limitations of the various terms which—as I have previously set forth—are involved in a contractual system with respect to the content of agreements, the means of securing assent, the scope of responsibility, and the societal interest. At both the legal and informal levels, then, these conditions and limitations vary in accordance with the societal functions performed by the contracting units, the various aspects of the situations in which they operate, and other similar considerations. Thus a private relationship between a physician and a patient, established to serve the interest of the patient's health, is sanctioned. However, the offering of certain types of health service is restricted partly by law and partly by informal institutionalization, and may be performed only by licensed and "adequately trained" physicians; and the acceptance of such services is, if it is legitimate restricted, in a more informal sense, to persons who are really "sick." There is abundant evidence that there is wide area in which illness is not so much an objective "condition" as a socially defined role.

Therefore, the problem of the content of contractual relations involves differentiating between role-categories that are regarded as the legitimate bearers of various social functions and those that are not. A consumer or client may contract for a very wide range of goods and services, but he is not completely free to choose the agencies with which he will contract, since institutional norms define the functions which certain agencies may perform.

In addition, the ways in which the terms of the contract are settled are institutionalized in various ways, and this influences the structure of the market. Economists have been particularly concerned with one type, the "commercial" market, where prices are arrived at on the basis of "competition," and where there is an institutionalized expectation that the right of the purveying agency to continue in operation is a function of its ability to meet expenses and to show a profit. Furthermore, it is the customer's expectation that the price he pays will cover the full cost of what he purchases. However, the structure of the market in which a large number of governmental, professional, and other services are purveyed, is quite different. Although a service may be entirely free in the monetary sense, the conditions of eligibility may be sharply defined, as in the case of those regulating admission to public hospitals. Or, as is often the case in private medical practice, there may be a sliding scale of costs, so that one participant in the contract, the patient—contrary to what is expected of the customer in the commercial market—fulfills only part of his obligation in that the fee he pays covers a portion of the costs of performing the service contracted for which ranges from far less than average unit cost to very much more.

Furthermore, there is the problem of the scope of the responsibility involved in such a relation. The Spencerian version of the idea of contract tended to assume that the question of the participants' abilities to "deliver" presented no complicated problem. The typical economic exchange in which the buyer has sufficient money and the seller sufficient goods is taken as the prototype. But this is by no means always the situation. As an illustration, let us again take a certain type of professional relationship. A sick person cannot be held responsible for ending his deplored condition simply by making a voluntary effort: his helplessness is a primary criterion by which his need of, and right to, professional service is determined. But he is responsible for recognizing his helplessness and for actively cooperating with therapeutic agencies in bringing about his recovery. These agencies, in turn, though their role may be defined in terms of technical competence, must recognize a wide variation in the capacities of individuals so that if there is a failure in certain cases, the physician is not held responsible, provided he has done his best. Another good example is found in education where because of the youth of the ignorant person, ignorance is not considered culpable. Nor is a child expected to educate himself without the help of schools. He is, however, expected to work hard in acquiring his education within the framework of the school. And some children are harder to educate than others, and failures are not treated as being always or wholly the teacher's fault. There are elaborately institutionalized norms covering fields such as these.

The protection of the interest of society in contractual relations is more diffusely institutionalized; it is, in a sense, an aspect of all the norms in this area. At the legal level, however, there are a number of provisions which enable the courts and other governmental agencies that represent the public interest to intervene in order to prevent or modify such arrangements. Because of its very nature, the institutionalization of a contractual system involves the imposition of a whole system of limitations on the powers of government. But the residual opportunities for private interests to exploit their freedom against the rest of the society require the maintenance of a delicately balanced equilibrium of integration.

The monetary mechanism is essential because, in the first place, the division of labor cannot develop very far if all exchanges are restricted to the level of barter. In a fully developed system, money has four primary functions. It serves, first, as a measure of the economic value of resources and products. It is in this connection that we speak of the gross national product as a monetary sum. Second, it serves as a standard for the rational allocation of resources, for comparing cost and outcome. Only in the "business" sector, where productive function in the economic sense has primacy, is the monetary standard the primary one applied. But in other functional areas, too, such as education or health, monetary cost is a very essential evaluative mechanism in that it is, from the point of view of the unit, the basis for evaluating one major component in the conditions necessary to accomplish whatever goal is involved, and is, from the point of view of the system at large, a measure of the sacrificed uses to which the resources in question might have been put.

It is thus essential to discriminate profitability as a measure of the worthwhileness of a function from the use of monetary cost as one component of the conditions that must be weighed in arriving at a judgment of worthwhileness. The capacity somehow to cover monetary cost, the ability to raise the money somehow, is, of course, a necessary limiting condition of those functions which require resources that are acquired through the market.

In serving as a measure and standard, money does not circulate; nothing changes hands. In performing its other two functions, however, money is a medium of exchange. In the first of these, money is an essential facility wherever the attainment of goals is dependent on resources accessible through market channels. Not only is it necessary to have it, but, it must be noted, in a ighly developed market system, there is an extraordinarily wide range of choices open to the unit that possesses sufficient funds. The other mediating function of money is to serve as a reward. Here the reference is in the nature of the case comparative and relative; what counts is the amount of monetary income received by one unit or resource as compared with that received by another. It is this function of money that is the primary focus of the regulation of the process of allocation of resources, in so far as this is the result of market transactions. The basic principle is the economic one: A resource will flow to that one of the situations in which it is utilized that offers the highest relative reward, the reward being, in this case, monetary.

Here again it is essential, however, to insist on the same basic distinction which was made in connection with the standards of allocation. Money is not the sole component of the complex of rewards. It has primacy over other components only when the function of economic production has primacy over other functions, that is, in the "business" sector of the organizational and occupational system. It is essentially for this reason that the monetary remuneration for human services in that sector is higher than other sectors such as government, education, and so on. But even where other components of reward—political power, integrative acceptance or solidarity, or cultural prestige—have primacy within a given subsystem, it is essential that the monetary remuneration correspond to the quality of the services performed, as determined on the basis of the dominant criteria for that subsystem. In the academic profession, for example, contrary to the situation in the business occupations, the amount of one's income is not a valid measure of one's relative prestige in the general occupational system. Within the profession, however, and especially within the same faculty, there is strong pressure to establish a correspondence between professional competence and the salaries paid. Failure to do so is a prime source of integrative strain.

I have taken the space to discuss the relation among the allocation of fluid resources, the institutionalization of contract, property, and occupation, and the market and money in some detail because such an analysis is more comprehensive than any Durkheim was in a position to give, and thus provides a large setting in which to evaluate the true importance of his basic in sights about organic solidarity. His crucial insight is that there must be, in this area, a whole complex of institutionalized norms as a condition of the stability of a functionally differentiated sys tem. In *De la division du travail social*, Durkheim did not go very far in analyzing the motivations underlying adherence to such norms. But he was entirely clear on one central point, namely that this adherence on the part of the acting unit in the system could not be motivated primarily by considerations of expedien utility. This is the basic reason why the concept of the *conscience collective* as consisting in "beliefs and sentiments held in com mon" is of such central importance. In his later work, he took three major steps bearing on this question of motivation. Before attempting to outline these, however, it is well to discuss briefly the relation of the *conscience collective* to organic solidarity and the relation of organic and mechanical solidarity to each other.

Concerning the first of these two problems, Durkheim seems to have been genuinely confused, for he failed to clarify the struc tural distinction between values and norms, which I have pre sented earlier, and did not see that this distinction applies and is relevant equally to organic and mechanical solidarity. Instead, he got bogged down in the identification of mechanical solidarity with a lack of differentiation of structure, and hence with the similarity of roles which are personal expressions of the commu nity of beliefs and sentiments. Consequently, he had no clear criteria for defining the relation of functionally differentiated norms to the *conscience collective*. Durkheim's treatment of the conception of the "dynamic density" of a social system and its relation to competition, represents, as Schnore has pointed out,[8] a valid attempt to solve the problem of the processes of structural differentiation, but he did not succeed in linking it to his master concept of the *conscience collective*.

It is now possible to state his fundamental relation more adequately: As noted above, the crucial component of the *con science collective* is common societal values. Commitment to such values, carefully interpreted with reference to the object concerned—that is, the society as such—and to the level of generality or specification, is one major component of the general phenomenon of institutionalization. Institutionalization is, in turn, the primary basis, at the level of the integration of the social system, of Durkheim's "solidarity." But with respect to any fundamental function of the social system, values must be specified in terms of their relevance to that particular function. Furthermore, values must be brought to bear on the legitimation of the differentiated institutionalized norms that are necessary to regulate behavior in the area of that function—to regulate it, on the one hand, in relation to the concrete exigencies under which it operates, and, on the other, in relation to the interest of the society as a system. Legitimation itself, however, is not enough; in addition, there must be the functions of defining jurisdiction, of defining and administering sanctions, and of interpreting the norms themselves.

This basic complex of relationships and functions can be quite clearly worked out for the division of labor as an economic phenomenon and for the institutions clustering around it. This complex was Durkheim's primary reference; and, except for the fact that his formulation of its relation to the *conscience collective* is ambiguous, he made an excellent start on analyzing it. But he did not see that the properties of the contractual complex are directly paralleled by those of the complex involving mechanical solidarity. I have suggested that this parallel primarily concerns the relations between common values and the institutionalization of political function in the society. Here also, the values must be specified at a concrete level in order to legitimize not only society in the broadest sense, but also the type of organization which is institutionalized in it for the attainment of collective goals. This organization is, however, a differentiated functional area which in certain fundamental respects is parallel to, or cognate with, that of the mobilization of fluid resources. Furthermore, it involves differentiated structures within itself at the norm, collectivity, and role levels. Hence the relation of values to norms is essentially the same in this area as in the economic. The norms must be legitimated, but, in addition, jurisdictions must be defined, sanctions specified, and norms interpreted. The *conscience collective* does not perform these functions directly or automatically. The differentiated normative complex which centers on the institutionalization of leadership and authority parallels the complex which centers on contract, property, and occupational role in the economic area. Power is a measure and medium that in those respects which are relevant is parallel to money.

Durkheim's treatment involves a further complication, namely, the problem of evolutionary sequence. He made two crucially important points in this connection. The first is that the development of the patterns of organic solidarity that are connected with an extensive division of labor presupposes the existence of a system of societal integration characterized by mechanical solidarity. The second is that the economic division of labor and an elaborated and differentiated governmental organization develop concomitantly. It is not a case of one's developing at the expense of the other.

Sound as these two insights were, Durkheim's association of mechanical solidarity with a lack of structural differentiation inclined him toward identifying this association with primitiveness in an evolutionary sense, and prevented him from making the essential connection between common values and the legitimation of the political order and organization in a more differentiated, modern type of society. The relation of modern political institutions to solidarity—very much like that of economic institutions to solidarity—was simply left hanging in the air.

I should like to suggest, therefore, a refinement of Durkheim's classification. If organic solidarity and mechanical solidarity are correlative terms, one should refer to the type of solidarity which focuses on the legitimation of political institutions, and the other to that type which focuses on economic institutions. Broadly speaking, we may say that, although the situation varies substantially with the type of social structure, both exist simultaneously in parts of the same social system, parts that can be distinguished on the basis of structure and through analysis; and there should be no general tendency for one to replace the other. The solidarity which exists prior to the development of any of the higher levels of social differentiation is not the same thing as this "political" type. The latter is closer to the principal referent of

Durkheim's mechanical solidarity, but I should prefer another term—"diffuse solidarity," for example. It is the common matrix out of which *both* the others have emerged by a process of differentiation.

Durkheim seems to have faced a very common difficulty in dealing with the processes of differentiation. When a component of a system retains the same name at a later, more highly differentiated phase in the development of the system that it had at an earlier, less differentiated one, the component carrying the original name will have less importance in the later phase. This follows inevitably from the fact that in the earlier phase it may have designated one of, say, four cognate components, and in the later phase one of eight. This diminishing of importance is often attributed to "a loss of functions" or "a decline in strength" on the part of the component named. Good examples in contemporary Western society are "family" and "religion." These names have been used throughout the successive phases of our development, but the components they have designated have not remained cognate. The modern urban family whose function of economic production has been transferred to occupational organizations is not cognate with the peasant household which is a principal unit of production, in addition to being, like the modern one, a unit for the rearing of children and the regulation of personality. In its capacity as a unit of production, the peasant family is, in fact, a "family firm," but the term "firm" is usually not applied to it.

One qualification of this argument, touching upon the hierarchical ordering of functions in social systems, should be made. This is that political organization, within an institutionalized framework of order, must indeed precede, in the developmental sequence, the emergence of a highly differentiated market type of economy. Hence there is some empirical justification, even within the framework I have sketched, for Durkheim's saying that mechanical solidarity precedes organic solidarity.

14

DOUBLE INTERCHANGES IN ECONOMY AND SOCIETY

WITH NEIL SMELSER

In the concrete case, the primary interchanges across each of the three open boundaries of the economy do not result from direct specific transactions;[1] there is an *intermediary mechanism* at each boundary, at least in differentiated systems.

At the $A_G–L_G$ boundary, goods and services are sold by firms and other suppliers for money payments which are drawn from the wages of households. There are two distinct exchanges: consumers' goods for money funds and labour services for money funds. Money is thus the intervening mechanism in the overall exchange. Furthermore, the unit of the economy which receives consumers' spending is usually not the primary source of the wage income of the household. The "employing units" and the "selling units" in the economy are directly united only by the market nexus.

There are two bases for this duality of interchange. The first is the division of labour. The consuming household cannot receive its total income of goods and services from the specialized organization which employs the breadwinner. The intervening monetary mechanism renders the gains from employment effective to control the acquisition of consumption goods.

The second basis is the divergence of interest arising from the fact that typical firms and typical households are primarily centred in different functional sub-systems of society and hence have different primary goals. Household members want to "live" according to a given pattern; the firm's goal is to "produce," secure rewards, and accumulate facilities to continue producing. Some mechanism must mediate between these two distinct orientations.

On the one hand, money represents the *generalization* of purchasing power to *control decisions* to exchange goods; on the other hand it symbolizes attitudes. The former is the "wealth" aspect of consumers' income, the latter the "prestige" aspect. If it cannot command goods and services money is not acceptable as wages; if it cannot symbolize prestige and mediate between detailed symbols and a broader symbolization it is not acceptable on other grounds. Only with this dual significance can money perform its *social* functions.

The duality of interchange, as shown in Figure 1, of course implies a duality of market structure for the consumers' goods market and the labour market. On each side of the firm-household exchange, therefore, are two independent sets of decisions. On the household side there is the decision of occupational choice and acceptance of specific employment *and* the decision to purchase kinds and quantities of goods and services. On the firm side there is the decision to offer employment in given quantities at given remuneration levels *and* the decision of how much to produce on what terms. Only through several delicate balances in-

FIGURE 1
**THE DOUBLE INTERCHANGE BETWEEN THE ECONOMY
AND THE PATTERN-MAINTENANCE SUB-SYSTEM**

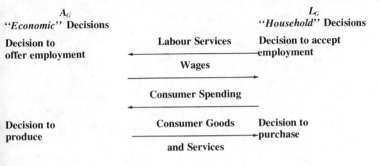

A_G		L_G
"Economic" **Decisions**		*"Household"* **Decisions**
Decision to offer employment	Labour Services ⟵	**Decision to accept employment**
	Wages ⟶	
	Consumer Spending ⟵	
Decision to produce	Consumer Goods and Services ⟶	**Decision to purchase**

volving both intra-system and boundary relationships are these four sets of decisions co-ordinated.

At the adaptive boundary, the input to the economy is the creation of capital funds by the polity. Their supply results from the exercise of one power component or output type (creation of generalized facilities). This supply is used to develop the economy's productive capacity and therefore to improve its level of adaptation.

At the same time, increased productive capacity involves an output of *productivity* or increased potential for providing facilities for societal system goals. This interchange between capital funds and productivity meets the adaptive needs of both economy and polity. The economy gains production potential and the polity gains power potential. Each sacrifices current production for future gains.

In a broad sense these performances and sanctions balance in this interchange, just as labour services and consumption goods and services balance at the latency-economy boundary. But at the adaptive boundary as well the exchange is mediated by an intervening mechanism.[1] The first basis for this mechanism is again the division of labour. The polity is not one big organizational unit; it includes (as units with political functions) governmental agencies, banks, insurance companies, individuals in lending capacities, firms, political parties, etc. Because of this differentiation, some *generalized* short-term sanction is necessary to reward the individual or collectivity for discreet and immediate performances. This sanction is a "measuring rod" to co-ordinate the two larger inputs of control of purchasing power and productivity. The second basis for the intermediate mechanism is the *symbolization of attitudes* and interests which differ in the respective sub-systems. In the case of the polity, the mechanism ties in closely with attitudes toward *power* (as opposed to prestige at the A_G–L_G boundary).

Presently we will discuss the nature of this intervening mechanism, and its mode of control. First, let us specify its form in balancing the control of productivity and the control of the creation of capital funds.

How does the polity "sanction" the production of productivity? These sanctions extend over a wide range of direct politico-legal encouragements and discouragements of the creation of productive enterprise. Concretely, these appear above all in governmental regulations and law codes. Probably the most direct sanctions are certain economic policies of the governmental authority, such as the tax exemption of ploughed-back profits, the general treatment of corporate taxes, direct subsidies, and protection of key industries by tariffs and subsidies. The primary emphasis of such sanctions is an *endorsement* of the industry or sector of the economy in question by the political authority; it is above all a guarantee that the industry or sector of the economy remains in good standing, especially with reference to its continuing contribution to the economy. One of the implications of these encouragements is that the industry or economic sector in question is adjudged a good credit risk. In return for these various encouragements, the relevant sector of the economy maintains or supplies productivity as a complex of facilities available for the pursuit of various system goals.

Certain other political policies, while not directly or predominantly encouragements to enterprise, often encourage the creation of productivity secondarily. A legal instance of such policies is the guarantee of "damages" to various enterprises in case of interference with their activity by any individual or collectivity. One aspect of fair trade, anti-trust and other attempts to regulate imperfect competition is what policy-makers consider to be encouragement of a more productive economy, even though the main focus of such attempts may be the integration of the economy itself or the regulation of the political activity of economic units, i.e., it is only partially economic in its effects.

At the second economy-polity interchange, how does the economy sanction the control over capital funds in the more immediate sense? It relinquishes to the suppliers of these funds certain *rights to intervene* by exercising control over the supply of capital funds. Sometimes these rights are restricted, e.g., the lender to an insurance company redeems his premiums only at a certain rate or at a certain time. In loans to firms various arrangements may be worked out as to the conditions of return of the principal. On the other hand, demand deposits are subject to no such restrictions; the right to intervene in the use of these funds is completely granted. The immediate interchange between polity and economy is therefore between the control of the creation of capital funds through credit and granting the suppliers of funds certain rights to intervene.

What common element (analogous to money as wage income and consumers spending at the A_G–L_G boundary) is shared by "encouragements to enterprise" and "rights to intervene" in credit supply? It seems to us that the mechanism of control is *primarily* political, i.e., the interchanges are not markets in the usual economic sense of the word. What the polity gives in encouraging enterprise and what it receives through the rights to intervene in credit is a sort of reputation, with special reference to the credit standing of the economic sector in question. For want of a better term, therefore, we will refer to the control mechanism at the boundary between polity and economy as "credit standing."

Credit standing is, strictly speaking, a form of power. It implies a *capacity to command* capital resources in exchange for securing the maintenance and/or increase of productivity by applying these resources to the productive plant rationally. To grant credit standing is indeed to encourage enterprise in so far as it places the recipient in the position to command actual purchasing power. On the other hand, to extend the corresponding rights to intervene implies that further extension of purchasing power to the recipient is controlled by the polity upon condition that certain results of the application of purchasing power be forthcoming.

If we think of the "encouragement of enterprise" as analogous to wage payments at the A_G–L_G boundary, then the encouragement of a certain economic sector is in effect to confer upon it a certain endorsement of its continuing existence by means of enhancing its credit standing. This credit standing may be "spent" by granting lenders rights to intervene in return for a supply of credit. Furthermore, like wages, the credit standing may be exhausted by means of excessive borrowing unless further encouragement is forthcoming from the relevant political agency.

We thus view this political endorsement, which we have referred to as "credit standing," as strictly analogous to money at the A_G–L_G boundary in so far as it is an intervening mechanism which in a more immediate sense controls the major outputs of polity and economy at the A_A–G_A boundary, and co-ordinates the "flows" of productivity and creation of credit, respectively. We will review the dynamics of this co-ordination briefly toward the end of the chapter when we point out formal parallels among all the external economic boundaries.

To summarize, we propose that the primary controls at the A_A–G_A boundary are political in our technical sense of the term. This is obviously a radical departure from traditional economic analysis, which has tended to treat the supply of capital funds as directly dependent, in one sense or another, on some money payment, usually interest. We wish to suggest an extensive modification of this view. What, therefore, is the role of monetary mechanisms at the double-interchange between economy and polity?

In one capacity "interest" is a direct payment, similar to wages, for the surrender of goods and services. In this capacity it is a generalized mechanism which *controls* the release of capital funds But the monetary mechanism has a symbolic aspect as well. On the one hand it represents the degree of the creditor's *rights to intervene,* or power to control the relinquished capital funds. The high interest rate which accompanies high risk symbolizes a diminution of the owner's power to control supply by intervention if loss of funds threatens. It symbolizes the supplier's power position much as the wage level symbolizes the prestige position of the earner. On the other hand, the interest rate represents one of the primary symbolic means of encouraging or discouraging enterprise. Operating primarily through monetary policy, a change in the interest rate symbolizes political concern with the state of productivity and its changes in the economy. Raising the interest rate is a signal that productivity must increase at a sufficiently higher rate in order to justify the current level of credit; lowering the interest encourages enterprise by symbolically communicating that the rate of productivity increase need not be so high. In any case manipulating the interest rate signifies certain political attitudes toward the state of the economy.

One significant failing of economic analysis has been to treat the interest rate only in the direct payment sense. We do not wish to minimize the monetary reward aspects of the interest rate. In cases of exorbitant rates and of equal risk with unequal terms the reward is significant. Most recent empirical work has shown however, that to treat interest simply as reward for capital supply is questionable.[2] We give the symbolic aspect more salience than is traditional. Changes in the interest rate (either fortuitous or directed by some central authority) are therefore analogous to a change of a traffic light. A rising interest rate—similar to a red or yellow flash—is less a "wage increase" and more a signal that rights to intervene are likely to be jeopardized by outright loss, by loss of value through inflation, etc.

In the case of the relation between the official bank rate and the volume of commercial credit this symbolic function is more conspicuous in Great Britain than in the United States. The virtual monopoly of commercial banking by five banks operating on a nation-wide basis means that policies of control are communicated by the requisite governmental agencies (Chancellor of the Exchequer and Bank of England) to the top management of these banks. The changed interest rate is not the cause of a policy change, but is a symbolization of it which helps in communicating its implications to a wider circle of lenders and prospective borrowers.

Besides interest, other monetary mechanisms play a special role in the interchange between control over productivity and encouragements to productivity. Often money returns to economic enterprises are directly concomitant—e.g., tax relief, "damages," subsidies, etc., further encouragement of productivity. In other cases, such as tariffs or direct control by injunctions, direct monetary reward from the polity is absent. In general, however, this particular balance between encouragements to productive enterprise and productivity is not in the usual sense a market between government interest and economic interest, if a market means that the direct sanction in power of monetary purchasing power operates to determine a "price."[3] Hence the primary significance of the monetary mechanism is again symbolic. It symbolizes attitudes and policies of the polity toward the supply and control of productive capacity for the pursuit of system goals.

FIGURE 2
THE DOUBLE INTERCHANGE BETWEEN THE
ECONOMY AND THE POLITY

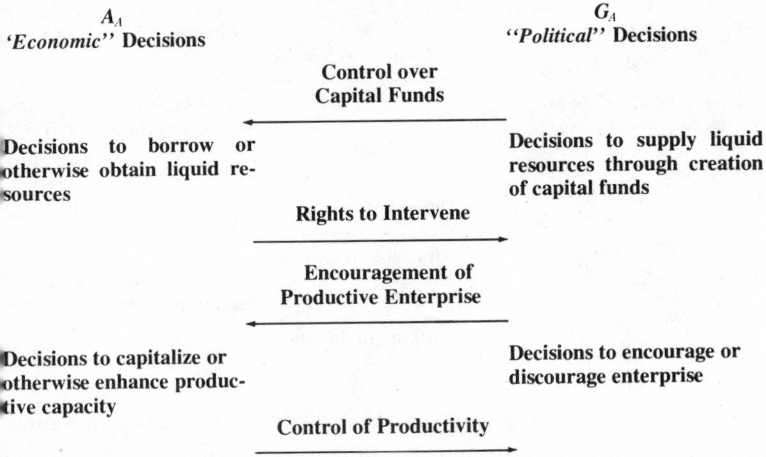

A_A		G_A
'Economic" Decisions		*"Political"* Decisions

	Control over Capital Funds	
Decisions to borrow or otherwise obtain liquid resources	←	Decisions to supply liquid resources through creation of capital funds
	Rights to Intervene →	
	Encouragement of Productive Enterprise ←	
Decisions to capitalize or otherwise enhance productive capacity		Decisions to encourage or discourage enterprise
	Control of Productivity →	

The power exigencies of system-goal attainment—the business of the polity are so salient that the direct encouragement of enterprise overshadows the market control elements of the monetary mechanisms in this exchange.

Figure 2 shows the double interchange between economy and polity. As in the economy-household boundary, there is a duality of structure in the "markets" and two partially independent sets of decisions on each side of the boundary interchange.[4]

At the economy's third open boundary, A_I-I_I, the overall exchange is between "organization" and new output combinations to the consuming public. The significance of entrepreneurial services is to adjust the proportions of the factors of production and thus integrate the functioning economy; the significance of new output combinations is integrative in so far as it impinges on the problems of the distribution of wealth and of the style-of-life symbolization with reference to the stratification of society. What is the intermediary mechanism in this exchange?

Entrepreneurial service is directly balanced by "profit," or monetary reward for introducing integrative services into the

FIGURE 3
THE DOUBLE INTERCHANGE BETWEEN
ECONOMY AND THE INTEGRATIVE SUB-SYSTEM

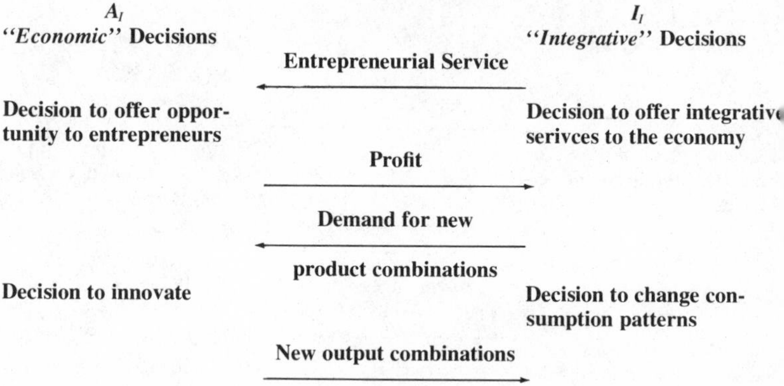

A_I
"Economic" Decisions

I_I
"Integrative" Decisions

Entrepreneurial Service

◄─────────────────────

Decision to offer oppor-
tunity to entrepreneurs

Decision to offer integrative
serivces to the economy

Profit

─────────────────────►

Demand for new

◄─────────────────────

product combinations

Decision to innovate

Decision to change con-
sumption patterns

New output combinations

─────────────────────►

economy. Above and beyond this reward aspect, this paymen
symbolizes the entrepreneur's strategic position in the integrative
system.

The balance for new output combinations from the economy is
the *demand for new product combinations,* which is analogous to
consumers' demand in the short run. In one sense this demand is
direct reward to the economy for producing such new combina
tions. It is also a symbol of the incorporation of new combinations
into various style-of-life patterns relevant to the symbolization of
the integration of society through stratification.

Figure 3 shows the double interchange at the A_I–I_I boundary
which we will develop further when we consider Schumpeter's
treatment of the functions of the entrepreneur.

This is perhaps an appropriate place for a general summary
statement of the relation between the analytical input-output
categories of the economy as we have developed them and con
crete social structures in our own and other societies.

In our conception of the relation between economy and soci
ety, the main outline of which we have just presented, it is inher
ent that the analytical boundaries will correspond to the lines of
differentiation between concrete roles and collectivities most
closely in those societies which are in general highly dif

ferentiated and which stress the economic aspects of their structure and functioning. For this reason as well as that of the accessibility of relevant information, we have found it convenient for the most part to choose illustrations from our own society and its recent history.

Even here, however, the lines of collectivity differentiation seldom if ever correspond *exactly* to the analytical boundary-lines between the economy and other functional sub-systems. Thus, given the high degree of differentiation in our society between occupational roles and familial roles, the line between household and firm—as mediated by the labour and consumer markets—is for many purposes a fair approximation of that between pattern-maintenance and adaptive functional sub-systems. But this organizational line is only an approximation. For instance, durable consumers' goods in the household should be treated analytically as capital goods, hence an important part of consumers' spending is analytically a process of capital investment. Correspondingly, an important part of housewives' activities within the household constitute labour services in the technical economic sense. Thus in both these respects the line between the pattern-maintenance system and economy lies *within* the household, even in our own society. By the same token the concrete role of the worker in the firm is never exclusively economic in functional significance; it involves a pattern-maintenance aspect, the preservation of which is, we will argue in the next chapter, one of the foci of the bases of trade unions in our society. It is true that the firm is characterized by the *primacy* of economic function and the household by the *primacy* of pattern-maintenance function, but this by no means implies that the firm is exclusively economic and the household totally non-economic in its significance.

Furthermore, consumption in the economic sense is by no means confined to the household in our society but is to some extent a function of *all* concrete role and collectivity units of the social structure. Even business firms in our society spend part of their income for style-of-life symbols directly comparable to those of households; office buildings and their appointments, the landscaping of the grounds of industrial plants and a variety of other phenomena belong in this context. In addition governmental units, universities and other non-household organizations are important consumers in the strict economic sense.

Similar considerations apply at the other open boundaries of our economy. Even with such highly differentiated financial institutions as in our own society, the line between economy and polity does not correspond in any simple way with the concrete boundaries between concrete collectivity or role units. Thus we treat the credit-creating banking organization as primarily a political unit though it is not usually an organ of government in our society. But clearly a bank has conspicuous economic aspects second in importance only to the political. It is thus governed to a more stringent degree by imperatives of solvency than are most households or units of government. Similarly, the large-scale self-financing of expansion by business firms means that these firms have undertaken considerable political functions. At the very least they have undertaken (usually with passive acquiescence) to withhold some of the property of the investing public from its owners in order to "plough it back." By building up their productivity, such organizations improve their credit standing. This standing may serve as a basis for seeking new funds from banks or governmental agencies or, more frequently, as the basis for justifying still further withholding of dividends from investors, thereby placing these investors (more or less involuntarily) in the role of credit-creators. The firm thus in effect borrows from its own security holders on the implicit plea that *it* has the power to convert their assets into increased productivity (hence increased capitalized value of their securities). The firm's high credit standing enables it to carry out these operations without exposing itself to unmanageable pressure for immediate dividend payments.

These imperfections of matching between the functional categories of boundary-interchange and the concrete social structure are apparent even in our own society. Similar considerations must weigh even more heavily when we analyse societies in which the level of differentiation is less advanced than in our own and/or in which the adaptive emphasis is substantially less strong.

To take an example of a less differentiated society, historically the great societies of the Oriental world have been characterized by an overwhelming majority (usually 80 per cent or more) of "peasants" in the working population engaged either in the production of food or closely related primary products such as textile fibres from the land. The typical organizational unit of such populations has been a *combination* household and productive unit in which the differentiation between occupational and familial roles does not hold. Economic considerations are certainly relevant to the analysis of behaviour in such a unit, but inevitably it is subject to constraints on giving primacy to economic considerations, constraints which the modern Western firm does not face.

An example of a fusion of economic and non-economic functions at a higher level of organization in the medieval European manor. As an economic unit it managed economic resources—the land, manpower and some capital and organization. At the same time it was a unit of formal political and military organization and of social integration by means of hereditary local ties and class status. If anything the manor's economic functions were subordinated to these latter functions as a rule. This is reflected in the marked economic "traditionalism" of medieval rural society. It is not without reason that the break-up of the manor, for instance through "enclosures," has been associated with the beginning of a new era of economic development.

Though the handicraft organization of the medieval towns was doubtless closer to economic primacy than the medieval manor on either peasant or gentry level, it was bound closely by non-economic constraints. Not only did the master craftsman himself work within his own household but his apprentices were treated virtually as adopted sons and even his journeymen were often partially integrated in a similar way. Furthermore the gild solidarity and the elaborate restrictions on competition for raw materials, labour or customers, establish beyond doubt that such craft organizations were very far from the functionally differentiated form of "business" organization, despite their elaborate "specialization."

Somewhat closer to such differentiation is the relatively recent "family business" of the type which has been particularly conspicuous in France. Here household, economic (managerial in a technical sense) and political (capital-holding) functions are fused in a single solidary kinship unit, membership in which is based on hereditary ascription (a strictly non-economic criterion) or on arranged marriage in which the probable effect on the firm's economic efficiency is scarcely the ruling consideration. Though such firms are "business" organizations producing for relatively free markets, they represent a lower level of differentiation of economic function than does modern large-scale American corporate industry.[5]

As a final example, modern totalitarian societies such as Soviet Russia bring most of the economy under exceedingly stringent governmental (hence in our sense primarily political) control. At least the proximate goal, in addition to consolidating the power-position of the régime itself, is to bring about the largest scale and most rapid possible process of economic development.[6] This represents above all a fusion between economy and polity in the dominant structure of a modern socialistic state, with the political element dominant. How stable, beyond the period of "forced draft" development, such a fusion may be is a crucial question about such societies; will certain "natural" tendencies for the economy to differentiate from the polity appear or will they be inhibited?

We have cited these examples of comparative organizational and institutional arrangements involving the economy in order to outline the relation between our type of functional analysis of the economy and the more concrete and empirical analysis of social phenomena, whether or not the latter are usually defined as "economic."

We hold that our generalized theoretical scheme, for the analysis of a society and of the economy as one of its sub-systems, is *not* bound to any particular structural type of society or economy. The analytical elements we have distinguished, and others we have been unable to discuss for reasons of space, are distinguishable as elements in *any* society, indeed in any social system. These analytical elements are not, however, equally closely related to the concrete structure of collectivities and roles in all societies. In general our functional sub-system categories correspond more closely to organizationally differentiated sectors of the social structure as the society approaches greater *structural* differentiation. But even here the correspondence is only approximate. Furthermore, the categories of economic theory apply more directly to the concrete social structure of a differentiated society and its processes as adaptive or economic values approach greater primacy over others. Only in societies which meet both these criteria do many of the more technical parts of economic theory apply directly to empirical analysis, e.g., in the analysis of price determination in specific markets.

Even in such societies, as we argue throughout this volume, close application to many empirical areas such as market imperfections can be attained only by supplementing economic theory with other elements of the general theory of social systems. But as we treat societies with a lower level of structural differentiation and with less economic emphasis, economic theory alone becomes less and less satisfactory as an analytical tool. The relative importance of the non-economic parts of the theory of social systems for the empirically "economic" problem areas increases until, in the case of "primitive" economies, it becomes overwhelmingly great.

15

ON THE CONCEPT OF INFLUENCE

It may plausibly be held that the development of research technology in the field of opinion and attitude study has outrun the development of theory. The intention of the present paper is to help to redress the balance by essaying a contribution in the theoretical area to try to bring to bear on the opinion field a more generalized conceptual scheme that has been worked out mainly in other connections.

First, let me state the main context of problems within the field on which I would like to concentrate. The first step beyond immediate description and classification of opinions is, of course, to attempt some analysis of determining factors, to answer such questions as why or under what conditions certain opinions are held or changed. It is within this area, rather than that of categories suitable for description and classification, that I wish to operate. To narrow the field still further, it is a question of whether anything can be said about *generalized* kinds of process or mechanism through the operation of which such determination, notably of change of opinions, comes about. It is as such a generalized mechanism by which attitudes or opinions are determined that I would like to conceive "influence," for the purposes of this paper.[1]

A further step in specification is to restrict my consideration to the problem of the operation of generalized mechanisms in the process of social interaction in its intentional forms. Thus, if a person's opinion has been changed by his experience of a natural event, such as a hurricane, or even by social events that could not conceivably be understood as intentionally oriented to having an effect on his opinions, such as a business depression, I shall not speak of these as "influence" in the present sense—similarly with the famous example of the alleged relation between a judge's legal opinions and the state of his digestion. Influence is a way of having an effect on the attitudes and opinions of others through intentional (though not necessarily rational) action—the effect may or may not be to change the opinion or to prevent a possible change.

General Mechanisms of Social Interaction: The Case of Money

What, then, is meant by a generalized mechanism operating in social interaction? There are various ways of approaching this question. Language is perhaps the prototype and can serve as a major point of reference. Having an effect on the action of others, thus possibly "influencing" them, through linguistic communication, is to present them with "symbolic" experiences in place of the concrete things or objects to which the symbols refer, which they "mean." Thus, a sign, "Beware the dog," may induce caution without the passer-by's actually seeing or hearing a dog. "Intrinsically," the language symbols do not have any caution-inducing properties; the black marks on the signboard have never bitten anyone, nor have they even barked.

In the well-known formulation of Jacobsen and Halle,[2] a language must be understood to involve two aspects: on the one hand, the use of language is a process of emitting and transmitting messages, combinations of linguistic components that have specific reference to particular situations; on the other hand, language is a *code* in terms of which the particular symbols constituting any particular message "have meaning." In these terms, a message can be meaningful and hence understood only by those who "know the language," that is the code, and accept its "conventions."

Language, as that concept is generally understood, is not an isolated phenomenon. In the field of social interaction, many mechanisms have properties so similar to those of language that it is not too much to say that they *are* specialized languages. Mathematical and artistic symbol systems are cases in point, but one that is both well known and lies close to our concern is money. Hence, for my purposes, I would like to say not merely that money resembles language, but that it *is* a very specialized language, i.e., a generalized medium of communication through the use of symbols given meaning within a code.[3]

I shall therefore treat influence as a generalized medium which in turn I interpret to mean a specialized language. I should like now to attempt, using money, because of its familiarity, as an illustration, to outline a paradigm of such a generalized medium, preliminary to stating the principal properties of influence as another such medium.

Seen in this light, money is a symbolic "embodiment" of economic *value,* of what economists in a technical sense call "utility." Just as the *word* "dog" can neither bark nor bite, yet "signifies" the animal that can, so a dollar has no intrinsic utility, yet signifies commodities that do, in the special sense that it can in certain circumstances be substituted for them, and can evoke control of relations with them in the special kind of process of social interaction we call economic exchange. This means that holders of objects of utility will, on occasion, be willing to relinquish control over them for money, and, conversely, holders of money will be able to acquire, by use of the money (its "expenditure"), control over objects of utility.[4]

The economic value called utility, however, is the basis of a type of *interest* in objects in the situation of action. It defines an aspect of their actual or potential meaning, under which rubric I wish to include not only what they "are" but what they "do," if they are actors, and what can be done *with* them, such as "consuming" them in the economist's sense, if they are commodities, or "utilizing their services," if they are persons. For symbolization to take place, it is necessary for the basis of this interest to be defined with sufficient clarity and specificity, just as the category of object "dog" must be adequately defined if the linguistic symbol is to designate it unambiguously. In the case of money, this involves a very high level of generalization, since the variety of objects of utility is immense; furthermore, it means a very strict quantification on a linear scale.

In addition to the relevant category of value for human actors on the one hand, the basis of interest in objects in their situation on the other, there are two further indispensable references in the conceptualization of a generalized symbolic mechanism. One of these is to the "definition of the situation," that is the categorization of objects in the situation with reference to their bearing on the type of interest in question. In the economic-monetary case, the situation consists in "objects of utility," that is those in which actors may have an economic basis of interest. Implementation of the interest consists in acquiring control over such objects to the extent that this is a condition of "utilizing" them. The "way" of acquiring such control is through exchange, which, if money is involved, may be called "market" exchange.[5]

In the case of money as a symbol, one of its meanings is clearly in the field of "procurement," of the opportunities of using it to gain access to and control over objects of utility. The first component of the situation needing definition, then, consists in the manifold objects that not only have utility but are available within the exchange system: thus certain objects of potential utility, such as full control of other human beings by owning them as chattels, are excluded in our property system. The second component concerns sources of supply, namely, units in the interaction system which, on the one hand, have control of such objects and, on the other, may be presumed to be willing to relinquish such control in exchange for other utilities, including especially money. The third component concerns the conditions on which terms of exchange can be settled, the most important one being the institutionalization of the offer of specific sums of money as a way of inducing transfer of control. And, finally, the fourth component concerns the question of the time relations involved in bringing the two ends of a chain of exchange of utilities together, for example the relinquishment of control over labor services to an employer, and the acquisition of control over consumer's goods.

By contrast with the two "pre-monetary" modes of exchange

mentioned above—ascriptive and barter exchange—money introduces altogether new degrees of freedom in all four of these respects. Thus, unlike the holder of a specific commodity in surplus—relative to his own wants—who wants to barter it for another commodity, the holder of money is not bound to find a specific partner who has what he wants and wants what he has. He has the whole range of the "market system" open with respect both to the items for which he wants to spend his funds and to the sources from which he might wish to purchase each item—so long as the market for the item is not monopolized. Exceedingly important, he is not bound to any particular time, since money, unlike virtually all commodities, does not intrinsically deteriorate through time and has minimal, if any, costs of storage. Finally, he has much greater freedom to accept or reject terms, and to negotiate them.

These freedoms, like all freedoms, are bought at a price. Money, being a symbol, is "intrinsically" worthless. Hence, in relinquishing control of objects of "real" utility for money, one risks never gaining an equivalent in return and being "stuck" with the symbol; similarly, if one relies on a sign rather than on actually seeing a dog, one risks being fooled, either by being alerted when there is no danger at all, or by being prepared to deal with a dog when in fact a tiger is lurking in the neighborhood.

There have doubtless been heroic figures in the history of market exchange who have risked everything on a conception of the sheer *value* of money without the existence of any institutionally established normative framework of rules according to which such a medium should be used. It seems clear, however, that, without such a framework, a *system* of market exchanges in which participants will regularly put major interests into monetary assets that, in our sense, are "intrinsically" worthless can hardly be expected to function. The most elementary of these rules is the condition of reciprocity in the acceptability of money. This may be formulated as follows: He who urges money on others in exchange for "real assets" must be willing in turn to accept money from others in exchange for his assets. Only mutual acceptability can make money a functioning medium rather than simply a way of getting something for nothing. From this central point, the network of norms that we ordinarily think of as the institutions of property and contract can be worked out. This is the fourth of the basic components of the complex that constitutes a generalized medium.

If a symbol or category of symbols is to function as a generalized medium in mediating the processes of social interaction, there must therefore be, I have contended, specific definition and institutional acceptance in four basic respects: (1) a category of *value*, of respects in which needs of the acting units are at stake; (2) a category of *interest*, of properties of objects in the situation of action that are important in the light of these values; (3) a *definition of the situation*, of the features of the actual situation that can be "exploited" in the implementation of the interest; and (4) a *normative framework* of rules discriminating between legitimate and illegitimate modes of action in pursuit of the interest in question. Only with institutionalization in all four respects can the risks inherently involved in accepting the "symbolic" in lieu of the "real" be expected to be widely assumed by whole categories of acting units.

Ways of Getting Results in Interaction

Because it is highly institutionalized and hence familiar, and because the conditions of its functioning have been very thoroughly analyzed by professional economists, I have used money as the example in terms of which to elucidate the nature and conditions of a generalized medium in the sense of this paper. In approaching a fuller analysis of the primary object of our concern, influence, a next step is to attempt to place both it and money in the context of a wider family of mechanisms. It is my view that money belongs in such a family, of which another well known member is power, in the broadly political sense. These mechanisms operate in social interaction in a way that is both much more specific and more generalized than communication through language. Furthermore, they have in common the imperative mood, i.e. they are ways of "getting results" rather than only of conveying information. They face the object with a decision, calling for a response such as the acceptance or rejection of a monetary offer.

These considerations indicate the approach. Such mechanisms

are ways of structuring *intentional* attempts to bring about results by eliciting the response of other actors to approaches, suggestions, etc. In the case of money, it is a matter of offers; in the case of power, of communicating decisions that activate obligations; in the case of influence, of giving reasons or "justifications" for a suggested line of action. How can these various modes of getting results be classified?

My suggestion is that there is a very simple paradigm of modes by which one acting unit—let us call him "ego"—can attempt to get results by bringing to bear on another unit, which we may call "alter," some kind of *communicative operation:* call it "pressure" if that term is understood in a nonpejorative sense.[6] It can be stated in terms of two variables, the cross-classification of which can then yield a fourfold typology. The first variable is whether ego attempts to work through potential control over the *situation* in which alter is placed and must act, or through an attempt to have an effect on alter's *intentions*, independently of changes in his situation. Let us call this the "channel" variable. Thus an offer in economic exchange operates situationally, in that it offers control either of an object of utility or of money, which in turn is exchangeable for control of such an object.

Offers are contingent—they say that, *if* alter will do something ego wants done, ego in turn will do something that is situationally advantageous to alter. There is, however, the limiting case in which ego confers a situational advantage on alter without giving him any option—this would be the pure case of the gift. This element of contingency, varying to the limit of no option, applies throughout the present typology.

The second variable concerns the nature of the contingent *consequences* for alter of ego's intervention in his action-complex, that is, in one aspect, the kind of decision with which alter is faced. So far as the element of contingency is involved, this concerns whether the *sanctions* contingently imposed by ego are positive or negative in their significance to alter, that is constitute advantages or disadvantages to him. Thus, in the case of economic exchange, ego *promises* that if alter will do what he wants, he in turn will do something which alter presumably wants, that is defines as advantageous. Giving him money or control of an object of utility are prototypical cases. On the other hand, ego may attempt to get alter to do something by saying, in effect, "You must, should, or ought to do so and so." Alter may then say, "But what if I choose not to?" If ego takes this approach and "means it," he must contend that in some sense the consequences of alter's choosing noncompliance (if he can "do anything about it") will be disadvantageous to alter. If the channel is situational, this will put him in the position of having to *threaten,* contingent on noncompliance, to do something disadvantageous to alter. On the other hand, he may give alter reasons why noncompliance will, independent of ego's intervention in the situation, prove to be unacceptable, so that *intentional* noncompliance cannot make sense to alter. Here the negative sanction would be internal or intentional, and not situational so far as alter is concerned.

The limiting case where alter is given no option is, in the situational-negative combination, compulsion: ego simply structures the situation so alter *must* comply.

Cross-classification of these two variables for the case of contingency yields the set of four types shown in our table. (1) Inducement is ego's attempt to get a favorable decision from alter by an offer of situational advantages contingent on ego's compliance with his suggestions. (2) Deterrence is ego's corresponding attempt to get compliance by invoking commitments in such a way that noncompliance exposes alter to a contingent threat of suffering a situational disadvantage.[7] (3) Activation of commitments is ego's attempt to get compliance by offering reasons why it would, from alter's own point of view, be "wrong" for him to refuse to act as ego wished. And, finally, (4) persuasion is ego's attempt to get compliance by offering reasons why it would, from alter's own point of view, independent of situational advantages, "be a good thing" for him to act as ego wished.

	CHANNEL	
Sanction	*Intentional*	*Situational*
Positive	Persuasion	Inducement
Negative	Activation of commitments	Deterrence

I should now like to suggest that this simple paradigm of modes of gaining ends in social interaction is matched by a paradigm of generalized media by which, in the appropriately structured type of interaction system, an enhanced capacity to gain such ends is made possible, provided the risks of acceptance of such a medium in the requisite situation are assumed. Seen in these terms, money should be regarded as a generalized medium of inducement, and influence as a generalized medium of persuasion. I shall try presently to elucidate further what the latter conception implies, but it will be useful first to put it in the context, not only of a comparison with money, but of this still more general classification of media.

Money and influence may be conceived to operate as positive sanctions in the above sense, money through the situational, influence through the intentional, channel. The negative medium corresponding to money on the situational side is then power in the political sense; on the intentional side, the negative medium corresponding to influence is generalization of commitments. The relation between the two pairs requires some elucidation.

Inducement and persuasion are ways of eliciting positively desired responses. Imposition of sanction and response correspond here. Deterrence, on the other hand, is intended to establish an inverse relation between sanctioned act and desired response. The purely negative side is the withholding of sanction in case of "compliance." What ego desires, however, is precisely compliance, the performance of obligation. He imposes sanctions only if "forced to."

It is hence not appropriate to define power simply as a generalized medium of deterrence, but rather of mobilizing the performance of binding obligations, with the conditional implication of the imposition of negative sanctions—in the situational case, "punishment"—in case of noncompliance. The intention of ego, however, is not to punish but to secure performance. Hence, we may speak of power as generalized capacity to secure performance of binding obligations in the interest of effective collective action (goal attainment). Parallel to this, on the intentional side (so far as alter is concerned), we may speak of the generalization of commitments as the capacity, through appeal to a subjective sense of obligation, to motivate fulfillment of relevant obligations without reference to any threat of *situational* sanctions (thus differentiating it from power). In this case, however, tendencies to noncompliance will be met with evaluative expressions on ego's part (disapproval of noncompliance) that are calculated to help activate alter's sense of obligation and threaten him with guilt feelings if he fails to comply.[8] We may then insert the four generalized media in the paradigm of sanctions, as follows:

Sanction	CHANNEL *Intentional*	*Situational*
Positive:		
Mode	Persuasion	Inducement
Medium	Influence	Money
Negative:		
Mode	Activation of commitments	Deterrence
Medium	Generalization of commitments	Power

Note: For readers familiar with the more general paradigm of the analysis of action on which various associates and I have worked for some years, it may be of interest to note that I conceive inducement and money to have primarily adaptive functions in the social system; deterrence and power, primarily goal-attainment functions; persuasion and influence, primarily integrative functions; and, finally, activation of commitments and the generalized commitments so activated, primarily pattern-maintenance functions.

Let us now attempt to get somewhat closer to the analysis of influence by calling attention to another aspect of the generalized media as mechanisms operating within the social system. This is the sense in which they bridge the gap between normative and factual aspects of the system in which they operate. This is to say that, from the point of view of the acting unit, whether it be individual or collectivity, there is one "direction" in which the medium serves as a means of furthering its interests, and this includes the structuring of conditions under which, in various contingencies, its interest is more or less secure. On the other hand, what from the acting unit's point of view are certain norms or rules to which it is subject in furthering its interest are, from the point of view of the system, a set of conditions under which process in it can be carried on stably, without disturbance to its integration and other essential functions.

In the case of money, the rock bottom of security for the unit is the possession of the proper quantity and combination of concrete objects of utility to the unit itself, namely, full "economic

self-sufficiency" in terms of "real assets." The next level is pos
session of objects such as gold, diamonds, land, which can be
exchanged in almost any contingency and the value of which is
not subject to deterioration. Institutionalized money has the ad
vantage of a far wider usefulness in exchange than such goods but
the disadvantage of vulnerability to disturbances in the system
Money, however, as we have insisted, is a symbol, the "mean
ing" of which (in this case, its economic value) is a function of its
mutual acceptability. In one direction, this acceptability is well-
known to depend on its convertibility into objects of rock-bottom
economic security, notably the monetary metal. Convertibility
however, is one thing, but frequent insistence on actual conver
sion is quite another.

The point is very simply that the insistence on actual conver
sion can be met only by measures that destroy the very degrees of
freedom that make money an advantageous mechanism from the
points of view *both* of the unit and of the system.[9] The mainte
nance of the degrees of freedom, however, is dependent on
minimum levels of compliance with the norms of the economic
complex with respect to the fulfillment of contractual obligations
and the rights and obligations of property. It is by this path that
we come to the conception that, while in one context the value of
money rests on its "backing" by convertibility into a secure utility, for example metal, in another and probably more important
context, it rests on the effective functioning of a ramified system
of monetary exchanges and markets. This, in turn, is one major
set of factors in the productivity of the economy of which these
markets are a central part. No economist would suppose that
such productivity can be created simply by adding to the supply
of monetary gold.

I suggest that this duality of reference is characteristic not only
of money as a mechanism, but of the whole set with which we are
concerned—indeed, more broadly, of language, law, and various
others. For the case of power, the basis of unit security corresponding to economic "real assets" consists in possession of
effective means of *enforcing* compliance (that is fulfillment of
wishes or performance of obligations) through implementing
coercive threats or exerting compulsion. In this context, it is well

known that physical force occupies a special place, a place which, it may be suggested, is parallel to monetary metal in the economic case. This is above all because force is the deterrent sanction par excellence. In turn, the most important aspect of this deterrence is very generally blocking channels of communication; for example, the most important feature of imprisonment is preventing the prisoner from communicating with others except in ways and through channels his custodians can control.

But just as possession of stocks of monetary gold cannot create a highly productive economy, so command of physical force alone cannot guarantee the effective fulfillment of ramified systems of binding obligations. The latter is dependent on such factors as the institutionalization of a system of norms in the fields of authority, and the legitimation of the power of leadership elements. The mutuality of the institutionalization of authority, on the one hand, and the acceptance of the legitimacy of its exercise, on the other, is the parallel of the mutual acceptability of "worthless" money in exchange. Clearly, the functioning of a *system* of power is preeminently dependent on the effective implementation of this normative structure. The analogue of economic productivity here may be said to be the *effectiveness of collective organization.*

Influence as a Symbolic Medium of Persuasion

Let us now attempt to apply this line of argument to the field of influence. There is a sense in which all four of the mechanisms under consideration here depend on the institutionalization of attitudes of trust. In the economic case, the actor relinquishes his interests (in commodities or labor) to the market, and the question is on what basis he can have confidence or trust that he will receive "fair value" in return for what he has relinquished. We have argued that there are two distinct foci of the problem of trust, namely, the convertibility of money into "real assets" and confidence in the functioning of the "system," which for the actor means the fulfillment of his more or less legitimate expectations from actual and potential exchange partners. Similarly, in the case of power, an actor may relinquish his coercive self-sufficiency: he cannot then defend himself adequately with his own strong right arm alone. In entrusting his security to a power *system,* there is on the one hand his possible identification with actual control of coercive means (in the last analysis, force), on the other his confidence that his expectations will be effectively fulfilled through agencies beyond his personal control, because the power *system* is effective.

In order to fit influence into this scheme, it is necessary to ask what influence symbolizes. In the case of money, it symbolized utility; in the case of power, effectiveness of collective action.[10] An answer seems to be given in our paradigm of interactive performance—sanction types. Influence is a means of *persuasion.* It is bringing about a decision on alter's part to act in a certain way because it is felt to be a "good thing" *for him,* on the one hand independently of contingent or otherwise imposed changes in his situation, on the other hand for positive reasons, not because of the obligations he would violate through noncompliance.

It then seems that, to correspond to the intrinsic "want-satisfiers," which the economist calls "goods and services," there should be a category of intrinsic "persuaders." The most obvious member of this category is "facts" from which alter can "draw his own conclusions." Ego, that is, can persuade by giving alter information which, given his situation and intentions, will lead him to make certain types of decisions.[11] It seems probable that information is indeed the proper parallel to commodities, with a special kind of information—the announcement of firm intentions of action on the part of significant others—the parallel to services.[12] Influence as a symbol, however, cannot be either of these, but must be more generalized relative to both.

The crucial thing to look for seems to be a symbolic act or component of action on ego's part which communicates a generalized intention on the basis of which trust in more specific intentions is requested and expected. This may operate in the realm of information. Here there must be some basis on which alter considers ego to be a trustworthy source of information and "believes" him even though he is not in a position to verify the information independently—or does not want to take the trouble. It can also operate in the realm of ego's intentions, and this is indeed a crucial matter; for example, agreeing to a contract is essentially an announcement of intentions which can perhaps be fulfilled only by a long series of performances over an extended period of time.

The monetary metal is not "just" one among many commodities; it is one with certain properties that favor security and maximum exchangeability. Similarly with force as an instrument of coercion-compulsion. Is there, then, any comparable "intrinsic" source of persuasion that has a special likelihood of inspiring trust? If, in answering this question, we remember that we are dealing specifically with social interaction, it seems reasonable to suggest that the most favorable condition under which alter will trust ego's efforts to persuade him (independent of specific facts or "inherently" trustworthy intentions) will be when the two stand in a mutual relation of fundamental diffuse solidarity, when they belong together in a collectivity on such a basis that, so long as the tie holds, ego *could not* have an interest in trying to deceive alter. We may then suggest that common belongingness in a *Gemeinschaft* type of solidarity is the primary "basis" of mutual influence, and is for influence systems the equivalent of gold for monetary and force for power systems.

This, however, can be only the security *base*. Just as a ramified monetary system cannot operate with an exclusively metallic medium, so a ramified influence system would be stultified if only close *Gemeinschaft* associates ever trusted each other beyond completely concrete levels of information and binding intentions. The degrees of freedom associated with the market are here matched by those of "communication" systems, e.g., freedom of the press and the like. Like any other interchange system, the stability of a free communication system is dependent on regulation by a set of institutionalized norms corresponding to those of property and contract. These have to do with the conditions normatively regulating types of association of people with each other, the kinds of obligations assumed in making assertions and giving opinions, and the kinds of obligations involved in statements of intention. Thus, the very fundamental principle of freedom of association may be said to be the normative principle in this sphere that corresponds to freedom of contract in the sphere of market organization; in both cases, of course, the freedoms are far from absolute, being subject to such restrictions as are imposed by the interests of third parties.

What then, can be said in general about the nature of these normative references? In the case of money, the reference, within the range of freedom of contract, is to value equivalences in the utility sense. Money functions here as the measure of value, and price is a statement of the assessed value of an exchangeable item. In the case of power, the reference is to authorization, in the sense that a unit with power is, within the given limits, authorized to make decisions that bind not only himself but certain categories of others and the relevant collectivity as a whole. Thus, the vote is an exercise of power, and, subject to the electoral rules, the aggregate of votes in an election will determine bindingly the incumbency of office.

In the case of influence, I suggest that the corresponding conception should be the normative justification of generalized statements about information or intention (*not* their empirical validation). The user of influence is under pressure to justify his statements, which are intended to have an effect on alter's action, by making them correspond to norms that are regarded as binding on both.[13] With reference to items of information, justification is necessary, since influence is a symbolic medium. The function of justification is not actually to verify the items, but to provide the basis for the communicators' *right* to state them without alter's needing to verify them; for example, ego may be a technically competent "authority" in the field. With reference to intentions, justification may be regulated by various aspects of status that are regularly invoked to indicate that such intentions should prove trustworthy when stated by persons in the category in question.[14] A very important category of the justification of influence is what is ordinarily meant by "reputation." The same statement will carry more "weight" if made by someone with a high reputation for competence, for reliability, for good judgment, etc., than by someone without this reputation or with a reputation for unreliability. The common component may be called "fiduciary responsibility." A unit wields influence in proportion as, in the relevant context, its unverified declarations of information and intention are believed to be responsibly made. This is the "reputational" parallel to financial credit standing.

Put in familiar sociological terms, the associational base of influence may be regarded as primarily particularistic. The question is *who* the wielder is in terms of his collectivity memberships. The normative reference, however, is primarily universalistic. It is not what he is saying, which is a "content" matter, but what "right" he has to expect to be taken seriously, over and above the intrinsic cogency of what he says.

I spoke above of influence as "based" on *Gemeinschaft* solidarity, on the elementary, diffuse kind of belonging-togetherness of which, in a society like ours, the family is the prototypical case. The relevance of associatedness in collectivities is not, however, exhausted by this limiting case. Indeed, we may say that at many levels being "one of us" is a factor enhancing influence, whether it be membership in a local community, an occupational or professional group, or any one of many others. For this reason, nonmembers of groups must exercise special care in matters concerning the affairs of the group, lest they be felt to be "interfering." An obvious case is a foreigner speaking about a nation's domestic politics, especially one holding an official position at home. If this is true, then, conversely, attempting to influence is to a degree an attempt to establish a common bond of solidarity, on occasion even to bring the object of influence into common membership in a collectivity. Thus, being subject to mutual influence is to constitute a "we" in the sense that the parties have opinions and attitudes in common by virtue of which they "stand together" relative to those differing from them. There are, of course, various other conditions for establishing a full collectivity besides openness to mutual influence among its members, but we can certainly say that this is a necessary, if not sufficient, condition of a stable collectivity.

There is a very clear relation between this point and the findings of the study *Voting,* by Berelson, Lazarsfeld and McPhee, concerning the importance for voting behavior of the solidary group structures in which individuals are involved, starting with their families, but going on to occupations and ethnic, religious, and other groupings.[15] The broad presumption seems to be that a person will tend to vote with others whom he defines as "my kind of people" and that it is the "cross-pressured" groups which are mostly likely to break away from this tendency—cross-pressuring being itself a consequence of the increasing role pluralism of a complex society. Indeed, this finding was one of the most important points on which it seemed to me possible to relate empirical studies of voting behavior to the broad scheme of analysis of social interaction that has been the point of departure of the present essay.[16]

Types of Influence

We may now approach the problem of classification of types or modes of influence. Here it is essential to bear in mind that the influence system is not a closed system. On the one hand, of course, it is used to get consent to particular attitudes and opinions that are to influence what particular commodities and services are to money. In this sense, we may think of influence as a "circulating" medium. To get consent, an "opinion leader" must expend some of his influence. He must therefore carefully husband it by choosing the occasions on which to intervene and the appropriate mode of intervention. The classic type of thriftless expenditure is illustrated by the nursery story about the repetition of the cry, "Wolf! Wolf!" so that when the wolf actually came, the warning was not believed. This is to say that by wasting his influence, the author of the cry had lost his influence, that is, his capacity to convince.

The circulating character of influence as a medium can be brought out more clearly if we break it down into types, since in each context it is easier to identify the nature of the flow in both ways than if it is treated on the more general level. I should like to suggest the following tentative classification: (1) "political" influence, (2) "fiduciary" influence, (3) influence through appeal to differential loyalties, and (4) influence oriented to the interpretation of norms. The fact that, in order to characterize the last two types, it is necessary to resort to cumbrous phrases rather than succinct single-word designations indicates clearly that the subject is rather undeveloped and needs elucidation. An important guide line for interpreting the first three types lies in the convertibility of each with one of the other three types of generalized media we have discussed.

1. When speaking of political influence, I mean it in an analytical sense, but one in which there is a directly significant relation between influence and power. The prototypical structural context is that of the democratic association, whether it be in the field of government at any one of several levels, or of private associations. The democratic association is characterized by a structure of offices the incumbents of which are authorized to take certain decisions binding on the collectivity as a whole and, hence, on its members in their respective capacities.[17] Such authorization is for action defined within constitutional norms, and there are also constitutional procedures by which incumbents of office are chosen, summed up as election and appointment.

The making of decisions binding on a collectivity I interpret to be an exercise of power, which includes the exercise of the franchise in the electoral procedure, since it is the aggregate of votes which determines who is elected to office. But both in seeking election and in office, officers and candidates are continually using other ways of getting the results they want besides the use of power in a strict sense. They are, of course, giving information and announcing intentions, in the detailed sense. They may well be offering inducements, making coercive threats outside the context of the power of office, and activating their own and others' commitments. But they are, above all, operating with influence, in our technical sense.

There are, as I conceive it, two main contexts in which this is the case. Because associations are typically differentiated on the axis of leadership-followership, we may use this axis here. One focus of influence, then, is the establishment of leadership position or reputation, either as incumbent of office or as explicit or implicit candidate, so that, for the followership in question, there will be a basis of trust going beyond the direct exercise of power, the giving of specific information and the like, and also beyond the manipulation of inducements, informal threats, etc. A leader, I suggest, must try to establish a basis on which he is trusted by a "constituency," in the symbolic sense of this discussion, so that when he "takes a position," he can count on a following "going along with him" on it, or even actively working for its implementation according to their respective capacities and roles. We often put this by saying that a leader "takes responsibility" for such positions. In any case, I would treat the concept of leadership as focusing on the use of influence, and the concept of office, on the use of power.

The other context is the obverse, that of the processes by which units not in a leadership position in the relevant respects can have and use influence oriented to having an effect on leadership. This is by and large the well-known field of "interest groups," very broadly in the sense of parts of the constituencies of parties and officeholders. The influence may be used in electoral processes, trying to establish terms on which electoral support—a form of power—will be given. Or, it may play on incumbents of office by trying to influence their decisions of policy. In either case, it is the use of a basis of presumptive "trust" and, hence, "right to speak" to try to swing a balance in favor of what the influencer advocates—or opposes—relative to alternatives, whether these be candidates or policies.

Political influence, then, we would conceive as influence operating in the context of the goal-functioning of collectivities, as generalized persuasion without power—i.e., independent of the use of power or direct threat,[18]—used, on the one hand, by units either exercising or bidding for leadership position and, on the other, by nonleaders seeking to have an effect on the decisions and orientations of leaders. Though political influence is analytically independent of power, we conceive the two to be closely interconnected. Very generally, leaders expect a major share of their influence to be translated into binding support, particularly through the franchise, and constituents in turn expect an important part of theirs to be translated into binding decisions congenial to them. But the independence of influence from power means that the influence system is an open one. To tie it to power in direct, matching terms would be to reduce the power-influence relation to a barter basis, and thus destroy the element of symbolic generalization we have treated as essential.

2. The second type of influence suggested has been called

"fiduciary." The relevant context here is not the effective determination of an attainment of collective goals, but the allocation of resources in a system where both collectivities and their goals are plural and the justification of each among the plural goals is problematical. The interests in control of resources and in attainment of goals are the classical instances of the operation of "interests" in social systems. In a more or less pluralistic system, the allocation of resources must, however, be subject to normative control; distributions must be justified by reference to norms more general than the mere desirability to the unit in question of getting what it wants. Furthermore, resources constitute, from the point of view of goal attainment, the principal opportunity factor that conditionally controls prospects of success. Hence, influence bearing on the allocation of resources is a particularly important field of trust.

There is a relation to money in this case which is in certain respects parallel to that to power in the case of political influence. This derives from the fact that, in a society in which the economy is highly differentiated relative to other elements of the social structure, money becomes the most important allocative mechanism, not only over commodities, but over human services. Hence, the focus of the fiduciary function is in the allocation of funds, because the possessor of funds is in turn in a position to claim, through market channels, control over the indicated share of "real" resources.

The interchanges we have in mind here do not constitute the use of money as a circulating medium, but rather as a measure of value. On the monetary side, an example is setting up a budget. The various interests that expect to share in a budget "assert their claims," and the budget-making agency reaches some kind of allocative ranking of these claims. This is the expression of need and of "right" in monetary terms. But both claims and accession of right in turn are subject to standards of justification, in our technical sense. These are never assertions of value as such, because the agency, dealing as it goes with scarce and allocable resources, must always consider situational exigency and competing claims. It operates, that is, at the level of norms, not of values. Those who assert claims may concretely, of course, use power to gain them; they may use inducements—in the extreme case, bribery—or various other means. But a special role is played by influence. A good example would be, in budgetary negotiations, the assertion of a highly qualified and trustworthy technical expert that to fulfill expectations he must have a certain specific minimum of resources at his disposal—an assertion that a budgetary officer, not himself an expert in the field, will find it difficult to contest. On the other hand, decisions of allocation in turn must be justified by reference to agreed standards of property priority in claims. Such standards, of course, are likely to be made most explicit where there is an unaccustomed stringency of resources and hence sacrifices must be justified. Just as the budgetary officer is often unable to judge the needs of the technical expert, so the latter, operating only in one specialized sector of the system, is not qualified to judge the urgency of the claims competing with his own. Hence the necessity for mutual influence to operate to cover this gap.

The case of a budget is the neatest case, because the relevant system is more or less closed by unitary organizational control of the resources and by power, in the strict sense, to make the allocative decisions binding. The same basic principles, however, apply in processes of allocation through free market channels. The economist's ideal of free competition is here the limiting case in which influence as an independent factor disappears. Here, then, it is in two areas that influence is most obviously operative. One is the establishment of norms by which the allocative process is regulated, as through tax legislation and the like; the other is through such modifications of "pure" market process as the involvement of voluntary contributions in allocation. The very term "fiduciary" is also most generally used for cases where certain "interested parties" cannot be expected to protect their interests without help, for example, administration of the property interests of minors by "trustees," i.e., people who can be trusted to apply acceptable standards even though their actions are not dictated by personal financial interest.

3. The third category has been called "influence through appeal to differential loyalties." Whereas in the political influence case the differentiation on the axis of leadership was the central

structural focus, and in the fiduciary influence case it was the problem of allocation of scarce resources, in this case it is the pluralistic structure of memberships in society. This operates at the level both of individuals in roles and of collectivities. The more highly differentiated the society is structurally, the more every concrete unit is a responsible member of a plurality of collectivities.[19] He is therefore in a position of having to balance the claims of these plural collectivities on his loyalties, i.e., a class of his normative commitments.

For the individual, particularly the adult male, the most important case is normally the relation between kinship and occupation, since for most men it is essential to participate in both, and in modern societies they are structurally independent of each other. Generally, in a reasonably stable situation, the broad lines of allocation of obligation are institutionally settled, but there are always areas of indeterminacy and of shift in the light of changing circumstances. Moreover, our society is rapidly changing, and one of the principal aspects of such change is the rise of new collectivities, and hence loyalties to them, and the decline of old ones. A large part of the population is thus faced with decisions about whether to take on new commitments or to sacrifice old ones, or both, or to shift balances among loyalties.

The commitments we have in mind are grounded in institutionalized values, which can, for purposes of analysis, be presumed to be shared by members of a society. But it is in the nature of a differentiated society that there is an important difference between asserting, however sincerely, the desirability of a value and, on the other hand, taking personal responsibility for its implementation, since the capacities and opportunities of units for effective contribution are inherently limited, and, moreover, some kinds of attempt would infringe the prerogatives of other units. It is with this problem that the present type of influence is concerned. It is a matter of the justification of assuming particular responsibilities in particular collectivity and subcollectivity contexts.

A person, then, will be faced by manifold demands for commitment through participation in collectivities, and will often be put in a position of having to justify the allocative decisions he makes. The normative structure (of "commitments") governing such processes then involves, on the one hand, appeals to common values and, on the other, assertion of norms governing the practical decisions of allocation of commitment among plural loyalties. The categories of influence, then, are, first, the plea that an actor ought, as a practical matter, to undertake such and such a collective responsibility (not merely that it is desirable that the function be effectively performed independently of *his* commitment; that is an assertion of its value), and second, the assertion of the norms it is held should govern such decisions, again at the level of practical allocation.

In one sense, this, like the last category of influence, concerns the allocation of "resources." But what I am here referring to as loyalties are not the same kind of resource as money and power, or the concrete utilities and modes of effectiveness controlled by them. From the point of view of the unit, the question is not with what means he will implement his commitments, but *whether he will undertake the commitment in the first place.* It is not, given that he "intends" to do something, a question of *how* he is to accomplish it, but rather whether he *ought*—in our sense of justification—to undertake it at all. Commitments in this sense surely constitute a societal resource, but, in the analysis of unit action, they concern the "orientational" side, not the situational side, of the action paradigm.[20]

As noted earlier in this paper, I consider generalized commitments to constitute a symbolic medium operating on the interaction process in the same basic sense that money, power, and influence do. Any promise by which the actor forecloses certain alternatives may be regarded as a *particular* commitment. By invoking a *generalized* commitment, however, the actor is enabled to command a series of more particular commitments, to be in a position to "activate" them in response to appropriate circumstances as we have said above. A good example is securing the acceptance of a job offer. Commitment to the job by the prospective employee then entails a commitment to perform a complex series of more particular acts as occasion arises, including commitment to accept certain types of authority within the organization.

Being grounded in values, generalized commitments in some sense involve the "honor" of the actors concerned, the more so the more generalized they are. They therefore cannot in general be altered lightly. Nevertheless, in a pluralistic and changing society, complete rigidity of commitments would introduce an intolerable rigidity into its structure. Commitments must therefore involve priority scales of seriousness, i.e., be referred to general standards, and there must be norms defining the situations in which particular commitments may be changed, not only new ones assumed but also old ones abandoned, even where this means the breaking of promises made and accepted in good faith. A good example here is the general norm that even in occupations where rules of tenure bind the employing organization, incumbents of such positions are generally considered entitled to resign subject only to giving "reasonable" notice. The category of influence with which we are now concerned operates in this range of flexibility of commitments and concerns the relation between the justification for change and the more generalized loyalties to fulfillment of commitments made.

4. The three types of influence so far discussed deal with the relations of the normative or integrative system to the other primary functional subsystems of the society, namely, what I should call the "polity," the "economy," and the "pattern maintenance" (in a structural aspect, the value maintenance) systems respectively.[21] The fourth and final type, which was referred to as influence oriented to the interpretation of norms, is internal to the integrative system. Here the prototype is the process of interpretation of legal norms in the appellate phase of the judicial process.

Since norms mediate between value commitments and particular interests and situational exigencies, they are, in formulation, in need of continual adjustment to the variations at these levels. Furthermore, since their primary function in the social system is integrative, the problem of consistency is a particularly important one. Hence, in a complex system of normative regulation, the interpretive function is highly important. A category of influence is organized about it of which the best example is the influence involved in the reputations of judges and lawyers. As in so many other fields, substantive arguments, i.e., particular justifications, of course play a central part. But there is the same need for symbolic generalization here as in the other fields. Another type of example of interpretive influence would be in the field of exegesis of ethical norms, which plays such an important part in many religious traditions.

This has been an exceedingly sketchy and tentative attempt to review a typology of the different contexts of the operation of influence. All, I think, are fields in which the general themes of the above analysis can be illustrated in sufficiently well-known terms to carry conviction of the reality and importance of the phenomena here called "influence." Let me reiterate that the critical common factor is a mechanism of persuasion that is generalized beyond appeal to particular facts, particular intentions, particular obligations and commitments, particular normative rules. The general suggestion is that, in the absence of a ramified system of influence in this sense, there would either be a much more pervasive atmosphere of distrust than in fact obtains, or the level of trust could be raised only by introducing more rigid specification as to who could be trusted in what specific ways, which would greatly limit the ranges of flexibility so important to a complex society.

Is Influence a Fixed Quantity in a Social System?

One further major topic is so essential to the general understanding of symbolic media that the discussion would be seriously incomplete without a brief treatment of it. It concerns a problem that has been particularly prominent in the history of the analysis of money and power, but the technical analysis of influence has been so primitive that it has scarcely arisen in that connection. It may be put in terms of the question whether any or all of these media are in general subject to a "zero-sum" condition of their operation.

At certain levels and in certain contexts it is obvious that this condition does hold. For a unit with fixed money income, increase of expenditure for one purpose must be balanced by reduction for one or more others. Similarly in power systems, electoral rules mean that a vote cast for one candidate must be denied to others, and persons in authority must choose between mutually incompatible alternatives in making many decisions. Important as this is, it is not, however, the whole story.

The most familiar case in the monetary field in which the zero-sum conception fails to apply is the creation of credit through banking. Money in one aspect is the most important object of property rights. Depositors in a bank in one sense "lend" their property to the bank. But, unlike most contracts of lease, they do not, even for a term, relinquish any of their rights: the main feature of a deposit is that it is repayable on demand, subject only to rules such as those regulating banking hours.

The bank, however, does not simply act as custodian for its depositors' funds. It lends a certain proportion to borrowers on contractual terms that enable the latter to "spend" them so long as they are presumptively in a position to repay at the term of the loan, and of course pay interest and any other charges. This means that *the same dollars* are functioning double as circulating media, so that the bank loans outstanding constitute a net addition to the quantity of the circulating medium.

This commonplace of economics has a very important implication. Clearly, an operating bank is in *one* important sense always formally "insolvent," in that its deposits are held on demand whereas its loans are on term. If all the depositors demand repayment at the same time, the bank cannot meet its obligations without outside resources. It usually keeps sufficient cash—and other resources—on hand to meet expected rates of withdrawal, with a margin of safety, but if it were completely "liquid," it would cease to be a bank. Financial panics are, precisely, occasions on which an abnormal rate of demand puts the bank in a difficult if not impossible position, in the extreme case forcing its "failure."

The question arises whether there are, with respect to the other media, phenomena analogous to those of banking and credit in the monetary field. The dominant opinion in the field of analysis of power seems to have been that there are not,[22] but this position has been questioned. The most appropriate context seems to be the relation between the grant of power to leadership in the democratic association and the use of that power by leadership.

Elected leaders may be said to be the recipients of a grant of power through the exercise of the franchise. This grant is, moreover, typically and in principle revocable, if not on demand, then at the end of a stated term of office, when the voter can transfer his support to a rival candidate. It could be argued, then, that this is a "deposit" of power, which is at the disposal of the depositors for the "purchase" of political benefits through the decisions made by the incumbents of office somewhere in the system, not necessarily this particular office. This would make it a "circulating" system where the amounts of power balanced.

It may be suggested, however, that this is only part of the story. Some of the power acquired through election to office may be "invested" in collective enterprises that are not direct responses to the interest demands of constituents, and this power in turn may be utilized by agencies other than constituents. Since power is in certain circumstances convertible into money, for example through taxation, it may be suggested that some of the use of tax funds, as in the support of scientific training and research, is a process of "investment" by officeholders—in both the executive and the legislative branches—that puts the funds at the disposal of scientists and educational institutions. If the electorate, like the bank's depositors, should demand immediate and strict accounting of power, the system would, like a good bank, turn out to be "insolvent" in the sense that these commitments could not be liquidated all at once. Often, however, politicians can shrewdly estimate the latitude it is safe to assume in making commitments other than those specifically demanded by the constituents on whom they are dependent. Politically organized collectivities, including government, can probably serve as agents of creative social change mainly by virtue of this type of mechanism, namely, the creation of increments of new power, since generating direct constituency demands for these changes may involve much more serious difficulties.

It would seem logical that the same reasoning should apply to influence. The case in which the zero-sum concept should particularly apply is political influence, because, on the economic analogy, this is a kind of "circular flow" situation in which the process of eliciting collective decisions in a ramified system is mediated.[23] The economic parallel lies in the markets for consumers' good and for labor.

In the field of influence, the analogy with banking and credit seems most obvious in connection with the allocation of loyalties. The postulate on which our whole analysis in this area is based is that it applies most clearly to a highly pluralistic social system in which the allocation of loyalties cannot be wholly based on direct assessment of the importance of the intrinsic issues involved, but that commitments are widely made in response to influence. If the quantity of influence is not fixed, but is expansible along the lines suggested by monetary credit, then it becomes possible for influence to operate as a mechanism by which a given capacity for power and commitments (in our technical sense) can be reallocated, in that the influence to command such commitments can be more or less directly and deliberately put in the hands of certain agencies.

My suggestion is that the principal way in which this is done in a society like the American is through voluntary associations that, unlike government even in its "democratic" aspect, are not primarily concerned with political functions—again in our technical sense. The "joiners" of such associations are analogous to depositors. They have, as we often put it, "lent their names" to the association and its leadership. But such an association often does more than simply collect increments of influence; it creates the effect of adding to the total amount of influence in circulation. This can occur in proportion as leadership exercises *independent* judgment in how to use the "name," not of individual members but of the association, to encourage commitments which they consider to be desirable, generally in quarters outside the membership itself.

Such associations may thus be considered to be a kind of "influence bank." Like money banks, they are formally "insolvent." Hence, if their members call for strict accounting—"You shall not use the name of the association without explicit consent of all the membership to the detailed implications"—this, of course, destroys the freedom of action of leaders, and leads to a deflation of "influence credit." The effect of this in turn is to deprive many agencies, dependent on the "backing" of such influence purveyors, of the basis on which they can "afford" to make important commitments. In more ordinary circumstances, however, leaders of such associations operate on a judgment of the acceptable margins of their independence. They do, in fact, make commitments of the association's name beyond the level of explicit authorization—though not of realistic expectation of "justification"—by the membership. In so doing, they add to the net amount of influence circulating in the system and have an effect on the distribution of commitments in the society in the direction of promoting the "causes" they hold to be desirable.

It should be clear from the above argument that phenomena analogous to deflation and inflation in the economic case should be found in the fields of power and influence as well. We have already indicated the direction that deflationary trends would take in these fields. In the field of power it is toward progressively increasing reliance on strict authority and coercive sanctions, culminating in the threat and use of physical force. In the field of influence it is toward undermining the basis of trust in reputations and fiduciary responsibility through increasing questioning of broader loyalties and rising insistence on narrow in-groupism.[24]

Inflationary process, on the other hand, is, for influence, the extension of claims to authoritative diagnoses of situations that cannot be validated with solid information and, on the other hand, the declaration of praiseworthy intentions that will not be backed by actual commitments when occasion arises. Unfortunately, there is no space here to develop these themes as they deserve.

It should go without saying that this essay has been very tentative indeed. It cannot claim to be more than the barest approach to the very complicated problems of this area. I hope, however, that it can serve as a useful basis not only for discussion but for the stimulation of serious research.

IV. CHANGE, EVOLUTION, AND MODERN SOCIETY

"Some Considerations on the Theory of Social Change" (1961) was one of Parsons's first systematic statements of the theory of evolutionary social change as a process of structural differentiation of functions accompanied by concomitant processes of reorganization. The latter include upgrading of capacities, new modes of including units in the larger social system, and reinterpretations of norms and values. In "Evolutionary Universals in Society" (1964), Parsons described some of the institutional forms of differentiation that appear to be universal in the evolutionary emergence of modern society.

"The Mass Media and the Structure of American Society" (1960) illustrates Parsons's use of evolutionary conceptions to criticize typical ideological attacks on modern society. Proper understanding of the differentiation of the institutions of communication provides a theoretical foundation for rebutting the claim that mass communication leads to social disintegration and cultural decline. "Archaic and Historic Societies," a selection from *The Evolution of Societies* (1977), suggests premodern social structures fundamentally exclude large portions of the population from participation in the cultural and institutional order. Hence, one of the principal problems of modernization is the inclusion of previously isolated and dependent groups. This idea adds yet another dimension to the theory of institutionalization; the process involves not merely the socialization of individuals but the incorporation of groups into the social system.

The final selection, "American Values and American Society," is also from *The Evolution of Societies*. In this passage, Parsons defends the health and resiliency of American society, arguing that the forces of modernization provide the means for insuring the democratic inclusion of all groups in the American societal community. This selection is introduced by a brief passage from *The American University* (1973) presenting Parsons's conception of American values.

16

SOME CONSIDERATIONS ON THE
THEORY OF SOCIAL CHANGE

I should like to concentrate my attention on one major type of change in social systems, that which is most closely analogous to the process of growth in the organism. This usually involves an element of quantitative increase in the "magnitude" of the system, in the social case, e.g., through increase in population, but it also involves what in an important sense is qualitative or "structural" change. The type of the latter on which I should like to concentrate is the process of structural differentiation and the concomitant development of patterns and mechanisms which integrate the differentiated parts. This, of course, is a classic sociological as well as biological problem, in the sociological case being central to Spencer's thought, but in its more modern phase above all associated with Durkheim.

One of the most fundamental canons of scientific method is that it is impossible to study everything at once. Since the basis of generalization in science is always the demonstration of relatedness in processes of variation (in one sense change), there must always somewhere be a distinction between the features of the phenomena under observation which do and which do not change under the relevant limitations of time and scope, and in the respects which are defined as important for the purposes in hand. The specificities of significant change could not even be identified

This paper was presented to the North Central States' Rural Sociology Committee, Chicago, Illinois, November 3, 1960. Reprinted by permission with deletions from "Some Considerations on the Theory of Social Change," *Rural Sociology* 26 (1961): 219–39.

if there were no *relative* background of nonchange to relate them to.

To me the concept of structure is simply a shorthand statement of this basic point. The structure of a system is that set of properties of its component parts and their relations or combinations which, for a particular set of analytical purposes, can both logically and empirically be treated as constant within definable limits. If, however, there is built up strong empirical evidence that treating such elements as constant for particular types of systems is helpful in understanding the patterning of variation of other elements, then this structure is not simply an arbitrary methodological assumption, but propositions about it and its limits of empirical stability become empirical generalizations which are just as important as are "dynamic" generalizations.

There are cases where structures are described in terms of problem statements involving no interest in what happens. These, however, are limiting cases of scientific analysis, though they are sometimes important ones, as witness the case of a map which simply delineates the relative locations of different topographical features of a terrain without any propositions about processes which might change them. But usually descriptions of structure constitute the primary reference-base for describing and analyzing processes. The classic concept of process is the motion of classical mechanics—but you cannot talk about motion without any categorization of the particle as "that which" moves, nor of space as a manifold of locations from which and to which a process of motion occurs.

Any ordinary system, therefore, is capable of description as on the one hand a structure, a set of units or components with, for the purposes in hand, stable properties, which of course may be relational, and on the other hand of events, of processes, in the course of which "something happens" to change some properties and some relations among them.

The concept of stability has obviously been used here as a defining characteristic of structure. The sense of the former term which must be distinguished from structure is that in which it is used to characterize a system as a whole, or some subsystem of such a system. In this present sense it is equivalent to the more specific concept of stable equilibrium—which in another reference may be either "static" or "moving." A system then is stable or (relatively) in equilibrium when the relation between its structure and the processes which go on within it, and between it and its environment, are such as to maintain those properties and relations, which for the purposes in hand have been called its structure, relatively unchanged. Very generally, always in "dynamic" systems, this maintenance is dependent on continuously varying processes, which "neutralize" either endogenous or exogenous sources of variability which, if they went far enough, would change the structure. A classic example of equilibrium in this sense is the maintenance of nearly constant body temperature by mammals and birds—in the face of continuing variation in environmental temperature and through mechanisms which operate either to produce heat, including slowing up its loss, or to slow down the rate of heat production or accelerate its dissipation.

Contrasted then with stability or equilibrating processes are those processes which operate to bring about structural change. That such processes exist and that they are of fundamental scientific importance is nowhere in question. Thus even in physics, whereas the mass of the atom of a particular element has been the prototype of the stable structural reference point, the discoveries of modern nuclear physics have now evolved a theory of change by which, through nuclear fission and/or fusion, the structures of "atomic identity" are transformed into others. The reason for insistence on the importance of keeping the concepts of structure and process and of stability and change analytically distinct is not a predilection in favor of one or the other item in each pair, but in favor of orderly procedure in scientific analysis.

As I see it now, the distinction between the two pairs of concepts is one of level of system reference. The structure of a system and of its environment must be distinguished from process *within* the system and in *interchange* between the system and its environment. But processes which maintain the stability of a system, internally through both structure and process, and in interchange with its environment, i.e., states of its equilibrium, must be distinguished from processes by which this balance between structure and more "elementary" process is altered in such a way as to lead to a new and different "state" of the system, a state which must be described in terms of an alteration of its previous structure.

These considerations constitute the major framework in which I should like to approach the analysis of change in social systems. I should like to attempt to discuss one type of change in the sense in which it has just been contrasted with stability, and therefore will presuppose that there is a system or set of systems to which the concept of equilibrium is relevant, but which are conceived as undergoing processes of change which as such are processes of upsetting the initial equilibrium state and later "settling down" into a new equilibrium state. I am, however, as noted above, treating this problem not for the highest-level equilibrium of societies as a whole, but for processes of change in subsystems of the society.

I

Let us start with the question of the structure of social systems and introduce both a formal and a substantive consideration. The formal one is that the structure of any empirical system may be treated as consisting in (1) *units,* such as the particle or the cell, and (2) *patterned relations* among units, such as relative distances, "organization" into tissues and organs. For social systems the minimum unit is the *role* of the participating individual actor (or status-role, if you will), and the minimum relation is that of patterned reciprocal interactions in terms of which each participant functions as an actor in relation to (orienting to) the others and, conversely, each is object for all the others. Higher-order units of social systems are collectivities, i.e., organized action systems of the role performance of pluralities of human individuals.

In social structure the element of "patterned relation" is clearly in part "normative." This is to say that from the point of view of the unit it includes a set of "expectations" as to his or its behavior on the axis of what is or is not proper, appropriate, or right. From the point of view of other units with which the unit of reference is in interaction, this is a set of standards according to which positive or negative sanctions can be legitimated. Corresponding to the distinction between role and collectivity for the case of units is that between norm and value for that of relational pattern. A value is a normative pattern which defines desirable behavior for a system in relation to its environment, without differentiation in terms of the functions of units or of their particular situations. A norm on the other hand is a pattern defining desirable behavior for a unit or class of units in respects specific to it and differentiated from the obligations of other classes.

The proposition that the relational patterns of social systems are normative, which is to say that they consist in institutionalized normative culture, can, in fact, be extended to the structure of units as well. One way of making this clear is to point out that what at one level of reference is a unit at another is a system. What we are calling the structural properties of the unit, therefore, are at the next level the relational patterns which order the relations between what in turn are the subunits making *it* up. Therefore, it is justified to assert, in the wider perspective, that the structure of social systems in general *consists* in institutionalized patterns of normative culture. It is of course further essential that these must be understood as applying at the two distinct levels of organization which we call that of units and relational pattern among units.

To return now to the paradigm of the stable system discussed above, process in a system must be conceived as a process of interchanging inputs and outputs between units (subsystems) of the system on the one hand, and between the system, through the agency of its units, and its environment on the other. There is thus a "flow" of such inputs and outputs as between all pairs of classes of units, whether the relation be internal or external. What I am calling the normative pattern governing the relationship is then to be conceived as regulating this flow. For stable interchange to go on there must on the one hand be flexibility for inputs and outputs to move, but there must also be ways of "channeling" this process to keep its variability within limits.

A prototypical case is the flow of transactions involving the exchange of things of "value," namely goods and services and money, which constitute a market process. The normative patterns on the other hand are the institutional patterns defining money itself, the norms of contract and of the aspects of property other than money, conceived as Durkheim did in the famous phrase about the noncontractual elements of contract. The equilibrium of a market system is dependent on the maintenance of limits, relative to a set of definable conditions, to the fluctuation in the rates of these flows. The stability of the *structure* of the market system in the present sense is on the other hand a matter of the stability of the normative pattern system, the institutions.

What, then, do we mean by the stability of an institutional complex? First, of course, is meant the stability of the normative pattern itself. The single term norm, especially if it is equated with "rule," is probably too narrow because it seems to imply a level of simplicity which permits description in a single proposition; this would patently not be true of the institutions of property or contract. Secondly, stability implies a minimum level of commitment of acting units, i.e., of dispositions to perform in accordance with the relevant expectations—rather than to evade or violate them—and to apply the relevant sanctions, positive or negative, to other units in response to performance, evasion, or violation. Third, institutionalization implies acceptance of an empirical and mutually understood "definition of the situation" in a sense of understanding of what the system of reference *is;* this can for example be ideologically distorted so as to make functioning impossible.

Finally, institutionalization means some order of integration of the normative complex in question in the more general one governing the system as a whole, at the normative level itself. Thus the doctrine of "separate but equal" proved to be dubiously integrated with the rest of the American system of constitutional rights formulated on the basis of the constitutional right to "equal protection of the laws." It can thus be said that the 1954 decision of the Supreme Court was a step in institutional integration, or at least that this was the primary problem before the court.

The concept of stable equilibrium implies that through integrative mechanisms endogenous variations are kept within limits compatible with the maintenance of the main structural patterns, and through adaptive mechanisms fluctuations in the relations between system and environment are similarly kept within limits. If we look at what is meant by stable equilibrium from the perspective of the principle of inertia,[1] then it becomes a problem to account for alterations in this stable state through disturbances of sufficient magnitude to overcome the stabilizing or equilibrating forces or mechanisms. Once a disturbance fulfilling these criteria is present, then, the problem is that of tracing its effects through the system, and defining the conditions under which new stable states can be predicted (or, retrospectively, accounted for).

There is a double reason why the boundary of the social system vis-à-vis the personality is particularly significant. In its most direct sense it is concerned with the "motivation" of the individual, in an analytical psychological sense, hence with his level of "gratification" and its negative, frustration. But *indirectly* the most critical point is that what is structurally the most critical component of social systems, what we call its institutionalized values, is institutionalized by way of its internalization in the personality of the individual. There is a sense in which the social system is "boxed in" between the cultural status of values and their significance to the integration of the individual personality.

I shall therefore postulate a change in the relation of a social system to its environment which in the first instance impinges on the definition of the situation for one or more classes of acting units within the system and then has further repercussions which can put pressure for change on the normative institutional patterns. The type of pressure I have specifically in mind is in the direction of differentiation.

Before attempting to outline a formal analysis perhaps it would be helpful to introduce an empirical example. A good one, of particular interest to rural sociologists and so important to the whole process of "modernization," is the differentiation of the collectivities in which occupational roles are performed from the kinship units in which the personal security of the individual and his "consumption" interests are anchored. The shift over from the family farm to the typical "urban" occupational situation of course involves this.

Even with such a seemingly simple case it is important to treat the question of system references with great care. Going on in the relevant sectors of the society in question there will be at least two processes of differentiation of operative units, namely, (1) at the collectivity level between kinship units and units which perform primarily "productive" functions in the society, which are mainly "specific-function" organizations. There may, however, be important intermediate cases like the classical family firm which at the ownership-management level is still "fused" but at the "employee" level has become differentiated. (2) At the role level, where the individual person who retains his membership in a kinship unit also comes to perform a role in a productive organization for which his services constitute important facilities. Not only should these two "operational" levels of the process of differentiation be distinguished, but it should be kept in mind that the same concrete process will presumably involve changes in the set of normative patterns governing each of the two units and the relations between them, and finally in the subsystem value institutionalized in these units, if not in the overall value system of the society, a possibility which is excluded from present consideration by our assumptions.

For present purposes it is not necessary to raise questions about "subsistence." It is enough that functions which have come to be organized about occupational roles were previously, so far as they were performed at all, performed within the kinship unit so that at the role level, e.g., the "husband-father" both "worked in the business" and "interacted" with his wife and children in his familial roles.

Some of the familiar things which must happen for the process to take place are (1) a loss of functions by the kinship unit, (2) a new pattern of organization of the functions which have come to be dissociated from the kinship unit, (3) a substitution of new ways of taking care of the needs of the kinship unit which are occasioned by this loss of service to it, (4) a way of organizing the terms of their relationships including the handling of the risks entailed in "cutting loose" from kinship in favor of employment in the new organization, and (5) a way of balancing the legitimation of both units at both the collectivity and the role levels so that the inevitable component of conflict of interest is "contained" within a pattern of mutual contribution to higher-order system functioning.

The new pattern of organization in this case is clearly the social structure of the employing collectivity. The loss of function from the point of view of the kinship unit is typically compensated by money income which in turn gives access to various needed goods and services through the market mechanism. The terms of employment are regulated by the contract of employment which is part of the larger complex comprising the institution of contract, whereas the market entails adequate institutionalization, among other things, of the money mechanism. Risks are handled by various devices, first the security of the particular employment, then alternatives of employment, then insurance, public responsibility, and so on. Conflict of interest is handled above all by the definition of the situation that employment is a channel for valued contribution to the welfare of the system in that the employing organization is conceived to be engaged in making such contributions. The alternative is definition of the relation of the organization to the family as one of "exploitation."

In the nature of the case at both collectivity and role levels there is *one* structural unit at the beginning of such a process of differentiation. It is, however, essential to look from both sides at the functional problem which is the setting for the process. The principle of inertia tells us that there will probably be resistance to the order of change which involves transfer of functions from within the original unit outside it to qualitatively different units; the transfer will quite literally be felt to be a loss.

Any number of factors may, however, make it difficult or impossible for this unit to cope with increasing "pressures." Leaving out the alternative of sheer disintegration—empirically important as that is—there is a highly important distinction to be made between differentiation and segmentation. Thus in American agricultural history, the combination of rapidly increasing population and availability of new lands led for a long period to very rapid increase in the number of family farms which is a case of segmentation. The typical process was, of course, with the establishment of new nuclear families by marriages, for the new couples to establish family farms of their own instead of trying to "fit into" the going enterprise of a farm run by one of the parental couples—though of course a large fraction in fact did just that. But given technological and market conditions it clearly would not work for the same farms to support indefinitely increasing numbers, however the allocation of belongingness between kin of husband and wife has worked out.

Differentiation, however, entails a process by which new kinds of unit, as distinguished from more of the same kind, come to be established. Here it is possible to state a very important principle, namely that the new kind of unit, e.g., collectivity or role, will subserve what, from the point of view of the adaptive exigencies of the system of which it is a part, is a *higher-order* function than did the unit out of which it differentiates and than does the "residual" unit left by the establishment of the new one.

If the process of change is to involve differentiation, then, a crucial if not the crucial question comes to be that of the availability and sources of the resources necessary to bring about, not only a structural change, but one which entails the genesis of capacities in the system for levels of performance which previously were not possible. The alternative is either segmentation or a process of disorganization. In general we can say that the process of differentiation must go concomitantly with a process of reorganization of the normative culture of the system, not only at the level of operative units, but at the level of norms and sub-system values. Though increases of "energy" may be required to bring about the process of differentiation, the crucial set of factors is likely to concern what we have been calling "organization."

It should finally be recalled that a source of disturbance may be either endogenous or exogenous, and that this applies to discrepancies between reality and normative expectation as well as to "conditional" factors.

With these preliminaries in mind, let us now attempt to outline in general terms the main steps in a cycle of differentiation, and then apply the analysis to the case of differentiation between household and producing collectivity.

We may start with the postulation of a deficit of input at the goal-attainment boundary of the social system which is postulated as undergoing a process of differentiation, e.g., the family household which also performs "occupational" functions. Looking at it from a functional point of view, it may be said that the "frustration" of its capacity to attain its goals, or fulfill its expectations, may focus at either of the functional levels which is important to it, namely its productive effectiveness or its effectiveness in performing what later come to be the "residual" family functions of socialization and regulation of the personalities of members, or of course some combination of the two. Secondly, it will of course concern the boundary between this and other subsystems of the society. In this case the important boundary conceptions are the markets for commodities and labor and the ideological "justifications" of the unit's position in the society, which may or may not take a prominently religious direction. But underlying this is the problem of input from the personality of the individual into the social system at the more general level; in the present case this is likely to be particularly important because familial and occupational roles are, for the personality of the adult, the most important foci of commitment to the performance of societal function. Third, there will be some balance between the two components of frustration just mentioned, namely with respect to the conditional components of facilities and rewards, and with respect to the normative components of expectation systems. The latter component is the indispensable condition of the process leading to differentiation.

The most important point to be made here is that, *whatever its source,* if a disturbance impinges on the goal-attaining subsystem of a social system, its effects will, in the first instance, be propagated in two directions. One of these concerns the functional problem of access to facilities for the performance of primary functions, namely the kind of facilities available and the terms on which they are available. The other direction concerns the kind of integrative support which the unit receives within the syystem, the senses in which it can be said to have a "mandate" to "do a job." Back of that, in turn, on a still higher level of control is the basic "legitimation" of its functioning. Support here may be defined as particularized to the specific unit or class of units. Legitimation on the other hand concerns more the functions than the particular unit and the normative more than the operative patterns.

These three problems fit into a hierarchy of control. The first is an adaptive problem and must be solved first if the groundwork of solution of the others is to be laid, and so on for the others. What is meant by "solution" in this case is provision of *opportunity* in a facilities sense for the higher level of functioning in question to be attained. Opportunity thus conceived is always double-barreled, in that it has a concrete resource aspect on the one hand, a normatively controlled "mechanism" or standard aspect on the other.

Another familiar sociological concept should be brought in here, namely ascription. Ascription is essentially the *fusion* of intrinsically independent functions in the same structural unit. Looked at in this way differentiation is a process of "emancipation" from ascriptive ties. As such it is a process of gaining "freedom from" certain restraints. But it is also the process of fitting into a normative order which can subject the now independent units to a type of normative control compatible with the functional imperative of the larger system of which they are a part. In differentiating, however, the unit gains certain degrees of freedom of choice and action which were not open to it before the process of differentiation had taken place. Moreover, this should be the case whichever side of the division is taken as a point of reference.

This point can be made clearer in terms of our illustrative example. The family farm producing for a market is, relative to anything like subsistence agriculture, already far along on the continuum of differentiatedness. But the resources available to its "management" cannot be dissociated from those belonging to the family household; it is a matter perhaps of relatively arbitrary decision on the part of the farmer what proportion of monetary resources he will allocate to operation of the farm, and what proportion he will "withdraw" for family consumption including, for instance, education of children.

The structural transition we have in mind would typically entail his change of status from that of proprietor of a farm to that of employee of a producing unit of some sort—whether it be agricultural or not. There has been a tendency to define this change as a derogation of status for the family head, but let us look at it from another point of view.

The family farm is in a position, as a family unit, of being ascribed to a particular source of income, namely the market for the sale of the products which it is feasible to grow in the location, with the type of land and other resources available. In "sloughing off" the productive function, the family becomes emancipated from ascription to "making a living" from the sale of its own agricultural products. The principal income earner—leaving aside for the moment other contributors—can fulfill his primary obligations to his family through any one of a much wider range of alternative sources of income, namely any organization which will accept him for employment, and of course pay him enough.

The obverse of this emancipation from ascription to a relatively particularized source of income is the freedom to offer a much wider variety of services in exchange for income. The labor force, that is to say, may become much more highly differentiated, and a wider variety of specialized talents may find employment. A new set of conditions are of course introduced, because the more important specialized talents often involve prerequisites of training and experience which cannot be universally taken for granted.

These two are the relatively "conditional" factors from the point of view of the household. We may say that it cannot afford to let the process of differentiation take place unless certain minima in these respects are if not guaranteed made highly probable. These probabilities are, in turn, dependent on two further sets of considerations which involve the more ramified relationship systems in which the process takes place. These are considerations in the first place of the nature of the labor market in which the income earner has to offer his services; above all the extent to which he is protected against pressures to accept particularly disadvantageous terms. There are three main mechanisms involved in modern labor markets at the operative level, though others may operate in other ways. These are of course competition between potential employers, the self-protective measures of employee groups, e.g., through collective bargaining, and establishment and enforcement of a normative order by "higher" authority, e.g., public agencies. The effect of regulation of terms by any combination of these factors is to emancipate the unit from exposure to particular pressures exerted by any one source of supply, e.g., of income. Through such means as the monetary mechanisms and credit instruments, there is also time-extension in that the employee is emancipated from the pressures of immediacy to a degree to which this may not be the case for the proprietor.

The above discussion is stated from the point of view of the family as a unit. For completeness it would be necessary to turn it around and raise the question of feasibility from the point of view of production by an organizational unit structurally differentiated from kinship groups. Here the primary functional problem of facilities would be that of access to an adequate labor force on the kinds of terms which would fit in with its exigencies. (For the family case I have taken the availability of consumers' goods for granted since the commercial family farm already procured them through the market.)

Let us now turn to the second context, that of support for the performance of function. This is the kind of context in which farming is regarded as a "way of life" rather than a "business." Typically occupational employment is justified by the higher level of efficiency of such organization in producing a higher standard of living, but this may be problematical when it involves ceasing to be "independent" and "working for ones own" rather than for an employer. On the other side there is the problem of "loss of function" of the family with the implication that the differentiated family is not "doing a worth-while job" but is coming to be a consumption unit alone—a question particularly coming to a head in the alleged concentration of the feminine role on "leisure" activities. We may follow through this context in terms of the problem of degrees of freedom, being careful to distinguish the two levels which above have been called support and legitimation.

The problem in which I am calling the context of support is the position of the family in locally significant "public opinion." The support of this unit is ascribed to the conception that acceptable status in the community is bound to proprietorship of an enterprise, with all its connotations about the place of property—the employed person is in some sense a second class citizen. It seems to follow that, just as in the context of facilities available to differentiating units the relevant frame of reference or "reference group" was the market, both for labor and for consumers' goods, in that of "support" it is the local community, since both residential unit and employing unit for the typical adult must be comprised within this. In the undifferentiated case the core structure of the local community in America consists in proprietary kinship units—in the first instance farm families, but the same structural patterns extend to small businesses and professional practices in market towns. In the differentiated case it is residential kinship units on the one hand, employing organizations on the other.

Since the basic "goals" of residential kinship units as such are in the nature of the case ascribed, namely as socialization of children and management of the personalities of members, the community gains in this respect an exceedingly important new range of freedom in the new levels and diversities of, in the above broad sense, "productive" achievement, which higher level organizations are capable of carrying out and which are beyond the capacities of kinship units. The typical family unit need no longer look to units of its own type of structure for these benefits, thus staying within the limits imposed by this structure, and members of the community can support the functions of the community *both* in the familial realm and in the productive without making their ascription to each other a condition.

This, however, is possible only if there are standards which regulate the terms on which the two categories of functions are related to each other. This, in part, concerns market relations; but a number of other things are also involved, such as obligations for contributing to the support of common community interests, both through taxation and through voluntary channels. There must be a new set of "rules of the game" according to which both sets of operating units can live in the same community without undue friction. One major focus of these balancing institutions lies in the field of stratification, above all perhaps because the larger scale of organization of producing units in the differentiated sense makes it impossible to preserve the basis of equality of kinship units of a family-farm community.

This leads over into the problem of legitimation which concerns

the justifications or questioning of the basic pattern of organization of socially important functions in terms of the institutionalized values of the system. Here the problem is that of
emancipating the formulae of legitimation from the organizational
particularities of the less differentiated situation. These considerations clearly get over into the ideological realm. For differentiation to be legitimated it must no longer be believed that only
proprietors are really "responsible" people, or that organizations
which are not controlled by locally prestigeful kinship units are
necessarily concerned only with "self-interest" and are not really
"contributing." On the other side, the family which has "lost
functions" can really be a "good family."

Perhaps the most important focus of this new legitimation is the
new conception of the adequate, socially desirable *man*, particularly as organized about the balancing of the two differentiated
spheres of performance and responsibility, in his occupational
role on the one hand, in his family on the other. If this is the case,
then clearly there are extremely important concomitant problems
of change in the feminine role. The first stage of these probably
concerns the ideological legitimation of a more differentiated
femininity than before, namely that even in a family which has
lost function it is justified for the woman to devote herself primarily to husband and children. A later phase involves various forms
of community participation and occupational involvement.

These three seem to be the main contexts in which the direct
impact of the impetus to structural change must work out if it is to
result in the differentiation of a previously fused structure. For
the sake of completeness it should be mentioned that there will be
certain other more indirect problem areas. One of these is that of
the sheer content of consumption tastes which is involved in a
change in the standard of living, and its relation to the occupational contribution of the income earner. A second is the problem
of the relation of values, at various levels of specification, not
only to the more immediate problems of the legitimation of the
various classes of structural units in the system, but to that of the
more generalized norms and standards which regulate their relations. Finally, the most indirect of all seems to lie in the field of
what Durkheim called organic solidarity. I interpret this to mean
the normative regulation of the adaptive processes and mecha-

nisms. As I see it, this is the primary link between what I have called support on the one hand and the realistic play of "interests" of the various units on the other.

The above discussion has dealt, in far too great a hurry, with several different "functional" contexts in which some kind of reordering has to take place if a process of differentiation, as this has been defined, is to be completed and the new structure stabilized. It is of the essence of the present view that in each of these there is involved a complex balance of input-output relationships such that too great a tipping in either direction with respect to any one such balance could make the difference between successful differentiation and its failure. The dismal complexity of the resulting picture is, however, somewhat mitigated by considerations of the hierarchy of control and hence of the fact that firm establishment of the "proper" patterns at the higher levels may make it possible to exercise control over rather wide ranges of variation at the lower.

The problem of the sequence of phases in such a process and the relations of these to the balances between resistance and more "progressive" factors has been—sketchily, to be sure—dealt with somewhere.[2] The essential point, perhaps, is that these balances must be adjusted in the favorable direction in a relatively determinate temporal sequence, if the successful outcome is to take place. Crucial as these problems are, there is no space to enter into them here.

Instead of this, in conclusion, I should like to attempt to summarize certain of the primary conditions of successful differentiation which also constitute in a sense characterizations of the outcome in the relevant respects. First there is what I have called the *opportunity* factor. This is the aspect of the structure of the situation which is most directly relevant to the process of differentiation as such. The operation of the process of course presupposes a need or demand factor, the source of disturbance to which reference was made above. The implementation of the process of differentiation in turn implies a leadership factor in that some individual or group should take responsibility, not only for routine "management" but for reorganization. The entrepreneur of standard economic discussion is a prototypical example.

But for there to be genuine differentiation there must be a process by which facilities, previously ascribed to less differentiated units, are freed from this ascription and are made available through suitable adaptive mechanisms for the utilization of the higher-order new class of units which are emerging. The proto-type of such facilities for the process considered above is that of labor services, freed from ascription to the household unit, but with their availability to the employing organization institutionally regulated in terms of the market system and the institutionalization of the contract of employment. The obverse is of course the accessibility, for the residual household units, of necessary facilities through the expenditure of money income on the markets for consumers' goods. Looked at then in structural terms the opportunity factor is essentially the possibility of institutionalizing the mutual access to facilities, in this case through the market mechanisms. In another type of case, for instance, it may be the mechanisms of communication.

The second main context of structural reorganization concerns the way in which the two new and differentiated classes of units are related to each other in the wider system, in the first instance from the point of view of the structure of collectivities. I have suggested, for the case of the producing household, that what is primarily involved here is a restructuring of the local community. The latter can no longer be an aggregate of proprietary kinship units, only supplemented by a few structures articulating it with the wider society, but it comes to be organized about the re-lationships between "residential" units and "employing" units. It is evident that this entails articulating the most important *differentiated* roles of the same individual, in the first instance of course the typical adult male.

This may be called the restructuring of the ways in which the particular unit, collectivity and role, is included in higher-order collectivity structures in the society. Since in the nature of the case any initial collectivity unit (or role unit) is part of a society, it is not a question whether it should or should not be included; for example, the case of absorption of immigrant kin groups into a host society is a different problem from that now under consideration. The point is rather that there must be a restructuring of collectivities on the level immediately above that of the initial unit, with either the incorporation of both the old (or "residual") unit and the new in an already available higher-order unit, or the creation of a new category of such units, or both. The essential point is that there must be established a new collectivity structure within which both types of units perform essential functions and in the name of which both can draw the kind of "support" discussed above. The problem is of course particularly acute for the newly emerging unit or class of units.

The third context in which normative components of structure have to be reorganized as part of a process of differentiation is that of the more general complexes of institutionalized norms which apply not to one collectivity structure but to many. The prototype here for large-scale and highly differentiated social systems is the system of legal norms, but it is not confined to that. Standards of performance or achievement, of technical adequacy, and the like are also involved.

In the case we have used for illustration, the standards in terms of which employing collectivities are legitimized are particularly important. Here it is important to recognize two different stages beyond that of the proprietary unit which was our original point of reference, namely that in which all productive roles are performed by household members. The next step has usually been the "family firm" in which the managerial and entrepreneurial roles were ascribed to kinship, but the "labor" roles were not. This of course is still very prominent in the "small business" sector of the American economy, and also in some other fields. But beyond this is the case where the organization is cut entirely loose from kinship. The most important legal aspect of this development has been the generalization of the idea of the corporation and its legitimation in many different fields, quantitatively of course most conspicuously the economic.

At the role level an important case is that of the standards of competence which become institutionalized as defining conditions of employment in certain classes of roles, behind which in turn lie levels of education. These, like legal norms, are independent of any particular employing collectivity or kinship group—in this sense both are universalistic. The rules of corporate organization define the kinds of things certain organized groups can do and the responsibilities they assume in organizing to do them; standards of education define the kinds of legitimate requirements of eligibility for certain types of employment which may be laid down, hence both the kinds of opportunities open to individuals of various classes, and the ways in which access to such opportunity is limited.

It has been suggested above that a process of differentiation, with the meaning we have given that term, involves the establishment of a unit having primary functions of a higher order, seen in terms of the system in which it operates, than was the function of the unit from which it differentiates. If this is the case, then the norms governing the performance of that function, including the relations of its performers to other units in the social structure, must be of a higher order of generality than before. This is what we mean by saying that they are more universalistic; they define standards which cannot, in their relevance, be confined to the lower-order function and the units performing it. This criterion is directly involved with the emancipation of resources from ascription. Competence as a qualification for a role, in a sense which denies the relevance of kinship membership, is prototypical. Thus we may speak of an *upgrading* of the standards of normative control of the more differentiated system as compared with the less differentiated one.

This whole discussion has been based on the assumption that the underlying value-pattern of the system does not change as a part of the process of differentiation. It does not, however, follow that nothing changes at the level of values. It is an essential proposition of the conceptual scheme used here that every social system has a system of values as the highest-order component of its structure. Its values comprise the definition, from the point of view of its members—if it is institutionalized—of the desirable type of system at a level independent of internal structural differentiation or of particularities of situation. This "system" involves both a pattern type and an element of content, namely a definition of what kind of system the pattern applies to. In our case there are the values of households and of employing-productive units. In what I am calling "pattern" terms they may be the same, e.g., both of them incorporating the general American pattern of "instrumental activism." But if these values are to be implemented in either type of system there must be specifications of the more general system to the type of function (not its particularities), and to the type of situation in which the unit operates.

Where differentiation has occurred, this means that the values of the new system, which includes both the new and the residual unit, must be different in the content component from that of the original unit, though not, under present assumptions, in the pattern component. The new values must be more extensive in the special sense that they can legitimize the functions of both differentiated units under a single formula, which permits each to do what it does and, equally essential, not to do what the other does. The difficulty of institutionalizing the more extensive values is evidenced by the widespread currency of what may be called romantic ideologies in this sense, the allegation that the "loss of function," which is an inevitable feature of what I call the residual unit after the differentiation has taken place, is a measure of failure to implement the value-pattern of the system. For example, the new dependence of households on occupational earnings from employing organizations is often interpreted as loss of a sense of responsibility for independent support. This to be sure is ideology, but as such is an index of incomplete institutionalization of restructured values.

The relation between the values of a higher-order social system and those of a differentiated subsystem may be said to be one of *specification* of the implications of the more generalized pattern of the more extensive system to the "level" of the subsystem, by taking account of the limitations imposed upon the latter by function and situation. In this sense a business firm may value "economic rationality" in a sense which comprises both productivity and solvency, with considerably less qualification for more extensive values than an undifferentiated family household can, and in a complementary sense the household can devote itself in economic contexts to "consumption."

The above is sufficient to indicate only a few highlights of a very complex problem area. In this paper I have dealt with only one aspect of the field of the theory of social change. I have had to do so very abstractly and with only a tiny bit of empirical illustration. It does, however, seem to me justified to draw the conclusion that the problems of this area are in principle soluble in empirical-theoretical terms. Above all we have at our disposal a conceptual scheme which is sufficiently developed so that at least at the level of categorization and of problem statement it is approaching the type of closure—logical of course—which makes *systematic* analysis of interdependencies possible. We can define the main ranges of variability which are essential for empirical analysis, and the main mechanisms through which variations are propagated through the system. We can quantify to the point of designating deficits and surpluses of inputs and outputs, and here and there we can come close to specifying threshold values beyond which equilibrium will break down.

This of course is not in the least to say that some neat package of operationally usable analysis has been completely worked out for such a complex process as a cycle of differentiation. Indeed, I have deliberately emphasized the theme of complexity, as exemplified by the insistence that at least four different components of the normative aspect of structure must be taken into account, in the sense that changes in all of them are parts of the process of differentiation. Though emphasizing complexity, however, I have also meant to indicate that there is sufficient definiteness and clarity at sufficiently high levels of theoretical generalization so that the conceptual scheme I have been presenting can function as a genuine kit of working tools for the sociological analyst. I hope this can legitimately be considered encouraging for the prospects of our science in the near rather than only the distant future.

17

THE MASS MEDIA AND THE STRUCTURE OF AMERICAN SOCIETY

WITH WINSTON WHITE

Raymond and Alice Bauer have made a careful and informative review of empirical research studies on the determinants and effects of the mass media.[1] Beyond this, the evidence they have adduced has led them into a critique of the so-called theory of mass society, which they speak of as the only available attempt at a generalized interpretation of the phenomena involved. Their findings indicate that there is not only a serious paucity of adequate research findings (which is one of the principal conclusions of this survey) but also an even greater lack of adequate theoretical analysis.

They note that in general the proponents of the theory of mass society operate both as commentators on the empirical state of the society and as evaluative critics of it. We think it extremely important, as do the Bauers, to distinguish between these two problems, and that by doing so it is possible to see the theory of mass society as an ideological position congenial to *certain groups* of intellectuals. The Bauers, for example, repeatedly point out the arbitrary ways in which these intellectuals place one of several possible interpretations on items of evidence and tend further to ignore or often distort evidence—in ideological fashion—that does not support their evaluative strictures.

As an alternative to the position of the intellectuals, we wish to suggest a line of theoretical analysis that attempts to fit the evidence on the mass media (and on "mass culture") with that avail-

Reprinted by permission from "The Mass Media and the Structure of American Society," *Journal of Social Issues* 26, no. 3 (1960):67–77.

able on other aspects of the society, and that interprets this evidence in the larger context of some of the major features of American social structure and trends of its change. It is only through such a consideration of a wider range of evidence and of the larger social system, we feel, that steps can be taken to reduce the admittedly serious dangers of ideological selectivity and distortion.

Our discussion takes up three main topics. We will first analyze the assumptions underlying the intellectuals' conclusions, and then point out the relation between those assumptions and the elements of ideological selectivity that result from them.[2] We will then suggest that the problems involved in the field of communications are analytically similar to those in two other fields—the system of economic markets and the system of political power and influence. Finally, we will attempt to state a more generalized formula for the patterns of social structure and sociocultural change into which all three of these problem areas seem to us to fit.

The Structure of the Intellectual Ideology

In an effort to account for the intellectuals' position, the Bauers have suggested that they are at the same time both "cultural élitists" and "social democrats." These labels pinpoint for us two points of reference from which the authors' analysis might be carried further.

On the one hand, there is the problem of cultural values and taste—of cultural standards, if you will. On the other hand, there is the problem of the social structure in which these standards are institutionalized; or put another way, it is the problem of the extent to which a given social structure allows for the expression and development (or frustration and deterioration) of desirable standards. The intellectuals have contended that cultural standards have deteriorated and that social structure has tended to become an aggregate of mass men, alienated from the meaningful ties that would uphold standards. The authors have challenged both of these conclusions with evidence about the upgrading and extension of standards in many areas and with evidence about the viability of primary-group relations.

The intellectuals deplore the "mass man's" alleged vulnerability to exploitation and his exposure to the mediocre. But underlying their discontent, the Bauers suggest, is their reluctance to let the guardianship of cultural standards slip out of their hands into those they consider less qualified. If the intellectuals do in fact hold both of these positions at once, how might one explain this seemingly inconsistent mixture of cultural conservatism and social liberalism?

We would agree with the Bauers that many intellectuals have explicitly or implicitly arrived at this conclusion. We do not feel, however, that all intellectuals have attempted to straddle the cultural and social fence in this manner; many have arrived at less ambiguous—although equally erroneous—conclusions. Behind these conclusions lie three distinct ideological sources, each with its own set of assumptions about social theory—about man's relation to society, to culture, and the like. These assumptions, as the authors point out, must be uncovered in order to understand and assess the intellectuals' positions. Tracing through these ideological patterns may clarify the problem. Two of them lie on the cultural side and one on the social side.

The ideology on the side of social structure assumes that man is essentially good and is only corrupted by social forces. Cultural standards are not seen as problematical but as epiphenomena of social conditions. Given a favorable social environment (e.g., the "right" economic-political institutions, the restoration of community ties, the elimination of "anonymous authority," etc.), desirable cultural standards will spring into efflorescence. But given the unfavorable conditions of a mass society, man is so alienated that he is unable to resist mass culture. He has, so to speak, no consumer sovereignty, and is compelled to "buy" whatever supply of culture is at hand. This point of view is more or less Marxian in its assumptions; Erich Fromm is one of its leading spokesmen.

The ideology on the cultural side assumes that man is conditionally good or evil and that his commitments to cultural standards cannot be taken for granted but must be vigilantly maintained. In this version, social structure is a non-problematical epiphenomenon of culture. Given the "right" cultural commitments, appropriate social institutions will follow along in due course. There are two ideological positions within this set of assumptions.

The élitist position, which the authors touch on, is that the highest cultural standards must be maintained by the agency of an élite and that high and folk culture alike should be borne by a gradation of classes. If standards are assured in this way (or, as we would put it, if they are ascribed to class and to region), then the social structure is safe. People know their place and what is expected of them. Without the guardianship of an élite, the demands of the untutored masses for a vulgarized cultural product will take over. T. S. Eliot and Ortega y Gasset have been spokesmen for this point of view.

Another important "cultural" ideology, however, is that held by those we will call the "moralizers." For them, social structure is even less problematical, in that buttressing by an elite and by a class structure is no longer felt to be necessary. The moralizers believe that standards must be maintained by individual responsibility. It is up to the individual to maintain his commitments to values, to hold the line on his own, as it were, against the seductions of mass society with its hedonistic flabbiness. It is in the hearts and minds of men that moral heroism (the intellectual's counterpart of the businessmen's rugged individualism) will shape the social fabric. Archibald MacLeish and Joseph Wood Krutch, for example, are notable spokesmen for this point of view. The élitists and the social-structure ideologists tend to regard the moralizers as hopelessly middle-brow, but it seems to us that any definition of "intellectuals" as social critics must include them.

Common to both types of "culture" ideologists—the élitists and moralizers alike—is the assumption that the individual does have "consumer sovereignty." The public gets what it wants (and deserves). Standards deteriorate because of the low quality of mass demand, not because of the low quality of supply.

Finally, those intellectuals whom the Bauers characterize as both cultural elitists and social democrats at the same time are, we suggest, ideologically analogous to, though of course not affiliated with, the Communist Party—an élite group that sets standards where, according to the ideology, there should be no need to. Further, the assertion of cultural autonomy by the mass of men, given favorable social conditions, is analogous to the withering away of the state. Either these intellectuals' beliefs are inconsistent in that they consider élite guidance necessary regardless of what kind of social conditions prevail, or they have embraced élitism as an intermediate means to hold the line until the proper social conditions can be attained, if ever.

None of these points of view is adequate, we believe, for analyzing the relationship between cultural standards and the social structure in which they are institutionalized. We have called them ideologies, for each in its own way is selective in its approach—tending to take for granted or to ignore factors that must be considered for proper analysis. As our further comments will spell out, we see the mass media as a mechanism operating in a "market" between the purveyors of cultural content and the public. And, as the Bauers have emphasized, it is not the only mechanism but one that operates in conjunction with others, such as informal primary-group relationships.

In such a "market,"[3] we maintain, both supply and demand operate without one always being subjected to the other. Our analysis has tried to show that the intellectuals are by no means in agreement on this issue. The élitists and moralizers believe that low-grade public demand lowers standards; the social-structure ideologists blame the quality of the supply, claiming that the public—or the masses, as they would say—cannot be expected to know better, social conditions being what they are.

It is with respect to standards that the issue comes to a head. The élitists regard standards as ascribed to class, with the highest standards maintained only through their agency. They are like parents who look on the public as their children, believing them incapable of acting responsibly without their surveillance.

The moralizers, on the other hand, tend to ignore the whole problem of the social context in which standards are defined. They believe that each individual, by exercising his autonomous "responsibility," can define his own standards independently of others, by means of "nonconformism" or "individualism." Standards, apparently, are given as in the utilitarian conception of "self-interest." Finally, for the social-structure ideologists, standards are taken for granted. Like autonomy and spontaneity, they spring full-born from the sane society.

Dwight MacDonald's metaphor of Gresham's law represents an

interesting combination of the above. For him, the "market" is purely one of runaway inflation which cannot be checked because standards are continually falling. Low-grade demand stimulates low-grade supply, and vice versa—like a reciprocating engine, as he puts it. With no élite in change of standards, he considers the situation hopeless.

Economic, Political, and Communications Systems

The context in which we wish to place our comparisons between mass communications and economic and political systems is that of the division of labor. Where the functions of units in a social system become sufficiently differentiated, it becomes impossible for the "producers" of an output—be it a commodity, an expression of political support, or a culturally significant message—to be ascriptively bound to the recipients, as would be the case, for example, for custom-made goods, feudal allegiance, or patronage of the arts. The offer of automobiles for sale or party appeals for votes are "broadcast" in a sense analogous to that of soap operas or symphony concerts. Their producers do not know in advance in detail who or how many the recipients will be, or what commitments they will be willing to make as a result of exposure, although market research can in all three cases narrow the range of uncertainty somewhat.

All such processes of differentiation lead to "alienation"—both for the producer from the ultimate use of his product and for the consumer from direct involvement with the source of his supply. Adam Smith's famous generalization about the economic efficiency of the division of labor can thus—with proper qualifications—be extended to these other two contexts: the "consumer" acquires degrees of freedom that would be impossible without such differentiation. At the same time, certain mechanisms of control become necessary if such a system is to be stable, and in fact bring about the degrees of freedom referred to. These controls center on *institutionalized* regulatory patterns—like contract and property in the economic sphere, leadership and authority in the political—and on institutionalized *media* such as money and political power (as exercised, for instance, through the franchise).

Let us consider first the degrees of freedom created by an economic market system, and then try to work out the parallels for political and communications systems. In so doing we hope to highlight those features of the latter that are analytically significant for the mass-media problem.

In contrast to a system of economic barter, the consumer who holds money funds in a highly differentiated market system has the following degrees of freedom: (1) in accepting money, e.g. in exchange for labor services, he is not *ipso facto* committed to buy what he wants to spend it for from any particular source of supply—he can "shop around"; (2) he is not committed to any particular composition of the "package" of items for which he spends it, but can select in terms of his wants at the time; (3) he is not committed to any particular terms of exchange but can shop and/or bargain over prices; and (4) he is not committed to any particular time of expenditure of his funds, but can extend his expenditures over time (indeed, the availability of interest puts a positive premium on delay).

This classification provides a convenient point of reference for identifying points of strain and certain possibilities of malfunctioning to which a market system is subject to a greater degree than one of ascriptive exchange or barter. All of these deviations have existed in fact in greater and less degree and in particular have figured prominently in critical discussions of "industrial" economies. Particularly prominent among these are the following: (1) Monopoly can restrict to varying degrees (and in the extreme case eliminate) the consumer's freedom of choice with respect to source of supply; indeed, one school of thought has alleged that its increase was an "inevitable" trend of a "capitalistic" economy. (2) Freedom to choose among a wide variety of products may be rendered valueless by an inherent process of product deterioration; the standards of handicraft excellence may give way to the shoddiness of mass-produced products, another point at which a prominent school of thought has alleged inevitability. (3) Freedom with respect to terms of exchange may be cancelled out by the inherently exploitative character of the market structure—a factor partly, but not necessarily wholly, deriving from monopoly. It has thus frequently been alleged that the "real" standards of living of consumers necessarily deteriorate at this point. Finally, (4) the freedom in time can be cancelled out by inflation, so that the longer one holds his dollar the greater the disadvantage of his position; inflation again has been held to be an inherent trend. The inference from this syndrome is that the economic welfare of some conceived "typical" individual is inevitably injured by the division of labor, markets, and industrialization—unless, as some think, it can be protected by socialism.

The broad answer, of course, is that, though all of these things can and do happen, such trends as have existed have not in general developed cumulatively to extremes in American society (to which present attention is confined). Thus to take one point, contrary to much opinion, it is impossible to prove that the degree of concentration in American manufacturing industry has increased appreciably over the past half century. If these trends have not gone to such extremes, there must be "countervailing" forces that lie in the mechanisms of control mentioned above. The prototypical problem statement here is Gresham's Law and both the Bauers and we must be grateful to Dwight MacDonald for having introduced this conception into the discussion. In the economic case it is simply not true empirically that, to paraphase the Communist Manifesto, "the history of all market and currency systems is a history of galloping inflation"—nor of monopoly, nor of product deterioration, nor of exploitation.

Exactly parallel problems may be identified in the political field. Political differentiation, we suggest, creates degrees of freedom analogous to those of the market as follows: (1) The analogy of economic source of supply is leadership agency, e.g. a party as the agency taking responsibility for collective decision-making if given requisite political support. A "free electorate" has a choice between such agencies and is not ascriptively bound to any one by its legitimacy. (2) The political analogy of products is policies. By virtue of his position in a political system, the individual or group is neither ascriptively committed to favoring particular policies nor committed to them—except in a minority of cases—by "barter deals," but is free to allocate such influence as he has between a significant range of alternatives. (3) Economic price is essentially a determination of *cost*. The political analogy is the obligations entailed by a commitment to a collective decision or policy. This means that there must be some balancing between the sharing of the benefits of what "gets done" and allocation of the burdens necessary to get it done, e.g. taxes. Finally, (4) in the political as in the economic case, differentiation makes it possible for leadership and followership both to enjoy greater flexibility with respect to time.

Elements of malfunctioning in such a differentiated political system which parallel those discussed in the economy can be identified as follows: (1) Parallel to economic monopoly is the concentration of political power to the point where effectiveness of choice among leadership elements is eliminated. A typical case of this view is Mills' contention[4] of the existence of a single unified "power elite." (2) The parallel to economic product deterioration is the alleged cumulatively increasing predominance in the political system of special and group interests over the public interest. It is suggested that the public does not get acceptable policies but only the effects of the "selfish" utilization of positions of political advantage to further special group interests. (3) The parallel to economic exploitation through the price system is the conception of progressively increasing exploitation of the "little man" by the "interests." Mills' conception of "cumulative advantage" seems to be the most explicit recent formulation of this view. Finally, (4) there is a political parallel to economic inflation. This is a process of progressive deterioration in the worth of general public commitments to the effective functioning of the political system through leadership. Various elements, that is to say, make "sacrifices," such as military service, only to find that the polity they devoted themselves to is becoming progressively less effective, more interest-dominated, time-serving, and the like.

The question of the balance between these disorganizing trends and countervailing factors in the American political system over the last half century, for instance, is clearly a complicated one. There has always been a left-wing school of thought which has given overwhelming preponderance to the former factors, Mills being the most prominent recent exponent. The relative effectiveness in meeting the crises of two world wars and the great depression, however, seem to most observers to indicate the operation of important countervailing factors. It seems legitimate to consider the theorists of "late monopoly capitalism" and those of the "power elite" as exponents of an ideology in the same sense in which we have attributed this to the theorists of mass culture.

We would like to consider the system of mass communications as a differentiated social system in the same sense that economic and political systems are, and a necessary one in a highly differentiated society of the American type. It involves the same order of specialization of function between "producing" and "consuming" units, and—most importantly—between different kinds of communication output. It also involves relative concentration of resources in the hands of larger producers, though the question of the degree of monopoly is not a simple one. It of course involves "alienation" of the recipient from control over the sources of communications. And it goes without saying that it involves both formal and informal mechanisms of control, the most important of which are institutionalized.

Such a system could be expected to produce degrees of freedom for the typical recipient analogous to those of the economic consumer or the member of the political public.

These may be sketched as follows: (1) Contrasted with the ascriptiveness of tradition is the range of alternative sources of communication output, newspapers, magazines, books, broadcasting stations and programs. This is far from unlimited, but unless restricted by totalitarian types of policies, far wider than in any traditional system. (2) There is a wide range of choice with reference to content, both with reference to types of content and to levels of quality within types. (3) There are freedoms with respect to "cost"—a conception, however, in need of clarification when used in this context. One component, of course, is money cost. Another, which figures in the Bauer study, is time spent by the consumer. Still another is something like "receptivity" to the line of influence suggested. For advertising, purchases can be a measure of this; for political campaigning, actual voting; but where literary tastes are at stake, measures are more difficult. (4) There is freedom with respect to time, in the sense of receiving and not receiving communications, and allocation of time between particular kinds. Among the most important points here is the fact that, given storage facilities, the printed word can be preserved for reference at any future time.

It is now our suggestion that the main interpretive contentions of the theorists of mass culture can be fitted into this classification, as modes in which allegedly relevant standards fail to be met. Thus (1) with respect to source, there is much complaint about the concentration of sources, especially with reference to newspapers and broadcasting. This tends to play down the very wide variety available in some fields of communication, e.g. local newspapers and book publishing, especially recently of paperbacks. (2) Perhaps the most prominent single contention is the parallel of economic product deterioration, namely the notion that mass communication inevitably leads to the predominance of *kitsch* over quality items. (3) The analogue of economic exploitation and cumulative advantage in the power system is the idea of the "manipulative" exploitation of the irrational through the mass communication media; the portrayal of violence and its alleged relation to delinquency is a good case in point. Finally, (4) we might suggest that the theme of "apathy" is the analogue of economic inflation, namely the contention that the communication "market" is so flooded with inferior items, from whatever cause, that the standards of the recipient tend to become undermined, his responses becoming automatized and undiscriminating.

Again, as in the previous instances, these malfunctionings can and do occur. The evidence the Bauers have marshalled, however, does not support the contention that such has been the case in American society; at the very least, it compels serious consideration for the position we are advancing that countervailing forces, such as institutionalized standards and favorable "market" conditions, do in fact prevail, to a significant degree.

Summary

In the field of communications, then, we suggest that structural changes have been occurring that are analytically similar to those more familiar in the economic and political systems and that these changes—in all three cases—have the consequences of what we call extension, differentiation, and upgrading.

With respect to communications in particular, fundamental to this process of change is the shaking up of older traditional ascriptions, among the most salient of which are those of stratification. The élitist system confined its audience, by and large, to its peers. It was not expected that the general public would, or could, in any way be interested—except perhaps for a diffuse admiration of the elegance of the upperclass way of life. One major consequence of the breaking down of ascriptive ties is the *extension* of accessibility to cultural content to ever wider circles of the population. In recent Western history, the most conspicuous example of this is the extension of education. Far wider groups than ever before are expected to appreciate elements of the great Western cultural heritage.

The second aspect of change is that of *differentiation*. The term "mass" media itself is misleading, suggesting that the media themselves are undifferentiated with respect to content and audience. Not only do different media (or often the same media) carry qualitatively different content and reach qualitatively different audiences, but the same individual, in many cases, uses a variety of media.

Just as economic and political systems—indeed, social structures in general—become more differentiated, so do the media themselves tend to differentiate. The news coverage, for example, of the news-magazine and the metropolitan newspaper enables the smaller community paper to specialize in local news. The advent of television has led to more specialization on the part of radio programming, witness the increase in musical programs.

With differentiation and specialization, one might expect, as in other systems, an increase of functional capacity in the communications system with the consequence of *upgrading*. If such is the case, one could expect a proportionately greater spread of the *higher* levels of culture than of the lower. Although the problems of evidence are formidable here, we would suggest, for example, that the advent of television has resulted in the upgrading of other "competing" media, itself coming in at the bottom of the qualitative ladder in certain respects (as successive waves of immigrants came in at the bottom of the occupational ladder, enabling previous arrivals to move up). Anyone watching old motion picture films on TV might well be impressed by their dismal mediocrity when compared with the contemporary films, a change that arises from something more than a mere shift in style. The growth of serious music programming on FM stations is also a case in point.

Perhaps one can suggest that both films and radio broadcasting have not only been "kicked upstairs" by TV competition, but that differentiation has led to an upgrading of taste. It is surely not too far-fetched to say that certain TV programs now fill a low-grade demand that previously turned to other media for satisfaction. This is not to say, however, that upgrading is *solely* a consequence of changes in the media of the "market" (the fallacy of a social-structure ideology). Upgrading is also dependent on raising the standards of the public in the sense of "building up" the level of their commitments to standards.[5] In addition to the extension of higher levels of education, this process is also effected through primary-group relations, where the individual learns not only to acquire new tastes but helps to define them as well. Even if his motivation arises purely from emulation or "status-seeking"—as some interpreters choose to suggest, brushing aside any realistic desire on the part of the individual to widen his range of experience—the *consequences* of this group interaction cannot be overlooked.

In conclusion, we hope that the combination of our treatment of the ideological problem with the parallel we have drawn between the selectivity of the mass-culture theorists and certain critics of the American economy and political system will serve to broaden the problem raised by the Bauers. By placing the mass-culture issue in a larger perspective, one can perhaps see that it is a special case of more general processes and that there is the same kind of problem in interpretation—not only of mass culture but of American society as a total system.

Most fundamental of the fallacies underlying the biases of the mass-culture theorists seems to us to be the assumption that this is an "atomized" mass society where the relations of one individual to another have become increasingly amorphous. Quite to the contrary, as Kornhauser[6] has pointed out, American society is one of the preeminent examples of a *pluralist* society in which—through the course of structural differentiation—an increasingly ramified network of criss-crossing solidarities has been developing. Nor is our conclusion to be taken as a defense of the status quo; American society has—in terms of our high expectations for it—many inadequacies. But, we believe, they cannot be "explained," much less confronted with any degree of sophistication, by the currently prominent theory of mass society.

18

ARCHAIC AND HISTORIC SOCIETIES

The second of the three main stages of societal evolution is the intermediate stage, characterized by the development of *written* language. There are cases in which predominantly primitive societies interpenetrate with literate cultures, one instance being the Nupe following their conquest by the Islamic Fullani. The Nupe are peripheral to an essentially foreign religio-cultural complex, whereas in a fully intermediate society, an *indigenous* literate tradition is constitutive of the culture. We distinguish two principal substages of intermediate society, the archaic and the advanced intermediate. By archaic, we mean the first stage in the evolution of intermediate society, that of craft literacy and cosmological religion. The advanced stage is characterized by full upper-class literacy and, on the cultural side, by an historic religion, one which has broken through to *philosophical* levels of generalization and systematization.[1] Such religions develop for the first time conceptions of a supernatural order differentiated from any order of nature.

An archaic cosmological religio-cultural system systematizes the constitutive symbolism of the society more than the cultural system of any primitive society. *This cultural elaboration depends on the literacy of priesthoods and their capacity to maintain a stable written tradition.* The literacy is, however, still esoteric and limited to specialized groups—hence, it is craft literacy. Besides the religio-magical, its specialized use is for

Reprinted with deletions from *The Evolution of Societies* by Talcott Parsons, © 1977, by permission of Prentice-Hall, Inc., Englewood Cliffs, N.J.

administrative purposes. Only in *advanced* intermediate societies is literacy centering about the mastery of a literary tradition a characteristic of all upper-class adult males—e.g., the upper-caste Hindus or the Chinese gentry. A cosmological cultural system is usually interpreted for the society by temple priesthoods. The priesthoods administer *cults,* the ritual benefits of which are no longer rigidly ascribed to underlying kinship and local community structures as in primitive societies. The temple itself may become a focus of the social organization—e.g., in economic connections. In general, the function of cultural legitimation has become differentiated, generalized, and, though closely bound to the highest echelon of the society (e.g., the king), entrusted to the priestly groups.[2]

On the political side, there is a parallel differentiation. *All* archaic societies have an administrative apparatus elaborated beyond the level of such societies as the Shilluk or Bemba. Both priestly and administrative functions are usually controlled by lineages rather than appointed individuals, particular statuses typically being hereditary. Moreover, the political and religious offices often overlap. They are, however, sufficiently distinct so that one can regard religious and secular stratification as being differentiated. Yet each tends to crystallize about a three-class pattern: the top, associated with the charisma of the monarch and the exercise of his combined religious and political authority; a middle group responsible for the more routine functioning of the society; and the mass of the common people, who are tillers of the soil. The last also includes craftsmen and even merchants, who become increasingly prominent with further development, particularly as functionaries of the great households or temples, standing in client-like relations with the leading proprietary lineages.[3]

Why is a written language necessary to societal evolution? Because along with stratification, a primitive society must develop *explicit cultural legitimation of differentiated societal functions* if it is to evolve, and a written language facilitates explicit cultural legitimation. Of course a written language does not mean universal literacy, not even upper-class literacy. More usually, *craft* literacy develops, that is, literacy monopolized by a priestly class. Their control over written records gives the priests an intellectual advantage over other upper-class elements, including the political leadership. One use they make of this advantage is to legitimate the authority of the rulers (or to withhold legitimation). As long as a literate priesthood continues to provide legitimation for the political rulers, the rulers are able to exercise more effective leadership of the society than is possible in primitive societies. This does not mean that the leadership is used to direct the society toward "better" goals, only that it can be more effectively mobilized toward *whatever* goals are established. Bear in mind that increased adaptive capacity does not imply moral superiority.

Historic Empires

The varieties of primitive and intermediate societies cannot usefully be regarded as comprising larger systems in the sense of the system of modern societies. This difference presents interpretive problems that will guide my discussion of advanced intermediate societies, problems the significance of which was demonstrated by Max Weber. The *range* of variation among advanced intermediate societies was wide—think of the contrast between the Chinese Empire at its height, the Indian caste system, the Islamic empires, and the Roman Empire! All these societies contained developed civilizations. Why, then, did the breakthrough to modernizations not occur in *any* of the Oriental advanced intermediate civilizations? Conversely, what constellation of factors were involved in its occurrence against the background of the most radical structural regression in the history of major societies—namely, the fall of the western Roman Empire and the reversion of its territories to archaic social conditions in the dark ages? This is the historical-interpretive perspective, as distinct from that of systematic theory which will guide my evolutionary analysis.

Advanced intermediate societies [e.g., China, India, the Islamic Empires, and Rome] developed independent political organizations on a large scale and integrated large populations and territories, but they had varying success in achieving stability and maintaining independence. All of them depended in some way upon cultural developments which separate them from the archaic type of society. With the partial exception of China, they have been involved with the world religions in a sense not applicable to any archaic society.

China and India were minimally influenced by the cultural movements which underlay Western society. India was influenced by Greek culture and by Judaism, via Islam, after the Islamic incursions, but such influences came late in its development. Islam and Rome were influenced by Israel and Greece.

[Archaic societies] were characterized by the comprehensiveness of their *cultural* innovations at the level of constitutive symbolism. They were the direct heirs of cultural movements called *philosophic breakthroughs*. The common feature of these movements—one that crosscut their differences in orientation—was the attainment of higher levels of generalization in the constitutive symbolism of their cultures. This attainment posed problems concerning the coming to terms of the new cultural orientations with the societal structures in which they arose or to which they were diffused.

I shall not analyze the processes that generated these breakthroughs or attempt to assess the relative roles of various cultural and social factors. The breakthroughs occurred within a relatively short time span in several different societies from the eastern Mediterranean (in Greece and Israel), through India, to China about the middle of the first millenium, B.C. My concern is with the implications of these changes for institutionalization in large-scale societies—on the scale that the major powers of the time had already achieved. For the breakthroughs of China and India, these implications were direct; but for those of Israel and Greece, they concern heir-societies, including Islam and Rome.

In the terms of our analytical scheme, the cultural breakthroughs—however they may have come about—affected the societal community structures of the societies in which they occurred or to which they were diffused. These cultural movements led to a differentiation between the order of representations of ultimate reality and the order of representation of the human condition. Any human being's pretension to divine status became out of the question; hence the institution of divine kingship was terminated with the archaic period. But the sharpness of the newly posed dichotomy between the supernatural and the natural orders accentuated the problem of defining the relation of human elements to the higher-order reality. This undermined the archaic tendency—conspicuous in Egypt—to proliferate status gradations. It tended to introduce a dichotomy between the human elements having, and those who have not, the capacity to act directly in terms of the new conception of the ultimate order. Hence, a new type of *two*-class structuring of the human society was a consequence of these cultural innovations. Society came to be divided between those who are, actually or potentially, qualified for the highest human standing relative to the cultural definition of the transcendent order and those who are excluded from such qualification, either inherently or until they meet specific conditions of eligibility.

The imposition of this dichotomy upon established societies involved complex readjustments, which worked out in different ways in the different cases. One generalization applies to all the societies in which this situation was introduced and in which its institutionalization was attempted on a large scale. There had to be eventual acceptance of the fact that the going society must include persons who could *not* meet the criteria of relatedness to the higher order of cultural standards that grounded the cultural definitions of desirable belonging. Chinese society had to include common people who were not "superior men"; India had the *Sudra* and outcasts who were not eligible for the discipline of religious enlightenment; Islam had the infidels who would not convert to the true faith; and Rome has the barbarians within her polity. By contrast, a trend in modern societies is the presumption of the possibility of including all persons subject to political jurisdiction in full membership status within the single societal community.

19

EVOLUTIONARY UNIVERSALS IN SOCIETY

Slowly and somewhat inarticulately, emphasis in both sociological and anthropological quarters is shifting from a studied disinterest in problems of social and cultural evolution to a "new relativity" that relates its universals to an evolutionary framework.

The older perspectives insisted that social and cultural systems are made up of indefinitely numerous discrete "traits," that "cultures" are totally separate, or that certain broad "human" universals, like language and the incest taboo, should be emphasized. Varied as they are, these emphases have in common the fact that they divert attention from specific *continuities* in patterns of social change, so that either traits or culture types must be treated as discretely unique and basically unconnected, and a pattern, to be considered universal, must be equally important to *all* societies and cultures. Despite their ostentatious repudiation of "culture-boundness," these perspectives have been conspicuously anthropocentric in setting off problems of man's modes of life so sharply from questions of continuity with the rest of the organic world. But the emphasis on human universals has also had a kind of "levelling" influence, tending to restrict attention to what is generally and essentially human, without considering gradations within the human category.

The "new relativity" removes this barrier and tries to consider human ways in direct continuity with the sub-human. It assumes

Reprinted by permission from "Evolutionary Universals in Society," *American Sociological Review*, June 1964, pp. 339–57.

that the watershed between sub-human and human does not mark a cessation of developmental change, but rather a stage in a long process that begins with many pre-human phases and continues through that watershed into our own time, and beyond. Granting a wide range of variability of types at all stages, it assumes that levels of evolutionary advancement may be empirically specified for the human as well as the pre-human phases.

Evolutionary Universals

I shall designate as an evolutionary universal any organizational development sufficiently important to further evolution that, rather than emerging only once, it is likely to be "hit upon" by various systems operating under different conditions.

In the organic world, vision is a good example of an evolutionary universal. Because it mediates the input of organized information from the organism's environment, and because it deals with both the most distant and the widest range of information sources, vision is the most generalized mechanism of sensory information. It therefore has the greatest potential significance for adaptation of the organism to its environment.

The evidence is that vision has not been a "one shot" invention in organic evolution, but has evolved independently in three different phyla—the molluscs, the insects, and the vertebrates. A particularly interesting feature of this case is that, while the visual organs in the three groups are anatomically quite different and present no evolutionary continuity, biochemically all use the same mechanism involving Vitamin A, though there is no evidence that it was not independently "hit upon" three times.[1] Vision, whatever its mechanisms, seems to be a genuine prerequisite of *all* the higher levels of organic evolution. It has been lost only by very particular groups like the bats, which have not subsequently given rise to important evolutionary developments.

With reference to man and his biological potential for social and cultural evolution, two familiar evolutionary universals may be cited, namely the hands and the brain. The human hand is, of course, the primordial general-purpose tool. The combination of four mobile fingers and an opposable thumb enables it to perform an enormous variety of operations—grasping, holding, and manipulating many kinds of objects. Its location at the end of an arm with mobile joints allows it to be maneuvered into many positions. Finally, the pairing of the arm-hand organs much more than doubles the capacity of each one because it permits cooperation and a complex division of labor between them.

It is worth noting that the development of the hands and arms has been bought at a heavy cost in locomotion: man on his two legs cannot compete in speed and maneuverability with the faster four-legged species. Man, however, uses his hands for such a wide range of behavior impossible for handless species that the loss is far more than compensated. He can, for instance, protect himself with weapons instead of running away.

The human brain is less nearly unique than the hand, but its advantages over the brains of even anthropoids is so great that it is man's most distinctive organ, the most important single source of human capacity. Not only is it the primary organ for controlling complex operations, notably manual skills, and coordinating visual and auditory information, but above all it is the organic basis of the capacity to learn and manipulate symbols. Hence it is the organic foundation of culture. Interestingly, this development too is bought at the sacrifice of immediate adaptive advantages. For example the brain occupies so much of the head that the jaws are much less effective than in other mammalian species—but this too is compensated for by the hands. And the brain is partly responsible for the long period of infantile dependency because the child must learn such a large factor of its effective behavior. Hence the burden of infant care and socialization is far higher for man than for any other species.

With these organic examples in mind, the conception of an evolutionary universal may be developed more fully. It should, I suggest, be formulated with reference to the concept of adaptation, which has been so fundamental to the theory of evolution since Darwin. Clearly, adaptation should mean, not merely passive "adjustment" to environmental conditions, but rather the capacity of a living system[2] to cope with its environment. This capacity includes an active concern with mastery, or the ability to change the environment to meet the needs of the system, as well as an ability to survive in the face of its unalterable features. Hence the capacity to cope with broad *ranges* of environmental factors, through adjustment or active control, or both, is crucial. Finally, a very critical point is the capacity to cope with unstable relations between system and environment, and hence with *uncertainty*. Instability here refers both to predictable variations, such as the cycle of the seasons, and to unpredictable variations, such as the sudden appearance of a dangerous predator.

An evolutionary universal, then, is a complex of structures and associated processes the development of which so increases the long-run adaptive capacity of living systems in a given class that only systems that develop the complex can attain certain higher levels of general adaptive capacity. This criterion, derived from the famous principle of natural selection, requires one major explicit qualification. The relatively disadvantaged system not developing a new universal need not be condemned to extinction. Thus some species representing all levels of organic evolution survive today—from the unicellular organisms up. The surviving lower types, however, stand in a variety of different relations to the higher. Some occupy special "niches" within which they live with limited scope, others stand in symbiotic relations to higher systems. They are not, by and large, major threats to the continued existence of the evolutionarily higher systems. Thus, though infectious diseases constitute a serious problem for man, bacteria are not likely to replace man as the dominant organic category, and man is symbiotically dependent on many bacterial species.

Two distinctions should be made here, because they apply most generally and throughout. The first is between the impact of an innovation when it is *first* introduced in a given species or society, and its importance as a continuing component of the system. Certain evolutionary universals in the social world, to be discussed below, initially provide their societies with major adaptive advantages over societies not developing them. Their introduction and institutionalization have, to be sure, often been attended with severe dislocations of the previous social organization, sometimes resulting in short-run losses in adaptation. Once institutionalized, however, they tend to become essential parts of later societies in the relevant lines of *development* and are seldom eliminated except by regression. But, as the system undergoes further evolution, universals are apt to generate major changes of their own, generally by developing more complex structures.

Unlike biological genes, cultural patterns are subject to "diffusion." Hence, for the cultural level, it is necessary to add a second distinction, between the conditions under which an adaptive advantage can develop for the first time, and those favoring its adoption from a source in which it is already established.

Prerequisites of the Evolution of Culture
and Society

From his distinctive organic endowment and from his capacity for and ultimate dependence on generalized learning, man derives his unique ability to create and transmit *culture*. To quote the biologist Alfred Emerson, within a major sphere of man's adaptation, the "gene" has been replaced by the "symbol."[3] Hence, it is not only the genetic constitution of the species that determines the "needs" confronting the environment, but this constitution *plus* the cultural tradition. A set of "normative expectations" pertaining to man's relation to his environment delineates the ways in which adaptation should be developed and extended. Within the relevant range, cultural innovations, especially definitions of what man's life *ought* to be, thus replace Darwinian variations in genetic constitution.

Cultural "patterns" or orientations, however, do not implement themselves. Properly conceived in their most fundamental aspect as "religious," they must be articulated with the environment in ways that make effective adaptation possible. I am inclined to treat the entire orientational aspect of culture itself, in the simplest, least evolved forms, as directly synonymous with *religion*.[4] But since a cultural system—never any more an individual matter than a genetic pattern—is shared among a plurality of individuals, mechanisms of *communication* must exist to mediate this sharing. The fundamental evolutionary universal here is language: no concrete human group lacks it. Neither communication nor the learning processes that make it possible, however, is conceivable without determinate̶ly organized relations among those who teach and learn and communicate.

The evolutionary origin of *social organization* seems to be kinship. In an evolutionary sense it is an extension of the mammalian system of bisexual reproduction. The imperative of socialization is of course a central corollary of culture, as is the need to establish a viable social system to "carry" the culture. From one viewpoint, the core of the kinship system is the incest taboo, or, more generally, the rules of exogamy and endogamy structuring relations of descent, affinity, and residence. Finally, since the cultural level of action implies the use of brain, hands, and other organs in actively coping with the physical environment, we may say that culture implies the existence of technology, which is, in its most undifferentiated form, a synthesis of empirical knowledge and practical techniques.

These four features of even the simplest action system— "religion," communication with language, social organization through kinship, and technology—may be regarded as an integrated set of evolutionary universals at even the earliest human level. No known human society has existed without *all* four in relatively definite relations to each other. In fact, their presence constitutes the very minimum that may be said to mark a society as truly human.

Social Stratification

Two evolutionary universals are closely interrelated in the process of "breaking out" of what may be called the "primitive" stage of societal evolution. These are the development of a well-marked system of social stratification, and that of a system of explicit cultural legitimation of differentiated societal functions, preeminently the political function, independent of kinship. The two are closely connected, but I am inclined to think that stratification comes first and is a condition of legitimation of political function.

The key to the evolutionary importance of stratification lies in the role in primitive societies of *ascription* of social status to criteria of biological relatedness. The kinship nexus of social organization is intrinsically a "seamless web" of relationships which, in and of itself, contains no principle of boundedness for the system as distinguished from certain subgroups within it. Probably the earliest and most important basis of boundedness is the political criterion of territorial jurisdiction. But the economic problem of articulation with the environment, contingent on kinship as well as other groups, is also prominent in primitive societies. In the first instance this is structured primarily through place of residence, which becomes increasingly important as technological development, notably of "settled agriculture," puts a premium on definiteness and permanence of location.

For present purposes, I assume that in the society we are discussing, the population occupying a territorial area is generally endogamous, with marriage of its members to those of other territorial groups being, if it occurs, somehow exceptional, and not systematically organized.[5] Given a presumptively endogamous territorial community, comprising a plurality of purely local groups, certain general processes of internal differentiation of the society can be explained. One aspect of this tends to be a prestige difference between central or "senior" lineage groups and "cadet" groups, whether or not the differentiation is on the basis of birth.[6] Quite generally, the latter must accept less advantageous bases of subsistence, including place of residence, than the former. At least this is apt to be the case where the residence groups become foci for the control of resources and as such are sharply differentiated from more inclusive political groupings. Thus a second aspect of an increased level of functional differentiation among the structures of the society tends to be involved.

Typically, I think, kinship status, in terms of both descent criteria and relative prestige of marriage opportunities is highly correlated with relative economic advantage and political power. This is to say that, under the conditions postulated, a tendency toward *vertical* differentiation of the society as a system overrides the pressure of the seamless web of kinship to equalize the status of all units of equivalent *kinship* character. This tendency is the product of two converging forces.

On the one hand, relative advantages are differentiated: members of cadet lineages, the kinship units with lesser claims to preferment, are "forced" into peripheral positions. They move to less advantaged residential locations and accept less productive economic resources, and they are not in a position to counteract these disadvantages by the use of political power.

On the other hand, the society as a system gains functional advantages by concentrating responsibility for certain functions. This concentration focuses in two areas, analytically, the political and the religious. First, the increased complexity of a society that has grown in population and probably territory and has become differentiated in status terms raises more difficult problems of internal order, e.g. controlling violence, upholding property and marriage rules, etc., and of defense against encroachment from outside. Second, a cultural tradition very close to both the details of everyday life and the interests and solidarities of particular groups is put under strain by increasing size and diversity. There is, then, pressure to centralize both responsibility for the symbolic systems, especially the religious, and authority in collective processes, and to redefine them in the direction of greater generality.

For the present argument, I assume that the tendencies to centralize political and religious responsibility need not be clearly differentiated in any immediate situation. The main point is that the differentiation of groups relative to an advantage-disadvantage axis tends to converge with the functional "need" for centralization of responsibility. Since responsibility and prestige seem to be inherently related in a system of institutionalized expectations, the advantaged group tends to assume, or have ascribed to it, the centralized responsibilities. It should be clear that the problem does not concern the balance between services to others and benefits accruing to the advantaged group, but the convergence of *both* sets of forces tending to the same primary structural outcome.

The development of written language can become a fundamental accelerating factor in this process, because in the nature of the case literacy cannot immediately be extended to total adult populations, and yet it confers enormous adaptive advantages. It also has a tendency to favor cultural or religious elements over the political.[7]

The crucial step in the development of a stratification system occurs when important elements in the population assume the prerogatives and functions of higher status and, at least by implication, exclude all other elements. This creates an "upper," a "leading" or, possibly, a "ruling" class set over against the "mass" of the population. Given early, or, indeed, not so early conditions, it is inevitable that membership in this upper class is primarily if not entirely based on kinship status. Thus, an individual military or other leader may go far toward establishing an important criterion of status, but in doing so he elevates the status of his lineage. He cannot dissociate his relatives from his own success, even presuming he would wish to.

Stratification in the present sense, then, is the differentiation of the population on a prestige scale of kinship units such that the distinctions among such units, or classes of them, become hereditary to an important degree. There are reasons to assume that the early tendency, which may be repeated, leads to a *two*-class system. The most important means of consolidating such a system is upper-class endogamy. Since this repeats the primary principle which, along with territoriality, delineates the boundaries of early societies, the upper class constitutes a kind of subsociety. It is not a class, however, unless its counterpart, the lower class, is clearly included in the *same* societal community.

From this "primordial" two-class system there are various possibilities for evolutionary change. Probably the most important leads to a four-class system.[8] This is based on the development of urban communities in which political-administrative functions, centralized religious and other cultural activities, and territorially specialized economic action are carried on. Thus, generalized "centers" of higher-order activity emerge, but the imperatives of social organization require that these centers, as local communities—including, e.g., "provincial" centers—cannot be inhabited exclusively by upper-class people. Hence the urban upper class tends to be differentiated from the rural upper class, and the urban from the rural lower class. When this occurs there is no longer a linear rank-order of classes. But so long as hereditary kinship status is a primary determinant of the individual's access to "advantages," we may speak of a stratified society; beyond the lowest level of complexity, every society is stratified.

Diffuse as its significance is, stratification is an *evolutionary* universal because the most primitive societies are not in the present sense stratified, but, beyond them, it is on two principal counts a prerequisite of a very wide range of further advances. First, what I have called a "prestige" position is a generalized prerequisite of responsible concentration of leadership. With few exceptions, those who lack a sufficiently "established" position cannot afford to "stick their necks out" in taking the responsibility for important changes. The second count concerns the availability of resources for implementing innovations. The dominance of kinship in social organization is inseparably connected with rigidity. People do what they are required to do by virtue of their kinship status. To whatever degree kinship is the basis of solidarity *within* an upper class, closure of that class by endogamy precludes kinship from being the basis of upper-class claims on the services and other resources of the lower groups. So long as the latter are genuinely within the same society, which implies solidarity across the class line, relations of mutual usefulness (e.g., patron-client relationships across class lines) on non-kin bases are possible—opening the door to universalistic definitions of merit as well as providing the upper groups with the resources to pursue their own advantages.

Social stratification in its initial development may thus be regarded as one primary condition of releasing the process of social evolution from the obstacles posed by ascription. The strong emphasis on kinship in much of the sociological literature on stratification tends to obscure the fact that the new mobility made possible by stratification is due primarily to such breaks in kinship ascription as that across class lines.

Stratification, of course, remains a major structural feature of subsequent societies and takes a wide variety of forms in their evolution. Since the general process of evolutionary change introduces a series of lines of differentiation on several bases, it is unlikely that a single simple prestige order will adequately represent the stratification system in more advanced societies. The "bourgeois" in the late European Middle Ages cannot be described simply as a "middle" class standing between the predominantly rural "feudal" classes and the peasantry. Nevertheless, statification tends to exert a pressure to generalized hierarchization, going beyond particular bases of prestige, such as political power, special sources of wealth, etc. This is precisely because it brings these various advantages together in their relations to the diffuse status of the kinship group, and through kinship inheritance exerts pressure to continue them from generation to generation. Thus, in the transition to full modernity, stratification often becomes a predominantly conservative force in contrast to the opportunities it provides for innovation in the earlier stages.

Cultural Legitimation

Specialized cultural legitimation is, like stratification, intimately involved in the emergence from primitiveness, and certainly the two processes are related. Legitimation could, perhaps, be treated first; in certain crucial respects it is a prerequisite to the establishment of the type of prestige position referred to above. The ways in which this might be the case pose a major problem for more detailed studies of evolutionary processes. Our task here, however, is much more modest, namely to call attention to the fact that without both statification and legitimation no major advances beyond the level of primitive society can be made.

The point of reference for the development of legitimation systems is the cultural counterpart of the seamless web of the kinship nexus with its presumptive equality of units. This is the cultural definition of the social collectivity simply as "we" who are essentially human or "people" and as such are undifferentiated, even in certain concepts of time, from our ancestors—except in certain senses for the mythical "founders"—and from contemporary "others." If the others are clearly recognized to be others (in an ideal type seamless web they would not be; they would be merely special groups of kin), they are regarded as not "really human," as strange in the sense that their relation to "us" is not comprehensible.

By explicit cultural legitimation, I mean the emergence of an institutionalized cultural definition of the society of reference, namely a referent of "we" (e.g., "We, the Tikopia" in Firth's study) which is differentiated, historically or comparatively or both, from other societies, while the merit of we-ness is asserted in a normative context. This definition has to be religious in some sense, e.g., stated in terms of a particular sacred tradition of relations to gods or holy places. It may also ascribe various meritorious features to the group, e.g., physical beauty, warlike prowess, faithful trusteeship of sacred territory or tradition, etc.

This usage of the term legitimation is closely associated with Max Weber's analysis of political authority. For very important reasons the primary focus of early stages beyond the primitive is political, involving the society's capacity to carry out coordinated collective action. Stratification, therefore, is an essential condition of major advances in political effectiveness, because, as just noted, it gives the advantaged elements a secure enough position that they can accept certain risks in undertaking collective leadership.

The differentiation inherent in stratification creates new sources of strain and potential disorganization, and the use of advantaged position to undertake major innovations multiplies this strain. Especially if, as is usually the case, the authors of major social innovation are already advantaged, they require legitimation for both their actions and their positions. Thus, a dynamic inherent in the development of cultural systems[9] revolves about the cultural importance of the question *why*—why such social arrangements as prestige and authority relations, and particular attendant rewards and deprivations, come about and are structured as they are. This cultural dynamic converges with the consequences of the stratification developments already outlined. Hence the crucial problem here is distributive, that of justifying advantages and prerogatives *over against* burdens and deprivations. Back of this, however, lies the problem of the meaning of the societal enterprise as a whole.

As the bases of legitimation are inherently cultural, meeting the legitimation need necessarily involves putting some kind of a premium on certain cultural services, and from this point of view there is clearly some potential advantage in specializing cultural action. Whether, under what conditions, and in what ways political and religious leadership or prestige status are differentiated from each other are exceedingly important general problems of societal evolution, but we cannot go into them here. A "God-King" may be the primary vehicle of legitimation for his own political regime, or the political "ruler" may be dependent on a priestly class that is in some degree structurally independent of his regime. But the main problems have to do with explicating the cultural basis of legitimation and institutionalizing agencies for implementing that function.

The functional argument here is essentially the same as that for stratification. Over an exceedingly wide front and relatively independently of particular cultural variations, political leaders must on the long run have not only sufficient power, but also legitimation for it. Particularly when bigger implementive steps are to be legitimized, legitimation must become a relatively explicit and, in many cases, a socially differentiated function. The combination of differentiated cultural patterns of legitimation with socially differentiated agencies is the essential aspect of the evolutionary universal of legitimation.

As evolutionary universals, stratification and legitimation are associated with the developmental problems of breaking through the ascriptive nexus of kinship, on the one hand, and of "traditionalized" culture, on the other. In turn they provide the basis for differentiation of a system that has previously, in the relevant respects, been undifferentiated. Differentiation must be carefully distinguished from segmentation, i.e., from either the development of undifferentiated segmental units of any given type within the system, or the splitting off of units from the system to form new societies, a process that appears to be particularly common at primitive levels. Differentiation requires solidarity and integrity of the system as a whole, with both common loyalties and common normative definitions of the situation. Stratification as here conceived is a hierarchical status differentiation that cuts across the overall seamless web of kinship and occurs definitely within a single collectivity, a "societal community." Legitimation is the differentiation of cultural definitions of normative patterns from a completely embedded, taken-for-granted fusion with the social structure, accompanied by institutionalization of the explicit, culture-oriented, legitimizing function in subsystems of the society.

Legitimation, of course, continues to present functional problems at later stages of evolution. The type associated with archaic religions is bound up with the relatively particularistic, arbitrary favor of divine patrons. A crucial step, represented by Bellah's "historic" religions, relates human society to a conception of supernatural order with which men must come to terms, rather than to particular divinities. Where a divinity is involved, like Jahweh, his relations with people are conceived in terms of an order which he makes binding on them, but to which, faith assures them, he will also adhere.

Bureaucratic Organization

A second pair of evolutionary universals develop, each with varying degrees of completeness and relative importance, in societies that have moved considerably past the primitive stage, particularly those with well institutionalized literacy.[10] These uinversals are administrative bureaucracy, which in early stages is found overwhelmingly in government, and money and markets. I shall discuss bureaucracy first because its development is likely to precede that of money and markets.

Despite the criticisms made of it, mainly in the light of the complexities of modern organizations, Weber's ideal type can serve as the primary point of reference for a discussion of bureaucracy. Its crucial feature is the institutionalization of the *authority of office*. This means that both individual incumbents and, perhaps even more importantly, the bureaucratic organization itself, may act "officially" for, or "in the name of," the organization, which could not otherwise exist. I shall call this capacity to act, or more broadly, that to make and promulgate binding decisions, *power* in a strict analytical sense.[11]

Although backed by coercive sanctions, up to and including the use of physical force, *at the same time* power rests on the consensual solidarity of a system that includes both the users of power and the "objects" of its use. (Note that I do not say *against* whom it is used: the "against" may or may not apply.) Power in this sense is the capacity of a unit in the social system, collective or individual, to establish or activate commitments to performance that contributes to, or is in the interest of, attainment of the goals of a collectivity. It is not itself a "factor" in effectiveness, nor a "real" output of the process, but a medium of mobilization and acquisition of factors and outputs. In this respect, it is like money.

Office implies the differentiation of the role of incumbent from a person's other role-involvements, above all from his kinship roles. Hence, so far as function in the collectivity is defined by the obligations of ascriptive kinship status, the organizational status cannot be an office in the present sense. Neither of the other two types of authority that Weber discusses—traditional and charismatic—establishes this differentiation between organizational role and the "personal" status of the incumbent. Hence bureaucratic authority is always rational-legal in type. Weber's well-known proposition that the top of a bureaucratic structure cannot itself be bureaucratic may be regarded as a statement about the modes of articulation of such a structure with other structures in the society. These may involve the ascribed traditional authority of royal families, some form of charismatic leadership, or the development of democratic associational control, to be discussed briefly below.

Internally, a bureaucratic system is always characterized by an institutionalized hierarchy of authority, which is differentiated on two axes: *level* of authority and "sphere" of competence. Spheres of competence are defined either on segmentary bases, e.g., territorially, or on functional bases, e.g., supply vs. combat units in an army. The hierarchical aspect defines the levels at which a higher authority's decisions, in case of conflict, take precedence over those of a lower authority. It is a general bureaucratic principle that the higher the level, the smaller the relative number of decision-making agencies, whether individual or collegial, and the wider the scope of each, so that at the top, in principle, a single agency must carry responsibility for *any* problems affecting the organization. Such a hierarchy is one of "pure" authority only so far as status within it is differentiated from other components of status, e.g., social class. Even with rather clear differentiation, however, position in a stratification system is likely to be highly correlated with position in a hierarchy of authority. Seldom, if ever, are high bureaucratic officials unequivocally members of the lowest social class.

Externally, two particularly important boundaries pose difficulties for bureaucracies. The first has to do with recruiting manpower and obtaining facilities. In ideal type, a position in a bureaucratic organization constitutes an occupational role, which implies that criteria of eligibility should be defined in terms of competence and maximal responsibility to the organization, not to "private" interests independent of, and potentially in conflict with, those of the organization. Thus high aristocrats may put loyalty to their lineage ahead of the obligations of office, or clergymen in political office may place loyalty to the church ahead of obligation to the civil government. Also, remunerating officials and providing facilities for their functions presents a serious problem of differentiation and hence of independence. The "financing of public bodies," as Weber calls it,[12] cannot be fully bureaucratic in this sense unless payment is in money, the sources of which are outside the control of the recipients. Various forms of benefices and prebends only very imperfectly meet these conditions, but modern salaries and operating budgets approximate them relatively closely.

The second boundary problem concerns political support. An organization is bureaucratic so far as incumbents of its offices can function independently of the influence of elements having special "interests" in its output, except where such elements are properly involved in the definition of the organization's goals through its nonbureaucratic top. Insulation from such influence, for example through such crude channels as bribery, is difficult to institutionalize and, as is well known, is relatively rare.

In the optimal case, internal hierarchy and division of functions, recruitment of manpower and facilities, and exclusion of "improper" influence, are all regulated by universalistic norms. This is implicit in the proposition that bureaucratic authority belongs to Weber's rational-legal type. Of course, in many concrete instances this condition is met very imperfectly, even in the most highly developed societies.

Bureaucracy tends to develop earliest in governmental administration primarily because even a modest approximation to the essential criteria requires a considerable concentration of power, which, as noted above, depends both on prestige and on legitimation. In the very important cases, like the *polis* of antiquity, where power is widely dispersed, private units of organization are not likely either to be large enough or to command sufficient resources to become highly bureaucratized. Perhaps the *oikos* organization of the interests of important aristocratic lineages in late antiquity constitutes one of the most important relatively early examples approximating private bureaucracy. The Western Church is clearly another, as are modern business firms.

The basis on which I classify bureaucracy as an evolutionary universal is very simple. As Weber said, it is the most effective large-scale administrative organization that man has invented, and there is no direct substitute for it.[13] Where capacity to carry out large-scale organized operations is important, e.g., military operations with mass forces, water control, tax administration, policing of large and heterogeneous populations, and productive enterprise requiring large capital investment and much manpower, the unit that commands effective bureaucratic organization is inherently superior to the one that does not. It is by no means the only structural factor in the adaptive capacity of social systems, but no one can deny that it is an important one. Above all, it is built on further specializations ensuing from the broad emancipation from ascription that stratification and specialized legitimation make possible.

Money and the Market Complex

Immediate effectiveness of collective function, especially on a large scale, depends on concentration of power, as noted. Power is in part a function of the mobility of the resources available for use in the interests of the collective goals in question. Mobility of resources, however, is a direct function of access to them through the market. Though the market is the most general means of such access, it does have two principal competitors. First is requisitioning through the direct application of political power, e.g., defining a collective goal as having military significance and requisitioning manpower under it for national defense. A second type of mobilization is the activation of nonpolitical solidarities and commitments, such as those of ethnic or religious membership, local community, caste, etc. The essential theme here is, "as one of us, it is your duty . . ."

The political power path involves a fundamental difficulty because of the role of explicit or implied coercion—"you contribute, or else . . ."—while the activation of non-political commitments, a category comprising at least two others, raises the issue of alternative obligations. The man appealed to in the interest of his ethnic group, may ask, "what about the problems of my family?" In contrast, market exchange avoids three dilemmas: first, that I must do what is expected or face punishment for noncompliance; second, if I do not comply, I will be disloyal to certain larger groups, identification with which is very important to my general status; third, if I do not comply, I may betray the unit which, like my family, is the primary basis of my immediate personal security.

Market exchange makes it possible to obtain resources for future action and yet avoid such dilemmas as these, because money is a generalized resource for the consumer-recipient, who can purchase "good things" regardless of his relations to their courses in other respects. Availability through the market cannot be unlimited—one should not be able to purchase conjugal love or ultimate political loyalty—but possession of physical commodities, and by extension, control of personal services by purchase, certainly can, very generally, be legitimized in the market nexus.

As a symbolic medium, money "stands for" the economic utility of the real assets for which it is exchangeable, but it represents the concrete objects so abstractly that it is neutral among the competing claims of various other orders in which the same objects are significant. It thus directs attention away from the more consummatory and, by and large, immediate significance of these objects toward their *instrumental* significance as potential means to further ends. Thus money becomes the great mediator of the instrumental use of goods and services. Markets, involving both the access of the consuming unit to objects it needs for consumption and the access of producing units to "outlets" that are not ascribed, but contingent on the voluntary decisions of "customers" to purchase, may be stabilized institutionally. Thus this universal "emancipates" resources from such ascriptive bonds as demands to give kinship expectations priority, to be loyal in highly specific senses to certain political groups, or to submit the details of daily life to the specific imperatives of religious sects.

In the money and market system, money as a medium of exchange and property rights, including rights of alienation, must be institutionalized. In general it is a further step that institutionalizes broadly an individual's contractual right to sell his services in a labor market without seriously involving himself in diffuse dependency relationships, which at lower status levels are usually in some ways "unfree." Property in land, on a basis that provides for its alienation, presents a very important problem. Its wide extension seems, except in a very few cases, to be a late development. The institution of contract in exchange of money and goods is also a complex area of considerable variation. Finally, money itself is by no means a simple entity, and in particular the development of credit instruments, banking and the like, has many variations.

These institutional elements are to a considerable degree independently variable and are often found unevenly developed. But if the main ones are sufficiently developed and integrated, the market system provides the operating units of the society, including of course its government, with a pool of disposable resources that can be applied to any of a range of uses and, within limits, can be shifted from use to use. The importance of such a pool is shown by the serious consequences of its shrinkage for even such highly organized political systems as some of the ancient empires.

Modern socialist societies appear to be exceptional because, up to a point, they achieve high productivity with a relatively minimal reliance on monetary and market mechanisms, substituting bureaucracy for them. But too radical a "demonetization" has negative consequences even for such an advanced economy as that of the Soviet Union.

A principal reason for placing money and markets after bureaucracy in the present series of evolutionary universals is that the conditions of their large-scale development are more precarious. This is particularly true in the very important areas where a generalized system of universalistic norms has not yet become firmly established. Market operations, and the monetary medium itself, are inevitably highly dependent on political "protection." The very fact that the mobilization of political power, and its implementation through bureaucratic organization, is so effective generates interests against sacrificing certain short-run advantages to favor the enhanced flexibility that market systems can provide. This has been a major field of conflict historically, and it is being repeated today in underdeveloped societies. The strong tendency for developing societies to adopt a "socialistic" pattern reflects a preference for increasing productivity through governmentally controlled bureaucratic means rather than more decentralized market-oriented means. But in general the money and market system has undoubtedly made a fundamental contribution to the adaptive capacity of the societies in which it has developed; those that restrict it too drastically are likely to suffer from severe adaptive disadvantages in the long run.

Generalized Universalistic Norms

A feature common to bureaucratic authority and the market system is that they incorporate, and are hence dependent on, universalistic norms. For bureaucracy, these involve definitions of the powers of office, the terms of access to it, and the line dividing proper from improper pressure or influence. For money and markets, the relevant norms include the whole complex of property rights, first in commodities, later in land and in monetary assets. Other norms regulate the monetary medium and contractual relations among the parties to transactions. Here relations between contracts of service or employment and other aspects of the civil and personal statuses of the persons concerned are particularly crucial.

Up to a point, the norms governing a bureaucratic organization may be regarded as independent of those governing property or those regulating the status of private persons in the same society.

As noted, however, there are also certain intrinsic connections, such as that between bureaucratic organization and the mobility of resources.

Although it is very difficult to pin down just what the crucial components are, how they are interrelated, and how they develop, one can identify the development of a general legal system as a crucial aspect of societal evolution. A general legal system is an integrated system of universalistic norms, applicable to the society as a whole rather than to a few functional or segmental sectors, highly generalized in terms of principles and standards, and relatively independent of both the religious agencies that legitimize the normative order of the society and vested interest groups in the operative sector, particularly in government.

The extent to which both bureaucratic organization and market systems can develop *without* a highly generalized universalistic normative order should not be underestimated. Such great Empires as the Mesopotamian, the ancient Chinese, and, perhaps the most extreme example, the Roman, including its Byzantine extension, certainly testify to this. But these societies suffered either from a static quality, failing to advance beyond certain points, or from instability leading in many cases to retrogression. Although many of the elements of such a general normative order appeared in quite highly developed form in earlier societies, in my view their crystallization into a coherent system represents a distinctive new step, which more than the industrial revolution itself, ushered in the *modern era* of social evolution.

The clear differentiation of secular government from religious organization has been a long and complicated process, and even in the modern world its results are unevenly developed. It has perhaps gone farthest in the sharp separation of Church and State in the United States. Bureaucracy has, of course, played an important part in this process. The secularization of government is associated with that of law, and both of these are related to the level of generality of the legal system.

Systems of law that are *directly* religiously sanctioned, treating compliance as a religious obligation, also tend to be "legalistic" in the sense of emphasizing detailed prescriptions and prohibitions, each of which is given specific Divine sanction. Preeminent examples are the Hebrew law of Leviticus, the later developments in the Talmudic tradition, and Islamic law based on the Koran and its interpretations. Legal decisions and the formulation of rules to cover new situations must then be based as directly as possible on an authoritative sacred text.

Not only does religious law as such tend to inhibit generalization of legal principle, but it also tends to favor what Weber called *substantive* over *formal* rationality.[14] The standard of legal correctness tends to be the implementation of religious precepts, not procedural propriety and consistency of general principle. Perhaps the outstanding difference between the legal systems of the other Empires, and the patterns that were developed importantly in Roman law, was the development of elements of formal rationality, which we may regard as a differentiation of legal norms out of "embeddedness" in the religious culture. The older systems—many of which still exist—tended to treat "justice" as a direct implementation of precepts of religious and moral conduct, in terms of what Weber called *Wertrationalität*, without institutionalizing an independent system of *societal* norms, adapted to the function of social control at the societal level and integrated on its own terms. The most important foci of such an independent system are, first, some kind of "codification" of norms under principles not *directly* moral or religious, though they generally continue to be grounded in religion, and, second, the formalization of procedural rules, defining the situations in which judgments are to be made on a societal basis. Especially important is the establishment of courts for purposes other than permitting political and religious leaders to make pronouncements and "examples."[15]

Something similar can be said about what I have called operative vested interests, notably government. Advantages are to be gained, on the one hand, by binding those outside the direct control of the group in question with detailed regulation, while, on the other hand, leaving maximum freedom for the group's leadership. This duality Weber made central to his concept of traditionalized fixity, on the one hand, and that of personal prerogative, reaching its extreme form in "sultanism," on the other.[16] Both aspects are highly resistant to the type of rationalization that is essential to a generalized universalistic legal system.

Though the Chinese Empire, Hindu law *(Manu)*, Babylonia, and to some extent, Islam made important beginnings in the direction I am discussing, the Roman legal system of the Imperial period was uniquely advanced in these respects. Though the early *jus civilis* was very bound religiously, this was not true to the same extent of the *jus gentium*, or of the later system as a totality. While a professional judiciary never developed, the jurisconsults in their "unofficial" status did constitute a genuine professional group, and they systematized the law very extensively, in the later phases strongly under the influence of Stoic Philosophy.

Though Roman law had a variety of more or less "archaic" features, its "failure" was surely on the level of institutionalization more than in any intrinsic defect of legal content. Roman society of that period lacked the institutional capacity, through government, religious legitimation, and other channels, to integrate the immense variety of peoples and cultures within the Empire, or to maintain the necessary economic, political, and administrative structures.[17] Roman law remained, however, the cultural reference point of all the significant later developments.

The next phase, of course, was the development of Catholic Canon Law, incorporating much of Roman law. A major characteristic of the Western Church, Canon law was not only very important in maintaining and consolidating the Church's differentiation from secular government and society, but, with the Justinian documents, it also preserved the legal tradition.

The third phase was the revival of the study of Roman secular law in Renaissance Italy and its gradual adoption by the developing national states of early modern Europe. The result was that the modern national state developed as, fundamentally, a *Rechtsstaat*. In Continental Europe, however, one fundamental limitation on this development was the degree to which the law continued to be intertwined and almost identified with government. For example, most higher civil servants were lawyers. One might ask whether this represented a "legalization of bureaucracy" or a bureaucratization of the law and the legal profession. But with elaborate bodies of law, law faculties as

major constituents of every important university, and the prominence of university-trained legal profession, Continental European nations certainly had well institutionalized legal systems.

In England, however, the development went, in a highly distinctive way, still farther. Although the differentiation of English
Common Law from Continental Roman law had late Mediaeval
roots, the crucial period was the early 17th century, when Justice
Coke asserted the independence of the Common law from control
by royal prerogative. With this, the establishment of the organizational independence of the Judiciary was the crucial symbolic
development. Substantially, the Common Law came to emphasize the protection of personal rights,[18] the institution of property
in private hands, and both freedom of contract and protection of
contractual interests far more strongly than did the Continental
law. Common Law also emphasized the development of institutions, including both the adversary system, in which parties
are highly independent of the Court, and procedural protections.[19]

Significantly, these Common Law developments were integral
parts of the more general development of British institutions associated with the Puritan movement, including the later
establishment of the independence of Parliament and the development of physical science.

This development of English Common Law, with its adoption
and further development in the overseas English-speaking world,
not only constituted the most advanced case of universalistic
normative order, but was probably decisive for the modern
world. This general type of legal order is, in my opinion, the most
important single hallmark of modern society. So much is it no
accident that the Industrial Revolution occurred first in England,
that I think it legitimate to regard the English type of legal system
as a fundamental prerequisite of the first occurrence of the Industrial Revolution.

The Democratic Association

A rather highly generalized universalistic legal order is in all
likelihood a necessary prerequisite for the development of the last

structural complex to be discussed as universal to social evolution, the democratic association with elective leadership and fully enfranchised membership. At least this seems true of the institutionalization of this pattern in the governments of large-scale societies. This form of democratic association originated only in the late 18th century in the Western world and was nowhere complete, if universal adult suffrage is a criterion, until well into the present century. Of course, those who regard the Communist society as a stable and enduring type might well dispute that democratic government in this sense is an evolutionary universal. But before discussing that issue, I will outline the history and principal components of this universal.

Surely it is significant that the earliest cases of democratic government were the *poleis* of classical antiquity, which were also the primary early sources of universalistic law. The democratic *polis,* however, not only was small in scale by modern standards (note Aristotle's belief that a citizen body should never be too large to assemble within earshot of a given speaker, of course without the aid of a public address system), but also its democratic associational aspects never included a total society. It is estimated that during the Periclean age in Athens, only about 30,000 of a total population of about 150,000 were citizens, the rest being metics and slaves. And, of course, citizen women were not enfranchised. Thus even in its democratic phase the *polis* was emphatically a two-class system. And under the conditions of the time, when Roman society increased in scale away from the *polis* type of situation, citizenship, at least for large proportions of the Empire's population, was bound to lose political functions almost in proportion to its gains in legal significance.

The basic principle of democratic association, however, never completely disappeared. To varying degrees and in varying forms, it survived in the *municipia* of the Roman Empire, in the Roman Senate, and in various aspects of the organization of the Christian Church, though the Church also maintained certain hierarchical aspects. Later the collegial pattern, e.g., the *college* of Cardinals, continued to be an aspect of Church structure. In the Italian and North European city-states of the late Middle Ages and early modern period, it had its place in government, for example in "senates," which though not democratically elected, were internally organized as democratic bodies. Another important case was the guild, as an association of merchants or craftsmen. In modern times there have, of course, been many different types of private association in many different fields. It is certainly safe to say that, even apart from government, the democratic association is a most prominent and important constituent of modern societies.

At the level of national government, we can speak first of the long development of Parliamentary assemblies functioning as democratic associations and legislating for the nation, whose members have been to some degree elected from fairly early times. Secondly, there has been a stepwise extension of both the franchise for electing legislative representatives and the legislative supremacy of their assemblies, following the lead of England, which developed rapidly in these respects after 1688. Later, the French and American Revolutions dramatized the conception of the total national community as essentially a democratic association in this sense.

There are four critically important components of the democratic association. First is the institutionalization of the leadership function in the form of an elective office, whether occupied by individuals, executive bodies, or collegial groups like legislatures. The second is the franchise, the institutionalized participation of members in collective decision-making through the election of officers and often through voting on specific policy issues. Third is the institutionalization of procedural rules for the voting process and the determination of its outcome and for the process of "discussion" or campaigning for votes by candidates or advocates of policies. Fourth is the institutionalization of the nearest possible approximation to the voluntary principle in regard to membership status. In the private association this is fundamental—no case where membership is ascribed or compulsory can be called a "pure" democratic association. In government, however, the coercive and compulsory elements of power, as well as the recruitment of societal communities largely by birth, modify the principle. Hence universality of franchise tends to replace the voluntary membership principle.

Formalization of definite procedural rules governing voting and the counting and evaluation of votes may be considered a case of formal rationality in Weber's sense, since it removes the consequences of the act from the control of the particular actor. It limits his control to the specific act of casting his ballot, choosing among the alternatives officially presented to him. Indirectly his vote might contribute to an outcome he did not desire, e.g., through splitting the opposition to an undesirable candidate and thus actually aiding him, but he cannot control this, except in the voting act itself.

Besides such formalization, however, Rokkan has shown in his comparative and historical study of Western electoral systems, that there is a strikingly general tendency to develop three other features of the franchise.[20] The first of these is universality, minimizing if not eliminating the overlap between membership and disenfranchisement. Thus property qualifications and, most recently, sex qualifications have been removed so that now the main Western democratic polities, with minimal exceptions, have universal adult suffrage. The second is equality, eliminating "class" systems, like the Prussian system in the German Empire, in favor of the principle, one citizen, one vote. Finally, secrecy of the ballot insulates the voting decision from pressures emanating from status superiors or peers that might interfere with the expression of the voter's personal preferences.

Certain characteristics of elective office directly complementary to those of the franchise can be formulated. Aside from the ways of achieving office and the rules of tenure in it, they are very similar to the pattern of bureaucratic office. The first, corresponding to the formalization of electoral rules, is that conduct in office must be legally regulated by universalistic norms. Second, corresponding to the universality of the franchise, is the principle of subordinating segmental or private interests to the collective interest within the sphere of competence of the office. Third, corresponding to equality of the franchise, is the principle of accountability for decisions to a total electorate. And finally, corresponding to secrecy of the ballot, is the principle of limiting the powers of office to specified spheres, in sharp contrast to the diffuseness of both traditional and charismatic authority.

The adoption of even such a relatively specific pattern as equality of the franchise may be considered a universal tendency, essentially because, under the principle that the membership rightfully chooses both the broad orientations of collective policy and the elements having leadership privileges and responsibilities, there is, among those with minimal competence, no universalistic basis for discriminating among classes of members. As a limitation on the hierarchical structure of power within collectivities, equality of franchise is the limiting or boundary condition of the democratic association, corresponding to equality of opportunity on the bureaucratic boundary of the polity.

Especially, though not exclusively, in national territorial states, the stable democratic association is notoriously difficult to institutionalize. Above all this seems to be a function of the difficulty in motivating holders of immediately effective power to relinquish their opportunities voluntarily despite the seriousness of the interest at stake—relinquishment of control of governmental machinery after electoral defeat being the most striking problem. The system is also open to other serious difficulties, most notably corruption and "populist" irresponsibility, as well as *de facto* dictatorship. Furthermore, such difficulties are by no means absent in private associations, as witness the rarity of effective electoral systems in large trade unions.

The basic argument for considering democratic association a universal, despite such problems, is that, the larger and more complex a society becomes, the more important is effective political organization, not only in its administrative capacity, but also, and not least, in its support of a universalistic legal order. Political effectiveness includes both the scale and operative flexibility of the organization of power. Power, however, precisely as a generalized societal medium, depends overwhelmingly on a consensual element, i.e., the ordered institutionalization and exercise of influence, linking the power system to the higher-order societal consensus at the value level.

No institutional form basically different from the democratic association can, *not* specifically *legitimize* authority and power in the most general sense, but *mediate consensus in its exercise* by particular persons and groups, and in the formation of particular

binding policy decisions. At high levels of structural differentiation in the society itself and in its governmental system, generalized legitimation cannot fill this gap adequately. Providing
structured participation in the selection of leaders and formation
of basic policy, as well as in opportunities to be heard and exert
influence and to have a real choice among alternatives, is the
crucial function of the associational system from this point of
view.

I realize that to take this position I must maintain that communist totalitarian organization will probably not fully match
"democracy" in political and integrative capacity in the long run.
I do indeed predict that it will prove to be unstable and will either
make adjustments in the general direction of electoral democracy
and a plural party system or "regress" into generally less advanced and politically less effective forms of organization, failing
to advance as rapidly or as far as otherwise may be expected. One
important basis of this prediction is that the Communist Party has
everywhere emphasized its function in *educating* the people for
the new society.[21] In the long run its legitimacy will certainly be
undermined if the party leadership continues to be unwilling to
trust the people it has educated. In the present context, however,
to trust the people is to entrust them with a share of political
responsibility. This can only mean that eventually the single
monolithic party must relinquish its monopoly of such responsibility. (This is not to analyze the many complex ways in
which this development might proceed, but only to indicate the
direction in which it is most likely to move and the consequences
it must bear if it fails in taking that direction.)

Conclusion

This paper is not meant to present even the schematic outline of
a "theory" of societal evolution. My aim is much more limited: I
have selected for detailed attention and illustration an especially
important type of structural innovation that has appeared in the
course of social change. I have attempted to clarify the concept
"evolutionary universal" by briefly discussing a few examples
from organic evolution, namely, vision, the human hands, and the
human brain. I have interpreted these as innovations endowing

their possessors with a very substantial increase in generalized adaptive capacity, so substantial that species lacking them are relatively disadvantaged in the major areas in which natural selection operates, not so much for survival as for the opportunity to initiate further major developments.

Four features of human societies at the level of culture and social organization were cited as having universal and major significance as prerequisites for socio-cultural development: technology, kinship organization based on an incest taboo, communication based on language, and religion. Primary attention, however, was given to six organizational complexes that develop mainly at the level of social structure. The first two, particularly important for the emergence of societies from primitiveness, are stratification, involving a primary break with primitive kinship ascription, and cultural legitimation, with institutionalized agencies that are independent of a diffuse religious tradition.

Fundamental to the structure of modern societies are, taken together, the other four complexes: bureaucratic organization of collective goal-attainment, money and market systems, generalized universalistic legal systems, and the democratic association with elective leadership and mediated membership support for policy orientations. Although these have developed very unevenly, some of them going back a very long time, all are clearly much more than simple "inventions" of particular societies.

Perhaps a single theme tying them together is that differentiation and attendant reduction in ascription has caused the initial two-class system to give way to more complex structures at the levels of social stratification and the relation between social structure and its cultural legitimation. First, this more complex system is characterized by a highly generalized universalistic normative structure in all fields. Second, subunits under such normative orders have greater autonomy both in pursuing their own goals and interests and in serving others instrumentally. Third, this autonomy is linked with the probability that structural units will develop greater diversity of interests and subgoals. Finally, this diversity results in pluralization of scales of prestige and therefore of differential access to economic resources, power, and influence.

Comparatively, the institutionalization of these four complexes and their interrelations is very uneven. In the broadest frame of reference, however, we may think of them as together constituting the main outline of the structural foundations of modern society. Clearly, such a combination, balanced relative to the exigencies of particular societal units, confers on its possessors an adaptive advantage far superior to the structural potential of societies lacking it. Surely the bearing of this proposition on problems of rapid "modernization" in present "underdeveloped" societies is extremely important.

Certain cultural developments such as the "philosophic breakthroughs" that produced what Bellah calls the "historic" religions or the emergence of modern science in the 16th and 17th centuries, are of significance equal to the developments discussed above. Indeed, the level of institutionalization of scientific investigation and technological application of science in the present century has become a structural complex ranking in importance with the four I have described as essential to modernity.

In closing I wish to express the hope that the reader will not be too concerned with the details of my characterizations of particular evolutionary universals, my specific judgments about their concrete historical developments, or my detailed evaluations of their importance. These parts of the paper are meant primarily for illustration. I hope he will give particular attention to the *idea* of the evolutionary universal and its grounding in the conception of generalized adaptive capacity. If this idea is sound, empirical shortcomings in its application can be remedied by research and criticism.

20

AMERICAN VALUES
AND AMERICAN SOCIETY

WITH GERALD M. PLATT

The importance of the value-pattern of cognitive rationality for American society can be better understood by placing it in the context of the value-system of the society as a whole. We do hold that there is and has been a single, relatively well-integrated value-system institutionalized in the society which has "evolved" but has not been drastically changed. As such it must be considered at a high level of generality.

The value-patterns which are part of the structure of a society are those values which implicitly or explicitly define the desirable type of society or its subsystems. In the nature of the case, a value-system does not describe the concrete state of affairs of the system in which it is institutionalized: it is always a source of normative tension between the actual state of affairs and that conceived, in value terms, to be desirable.

Subject to these considerations, the phrase "instrumental activism" is an appropriate characterization, at a high level of generality, of the main value-pattern institutionalized in American society. Instrumental activism characterizes the desirable type of society, not other classes of objects which Americans regard as desirable. The society as a system tends to be evaluated, not as an end in itself but as *instrumental* to bases of value outside itself. Its desirability is to be judged in terms of its contribution to these

Reprinted with deletions by permission from *The Evolution of Society* by Talcott Parsons, © 1977, Prentice-Hall, Inc., Englewood Cliffs, N.J., and from *The American University*, by Talcott Parsons and Gerald M. Platt (Cambridge: Harvard University Press, 1973), copyright © 1973 by The President and Fellows of Harvard College.

*extra*societal grounds of value. The value orientation is *activistic* in the sense that, in the relation between the society and its environments, what is valued is not passive adjustment to the exigencies of the environment but increasing the sphere of freedom of action within the environment and ultimately control over the environment. Of course, the environments of a society are not only the physical world, the biosphere, and other societies but also the organisms and personalities of the constituent individual members and the cultural system. Normative tensions are inherent in this type of value-system. The activistic component exerts pressure in the direction of treating the society as a goal-oriented system, as is suggested by the discussion of national goals and the soul-searching over the apparent prevalence of apathy instead of commitment to collective goals. If the instrumental component could be led back, as it was in the earlier religious phase, to an explicitly transcendent goal (namely the mandate of God to establish His Kingdom on Earth), then instrumental and activistic considerations would coincide. The main evolutionary trend, however, has been in an individualistic direction; hence the goals to which the instrumental component applies have become those distributively allocated to individual citizens and to subcollectivities. Individualistic normative pressure operates against the types of centralization and hierarchy characteristic of societies oriented predominantly to collective goals. In Herbert Spencer's phrase, the tendency has been more to the "industrial" type of society rather than to the "militant."[1] This trend explains our evaluative concerns with equality and freedom, concerns that have persisted in varying forms from the days of the founding fathers. Concern with freedom and equality contrast with the collective discipline of the Calvinistic movements and, what in some respects is a cultural revival and extension of them, Communist versions of socialism.

The emerging pattern in modern societies is *institutionalized individualism*. An early delineator of this pattern was Durkheim in connection with his conception of organic solidarity. Organic solidarity referred to a differentiated society in which different individuals and groups performed different functions. Its members are at the same time integrated through common ties of loyalty to the society and to each other as fellow citizens. This carries with it the complication that the differentiated functions are the source of valued *contributions* to the welfare and implementation of the values of the society. On such grounds a normative justification both of certain freedoms and of certain inequalities can be accepted.[2] This pattern of institutionalized individualism requires a balance of solidarity on a basis of pluralistic differentiatedness and high valuation of the freedom and dignity of the individual, what Durkheim called the "cult of the individual,"[3] as well as commitment to standards of *justice* in balancing the treatment, rewards, and access to facilities of different individuals and subgroups of them.

The normative pressure of the institutionalized individualism pattern has encouraged active achievement for the society as a whole and for its various subunits. Nevertheless, a social structure has emerged which does not emphasize hierarchy in the interest of collective effectiveness but incorporates an associational emphasis: it provides freedom of action for numerous differentiated subgroups and individuals. Higher education is one important field of institutionalization of institutionalized individualism, a field in which the associational emphasis is particularly strong.

The general value-pattern of instrumental activism has underlain the development of Western civilization through its Christian heritage.[4] Though science, industry, and commerce have not been confined to Protestant societies, Max Weber's insight about the facilitating influence of ascetic Protestantism has been generally supported by later research.[5]

The United States constituted a Puritan version of Protestantism which had time to become consolidated before the large-scale Catholic immigration took place.[6] Moreover, the form of the Puritan heritage which came to predominate was the individualistic one that crystallized in the eighteenth century[7] before the Independence movement and the settlement of the American constitutional framework. Bear in mind that separation of church and state and nearly complete religious freedom as well as denominational pluralism were thereby achieved for the first time in Christian history. Within the Christian framework two selective choices characterized liberal Protestantism: (1) the concern for "this world," for the quality of life in secular society, as contrasted with withdrawal into devotional spirituality, and (2) the individualistic trend, the centering of religio-moral sanctions on the conduct and role of the individual, not the collective achievements of a "church militant."

We are not concerned here to go into the many subtle problems about the status of this inherited value-pattern.[8] Privatization of religion and other aspects of secularization may suggest that *any* religiously grounded values have ceased to have implications for American society. A basis for this view is the alleged decline of the Protestant ethic. We believe that this allegation rests on misinterpretation of the nature of societal value-systems and of their role in actual societal structure and process.[9]

In terms of our paradigm of functional analysis, the value-pattern of instrumental activism should exert normative pressure on the society to stress adaptive functions, that is, orientation to the environment as distinguished from orientation to internal pattern-maintenance or integrative functions. As between the two types of environment-oriented functions, the adaptive emphasis is primarily economic as distinguished from goal-attainment. (At the societal level goal attainment is *collective* goal attainment leading to political organization with a hierarchical flavor.)

Weber had the insight to see that, at the period of development he was considering, a special affinity existed between the ethic of Protestantism and a high valuation of economic productivity. This high valuation had something to do with the fact that Americans followed the British example as pioneers of the industrial revolution and, with their greater population and resources, became the world's premier industrial nation. It was not the profit motive in its blatantly hedonistic meaning that Weber stressed, but the *valuation* of contribution to production as a "calling." Monetary earnings were a *measure* of that contribution, not its ultimate motivation.

The American Societal Community

The United States' new type of *societal community*, more than any other factor, justifies assigning it the lead in the latest phase of modernization. It attains fairly successfully the equality of opportunity stressed in socialism. It presupposes a market system, a legal order relatively independent of government, and a nation-state emancipated from religious and ethnic control. The educational revolution was a crucial innovation with its emphasis on the associational pattern as well as on openness of opportunity. American society has gone farther than any comparable large-scale society in its dissociation from the older ascriptive inequalities and the institutionalization of an egalitarian pattern. Contrary to the opinion among many intellectuals, American society—and most modern societies without dictatorial regimes—has institutionalized a broader range of freedoms than had previous societies. This range is not greater than that enjoyed by small privileged groups as eighteenth-century European aristocracy, but it is broader than ever before for large masses of people.

Such freedoms begin with freedom from some of the exigencies of physical life: ill health, short life, and geographical circumscription. They include reduced exposure to violence for most of the population most of the time. Higher incomes and extensive markets enhance freedom of choice in consumption. There is also general access to services like education and public accommodations. There is freedom of marital choice, of occupation, of religious adherence, of political allegiance, of thought, of speech and expression. From a comparative and evolutionary perspective, the more privileged societies of the later twentieth century have successfully institutionalized the liberal values of a century ago.

There are flaws. One, surely, is war and the danger of war. We are dealing here with the nature of the societal community, however. The deficiencies of the new societal community type do not lie mainly in the older grievances against the tyranny of authoritarian regimes, especially of the monarchical variety, or the privileges of aristocracies. Nor do they lie in class antagonism and exploitation in the Marxian sense. The problems of inequality and social justice remain, but framing these problems in terms of bourgeoisie versus proletariat is no longer justified.

There is one context in which equality-justice complaints are justified in the United States: the existence of substantial poverty in combination with the large Negro minority that has suffered a long history of discrimination originating in slavery. Poverty is not exclusively a Negro problem. By most criteria the majority of the American poor is white, and a substantial nonwhite population is not poor. There is, however, a coincidence of the two aspects of the problem among ghetto blacks in the central cities. The older view of these problems stresses absolute deprivation, malnutrition, and disease. The conviction that *relative* deprivation is more important, that what hurts most is the sense of *exclusion* from full participation in the societal community has been growing among social scientists.[10] In our paradigm of social change we have stressed the connection between inclusion and adaptive upgrading—through rising income—but they are not identical. The connection does help to explain why, considering the recent reduction of legal and political discrimination, tensions over the race problem have intensified, not subsided. That mitigation of feelings of relative deprivation through inclusion is in a sense symbolic does not make it the less urgent.

In a second context, the problem of equality and social justice is more difficult to assess. The old grievances of tyranny, privilege, and class in the Marxian sense are less central than they once were. But there remains a sense that advantaged groups use their positions illegitimately to promote their interests at the expense of the common interest. In an earlier generation these grievances were defined in economic terms, as in Franklin D. Roosevelt's reference to "malefactors of great wealth." The tendency now is to invoke the symbol of power—in C. W. Mills' phrase, a "power élite" is now held responsible for our social ills. Members of the power élite are less likely to be defined as office holders than as sinister wire-pullers behind the scenes. Ideological complexes with paranoid themes are old, but the question of what lies behind this one nevertheless arises.

Indignation over the economic privileges of the rich does not seem to be a major source of the moral malaise in modern society; indeed, indignation seems less than at the turn of the century. There is consensus that those elements below the poverty line should be brought above it. Beyond that consensus, the problem of economic inequality becomes complicated. The trend has been one of reduction in conspicuous consumption among élite groups. Though not much has happened for a generation, the future trend will be toward greater equality.

In terms of power and authority, society has become more decentralized and associational rather than more concentrated. This trend again suggests an explanation of discontent in terms of relative rather than absolute deprivation. Bureaucracy has become a negative symbol, implying centralized control through rigid rules and authority. The trend is actually not toward increased bureaucracy, even if bureaucracy were not in process of transformation, but toward associationism. But many sensitive groups *feel* that bureaucracy has been increasing. This sense is also related to accusations against the "military-industrial complex" in the United States, which is associated with a pervasive sense of limitation on freedom; in extreme groups, recent gains in freedoms are denied.

In the expression of relative deprivation two symbols are prominent. One is community, widely alleged to have deteriorated in the course of modern developments.[11] The residential community has allegedly been privatized and many relationships have been shifted to the context of large formal organizations. However, bureaucratization is not actually sweeping all before it. Furthermore, the system of mass communications is a functional equivalent of features of *Gemeinschaft* society; it enables an individual selectively to participate according to his own standards and desires.[12] A second symbol is "participation," especially in the formula of "participatory democracy." Demands for it are stated as if power were the main desideratum, but the diffuseness of these demands casts doubt on this conclusion. The demands are actually another manifestation of the desire for inclusion, for full acceptance as members of solidary groups. Similar considerations seem applicable to the fear of *illegitimate* power. What form participation can take compatible with the exigencies of effective organization is a difficult problem.

This interpretation is compatible with the recent prominence throughout modern societies of student unrest associated with the development of mass higher education. The themes stressed by student radicals have resonance in society at large. Both negatively and positively power is a potent symbol; the wrong kind of power allegedly explains what is wrong in society, and "student power" is among the remedies advocated. Bureaucracy and related themes are associated with the wrong kind of power. A new concept of community, with respect to which participation is urged, is endowed with magical virtues.

I have stressed the importance in modern society of three revolutions. Each has been a center of tension, producing radical groups that opposed features of the existing social structure as well as revolutionary changes. The French Revolution, a phase of the early democratic revolution, spawned the Jacobins, the absolutists of Rousseauean democracy. The industrial revolution generated conflicts about which I have had a good deal to say; the socialists were the radicals of this phase. The student radicals of the New Left have begun to play an analogous role in the educational revolution.

We face a paradox. Revolutionaries resent hearing that they share any values with those whose immoral systems they seek to overthrow. As I have used the concept of values in analysis, however, it is legitimate to raise the question whether or not the basic value *patterns* of modern society, and especially of the United States, are being fundamentally challenged. Are the institutional achievements associated with the progressive values of the nineteenth century no longer relevant? Have they been repudiated by the new generation? In my opinion these values are taken for granted, not repudiated.[13] Modern society is indicted for not living up to its professed values, as demonstrated by the existence of poverty and racial discrimination and the persistence of war and imperialism. On the other hand, there is insistence that society should not be content with these value implementations but should introduce new ones.

Egalitarian themes suggest what the next phases may be; the two symbols of community and participation point a direction. The modern system, particularly in the United States, completed one phase of institutional consolidation, but it is also undergoing the ferment that accompanies the emergence of new phases. The strategic significance of the societal community to new phases seems clear. The emergence of important features of this community is recent. Furthermore, the United States has led the change, but its features will spread through all modern societies. A description of these features is therefore in order.

The principle of equality is being applied more pervasively than ever before. A societal community *basically* composed of equals seems to be the final development in the process of undermining the legitimacy of older, more particularistic and ascriptive bases of membership, such as religion (in pluralistic society), ethnic affiliation, region or locality, and hereditary in social status (in the aristocracy but also in more recent versions of class status). This theme of equality has many antecedents but first crystallized in conceptions of natural rights under the Enlightenment and found expression in the Bill of Rights of the American Constitution. The Bill of Rights has proved to be a time bomb; some of its consequences emerged long after its official adoption, dramatically through Supreme Court action but also more generally. Concern over poverty and race problems in the United States reflects the moral repugnance that the conception of an inherently lower class or an inferior race arouses in modern societies.

Some radical ideologies claim that genuine equality requires abolition of all hierarchical status distinctions. This version of community has been a persistently recurring ideal for many centuries. Such approximations to realistic institutionalization as have occurred, however, have always been on a small scale and of short duration. Too intensive a drive in this direction would disrupt larger-scale institutions of modern societies as law, markets, effective government, and competent creation and use of advanced knowledge. It would shatter society into primitive small communities. The direction of modern societal development is toward a new pattern of stratification. The historical bases of legitimate inequality have been ascriptive. The value base of the new egalitarianism requires a different basis of legitimation. In general terms, this basis must be *functional* to society conceived of as a system. Differential outcomes of the competitive education process must be legitimatized in terms of societal interest in the contributions of especially competent people; special competence is a function of both native ability and good training. A societal interest in economic productivity (with no presumption that every individual or collective unit that participates will be equally productive) implies special rewards for the economically more productive units. Similarly, effective organization is a functional necessity of complex collectivities and one of the factors in such effectiveness is the institutionalization of power, which has an inherently differential aspect.

Two modes of reconciliation exist between the value imperative of basic equality and the functional needs for competence, productivity, and collective effectiveness—all of which intersect in concrete areas of the social structure. The first is the institutionalization of *accountability,* one example of which is the accountability of elected officials to their constituencies. Economic markets perform analogous functions, though imperfectly, as do mechanisms for certifying competence in the academic world, the professions, and other fiduciary bodies. The second mode is the institutionalization of equality of opportunity so that no citizen shall for ascriptive reasons (race, social class, religion, ethnic affiliation), be barred from equal access to opportunities for performance, as in employment, or to opportunities for making effective performance possible, like health and education. This ideal is far from full realization, but the view, so prevalent today, that equality of opportunity is sheer mockery suggests that the ideal actually is being taken seriously. In earlier times the lower classes, or individuals disadvantaged on other ascriptive bases, took for granted that opportunities open to their betters were not for them, and they did not protest. The volume of protest is not a simple function of the magnitude of the evil.

Balancing value-commitments to equality against inequalities implied in functional effectiveness presents integrative problems to modern societies because many of the historic bases of hierarchical legitimation are no longer available. This difficulty is compounded by the appearance of the problem not in one overarching sphere but in many different spheres. There are many bases for functional inequality; the classification competence-economic efficiency-collective effectiveness constitutes only an elementary framework. There must be integration not only between claims to special prerogatives and the principles of equality but also among different kinds of claims to special prerogatives in a pluralistic social system.

This integration is the focus of emerging institutions of stratification. None of the inherited formulas purporting to describe modern stratification is satisfactory. The basis is not, except in special instances, national or ethnic membership. It is neither aristocracy in the older sense nor class in the Marxian sense. It is still incompletely developed and essentially new. The integration of such a societal community must depend upon mechanisms that center around the attachment of generalized prestige to specific groups and to the statuses that they occupy, including the office of bearers of authority in collectivities. The prestige of such groups and statuses must be rooted in combinations of factors rather than in any one, like wealth, political power, or even moral authority. *Prestige* is the communication node through which factors essential to the integration of the societal community can be evaluated, balanced, and integrated in an output, *influence*. The exercise of influence by one unit or set of units can help to bring other units into consensus by justifying allocations of rights and obligations, expected performances, and rewards in terms of their contributions to a common interest. The common interest is that of the society conceived as a community.

The concentration on the societal community that has characterized the present chapter should be balanced by a recognition that values potentially transcend any particular community. That is why this book has been concerned with the *system* of modern societies rather than with any one society. The processes that transformed the societal community of the United States and promise to continue to transform it are not peculiar to this society but permeate the modern—and modernizing—system. Only on such an assumption of commonality is it understandable that European societies with no racial problems of their own can feel justified in taunting Americans about their callousness in the treatment of blacks or small independent countries in raising outcries of imperialism. From the vantage point of common membership in the modern system, the *intersocietal* institutionalization of a new value system, including its relevance to stratification, is worth studying.

The foci of conflict and thus of creative innovation in the modern system are not mainly economic in the sense of the nineteenth-century controversy over capitalism and socialism, nor do they seem political in the sense of the problem of the justice of the distribution of power, though both these conflicts are present. A cultural focus, especially in the wake of the educational revolution, is nearer the mark. The indications are that the storm center is the societal community. There is the relative obsolescence of many older values like hereditary privilege, ethnicity, and class. There are also unsolved problems of integrating the normative structure of community with the motivational basis of solidarity, which remains more problematic. The new societal community, conceived as an integrative institution, must operate at a level different from those familiar in our intellectual traditions; it must go beyond command of political power and wealth and of the factors that generate them to value commitments and mechanisms of influence.

NOTES

Preface

1. See Parsons, "The Relations between Biological and Socio-Cultural Theory," in *Social Systems and the Evolution of Action Theory* (Glencoe, Ill.: Free Press, 1977), pp. 118–21.

2. Ibid., pp. 22–76.

Introduction

1. Parsons, "The Kinship System of the Contemporary United States," *American Anthropologist* 45 (1943): 22–38.

2. Max Weber, *The Theory of Social and Economic Organization*, trans. A. M. Henderson and Talcott Parsons (New York: Oxford University Press, 1947).

3. Parsons, *The Structure of Social Action* (New York: McGraw Hill, 1937).

4. Parsons, "Capitalism in Recent German Literature: Sombart and Weber," *Journal of Political Economy* 36 (1928): 641–61.

5. Parsons, "The Professions and Social Structure," *Social Forces* 17 (1939): 457–67; "An Analytical Approach to the Theory of Social Stratification," *American Journal of Sociology* 45 (1940): 841–62; "Age and Sex in the Social Structure of the United States," *American Sociological Review* 7 (1942): 604–16; "The Kinship System of the Contemporary United States."

6. Parsons, *The Social System* (Glencoe, Ill.: Free Press, 1951); *Toward a General Theory of Action*, ed. with Edward A. Shils (Cambridge, Mass.: Harvard University Press, 1951); *Economy and Society*, with Neil Smelser (New York: Free Press, 1956); "An Outline of the Social System," in *Theories of Society*, ed. Parsons et al. (New York: Free Press, 1961), pp. 30–79.

7. Parsons, *Social System*, dedication page.

8. Parsons, *Structure of Social Action*, p. 10.

9. Parsons, "The Role of Theory in Social Research," *American Sociologial Review* 3 (1938): 15.

10. Ibid., pp. 14–15.

11. Parsons, *Structure of Social Action*, p. 28.

12. Parsons, "The Place of Ultimate Values in Sociological Theory," *International Journal of Ethics* 45 (1935): 282.

13. Parsons, *Structure of Social Action*, p. 732.

14. Ibid., pp. 100–102.

15. Parsons, *Social System*, pp. 58–67.

16. Parsons, *Structure of Social Action*, p. 399.

17. Parsons, *Social System*, p. 37.

18. Dennis Wrong, "The Oversocialized Conception of Man," *American Sociological Review* 26 (1961): 183–93.

19. Parsons, "Social Classes and Class Conflict in the Light of Recent Sociological Theory," in *Essays in Sociological Theory*, rev. ed. (Glencoe, Ill.: Free Press, 1954), pp. 323–35.

20. Ibid., p. 323.

21. Parsons, "A Paradigm of the Human Condition," in *Action Theory and the Human Condition* (New York: Free Press, 1978), pp. 352–433.

22. Ibid., p. 363.

23. Robert F. Bales, *Interaction Process Analysis* (Cambridge, Mass.: Addison-Wesley, 1950); Parsons et al., *Working Papers in the Theory of Action* (Glencoe, Ill.: Free Press, 1953), chapter 5. For a relatively uncomplicated presentation of the four-function scheme see Parsons's "General Theory in Sociology," in *Sociology Today*, ed. Robert K. Merton et al. (New York: Basic Books, 1959), pp. 3–38. For the most advanced treatment of the relation between the pattern variables and the four-function scheme and the continuities between the two paradigms, see Parsons, "Pattern Variables Revisited: A Response to Professor Dubin's Stimulus," in *Sociological Theory and Modern Society* (New York: Free Press, 1967), pp. 192–219.

24. Parsons, *Family, Socialization, and Interaction Process*, with Robert F. Bales et al. (New York: Free Press, 1955); "A Revised Analytical Approach to the Theory of Social Stratification," in *Essays in Sociological Theory*, rev. ed. (Glencoe, Ill.: Free Press, 1954), pp. 386–439.

25. Parsons, "On Building Social System Theory: A Personal History," *Social Systems and the Evolution of Action Theory* (New York: Free Press, 1977), p. 25.

26. Parsons, "Religion in Postindustrial America: The Problem of Secularization," *Social Research* 41 (1974): 300–22.

27. Parsons, "Durkheim's Contribution to the Integration of Social Systems," in *Sociological Theory and Modern Society*, pp. 3–34.

28. Parsons, *Economy and Society*, pp. 70–85.

29. Parsons, "On the Concept of Political Power," in *Sociological Theory and Modern Society*, p. 308.

30. Parsons, "On the Concept of Influence," in *Sociological Theory and Modern Society*, pp. 355–82.

31. Parsons, "On the Concept of Value-Commitments," in *Sociological Inquiry* 38 (1968): 135–60.

32. Parsons, "Some Considerations on the Theory of Social Change," in *Rural Sociology* 26 (1961): 219–39.

33. Parsons, *The Evolution of Societies*, ed. Jackson Toby (Englewood Cliffs, N.J.: Prentice-Hall, 1977), pp. 161–214.

34. Parsons, *The American University*, with Gerald M. Platt (Cambridge, Mass.: Harvard University Press, 1973); "A Paradigm of the Human Condition."

35. On the natural side see Parsons, "The Relations between Biological and Sociocultural Theory," with A. Hunter Dupree, in *Social Systems and the Evolution of Action Theory;* on the idealistic side see "A Paradigm of the Human Condition."

36. Parsons expressed considerable disappointment that so much critical attention was directed toward his earliest work, particularly *The Structure of Social Action*. See his "Comment on Burger's Critique," in *American Journal of Sociology* 83 (1977): 335–39. Among the more important critiques are Jeffrey C. Alexander, "Formal and Substantive Voluntarism in the Work of Talcott Parsons: A Theoretical and Ideological Reinterpretation," in *American Sociological Review* 43 (1978): 177–98; Harold Bershady, *Ideology and Social Knowledge* (New York: Wiley, 1973); Max Black, ed., *The Social Theories of Talcott Parsons* (Englewood Cliffs, N.J.: Prentice-Hall, 1961); Thomas Burger, "Talcott Parsons, the Problem of Order in Society, and the Program of an Analytical Sociology," in *American Journal of Sociology* 83 (1977): 320–34; Francesca Cancian, *What are Norms?* (Cambridge: Cambridge University Press, 1975); Lewis Feuer, "The Social Theories of Talcott Parsons: A Critical Examination," in *Journal of Philosophy* 59 (1962): 182–93; Daniel Foss, "The World View of Talcott Parsons," in *Sociology on Trial*, ed. Maurice Stein and Arthur Vidich (Englewood Cliffs, N.J.: Prentice-Hall, 1963), pp. 96–126; Anthony Giddens, "Power in the Recent Writings of Talcott Parsons," in *Sociology* 2 (1968): 257–72. Alvin Gouldner, *The Coming Crisis of Western Sociology* (New York: Basic Books, 1970); Harold Kaplan, "The Parsonian Image of Social Structure and Its Relevance for Political Science," in *Journal of Politics* 30 (1968): 885–909; David Lockwood, "Some Remarks on 'The Social System,'" in *British Journal of Sociology* 7 (1956): 134–46; C. Wright Mills, *The Sociological Imagination* (New York: Oxford University Press, 1959).

37. See Richard A. Lanham, *Style: An Anti-Textbook* (New Haven, Conn.: Yale University Press, 1974), pp. 69–78.

38. Mills, *Sociological Imagination*, pp. 25–49.

39. Parsons, "Social Classes and Class Conflict in the Light of Recent Sociological Theory"; see also *Theories of Society,* pp. 94–95.
40. Parsons, *The System of Modern Societies* (Englewood Cliffs, N.J.: Prentice-Hall, 1971), p. 142.
41. Ibid., p. 115.
42. Ibid., pp. 142–43.

Chapter 1

1. A. C. Pigou, ed., *Memorials of Alfred Marshall,* p. 108.
2. Talcott Parsons, *The Structure of Social Action* (New York: McGraw Hill, 1937).

Chapter 4

1. Thomas Hobbes, *The Leviathan,* Everyman ed., p. 24.
2. Ibid., p. 24.
3. Ibid., p. 43.
4. Ibid., p. 63.
5. Ibid., p. 66.
6. Ibid., p. 65.

Chapter 8

1. Cf. Talcott Parsons and Edward A. Shils, eds., *Toward a General Theory of Action* (Cambridge: Harvard University Press, 1951). Also Talcott Parsons, *The Social System* (New York: Free Press, 1951).
2. Durkheim's insights were first clearly stated in a paper, "Determination du Fait moral," published in the *Revue de Metaphysique et de Morale* in 1906, and were much further developed in *Les Formes elementaires de la Vie religieuse,* his last book (Paris: F. Alcan, 1912).
3. This view has certainly been modified in subsequent psychoanalytic thinking, but it is the major framework within which Freud introduced the concept of the superego.
4. This is in no way meant to suggest that there is *no* element of constitutional bisexuality, but only that *some* things Freud attributed to it may be explicable on other grounds.

Chapter 13

1. I have always considered the focal point of Durkheim's early work in this respect to lie in "Organic and Contractual Solidarity" (book 1, chap. 7), *The Division of Labor in Society,* trans. George Simpson (Glen-

coe, Ill.: Free Press, 1947). It starts as a critique of Spencer but actually goes clear back to Hobbes.

2. One reason for this is that the hypothetical turning-over of absolute authority to an unrestricted sovereign was empirically incompatible with the existence of the liberal governmental regimes that were a common-place in the Western world of Durkheim's time. On this phase of the history of thought the best source is still, without question, Elie Halévy, *The Growth of Philosophic Radicalism,* trans. Mary Morris ([1901–4] New York: Macmillan Co., 1928).

3. Durkheim does not, of course, in his more general discussion, confine himself to contract at the legal or other levels. He relates organic solidarity also to domestic, commercial, procedural, administrative, and constitutional law. Cf. *The Division of Labor in Society,* p. 122.

4. *De la division du travail social* (Paris: Felix Alcan, 1893), p. 46.

5. "The acts that it [repressive law] prohibits and qualifies as crimes are of two sorts. Either they directly manifest very violent dissemblance between the agent who accomplishes them and the collective type, or else they offend the organ of the common conscience."—*The Division of Labor in Society,* p. 106. The context makes clear that by the "organ" Durkheim means the government.

6. There is, of course, a sense in which the criminal law also lays down norms. Essentially, these norms concern the minimum standards of be-havior which are considered acceptable on the part of members of the society—regardless of their differentiated functions—who are not dis-qualified by mental incapacity, and so on. In a highly differentiated society, however, the largest body of norms increasingly concerns the re-lations between differentiated functions in the fields Durkheim enumer-ated; namely, contract, family life, commerce, administration, and the constitutional structure of the collectivity.

7. Talcott Parsons, *The Social System* (Glencoe, Ill.: Free Press, 1951), pp. 36–45.

8. Cf. Leo F. Schnore, "Social Morphology and Human Ecology," *American Journal of Sociology* 63 (1958): 620–34.

Chapter 14

1. E.g., labour services are not exchanged directly for consumers' goods.

2. Cf. H. O. Henderson, "The Significance of the Rate of Interest," *Oxford Economic Papers,* no. 1 (October 1938), pp. 1–13; J. E. Meade and P. W. S. Andrews, "Summary of Replies to Questions on Effects of Interest Rates," ibid., pp. 14–31.

3. Of course, in one sense the polity must "pay a price" to encourage productive enterprise in order to gain productivity. The *basis* of this price, however, is not the offer of purchasing power which the economy

may or may not accept in return for a given increment of productivity. The order of control is different; the monetary mechanisms are a *symbol* of the encouragement or discouragement which the polity uses as sanction.

4. Commonly the two sets of decisions on the polity side are located in different agencies. The exchange between capital funds and rights to intervene is closely associated with banking, insurance and other fiduciary agencies, though government historically has been involved in controlling these agencies and taking a direct hand in the interchange. The balance between productivity and encouragement of productive enterprise, on the other hand, is structurally linked to the governmental and judicial elements of the polity.

5. Cf. David Landes, "French Business and the Businessman: A Social and Cultural Analysis," in E. M. Earle, ed., *Modern France,* 1951. We are also indebted to personal discussion with Mr. Jesse R. Pitts.

6. What the more ultimate goals may be, e.g., promotion of the world revolution or a maximal standard of living for all, etc., is not immediately essential for our argument.

Chapter 15

1. It is taken for granted here that there is no formal standardization of terminology in this field, and that, hence, there is inevitably an element of arbitrariness involved in giving technical meaning to a term in such general usage as "influence." I make no apology for doing this, since in the social sciences the only alternative in this and many other cases is coining neologisms, the objections to which are overwhelming.

2. Roman Jacobsen and Morris Halle, *Fundamentals of Language* (The Hague: Mouton & Co., 1956).

3. This perspective on money as a language is strongly suggested by the usage of the classical economists (e.g. Adam Smith, Ricardo, and J. S. Mill), when they spoke of the dual nature of money, first, as a "medium of exchange" (message transmission) and, second, as a "measure of value" (code).

4. It is important to note that the linguistic parallel holds here. The experience of an encounter with a ferocious dog can be "converted" into words, in that, for example, the person frightened can tell another about it in the absence of the dog and evoke in him appropriate reactions. Conversely, in our example above, linguistic warning can evoke an attitude set appropriate to dealing with such an animal in the absence of direct experience of the dog. The linguistic symbols do not have the properties either of dangerousness or of capacity to cope with danger, but they can *mediate* the action process by "orienting" an actor to danger.

5. There are two modes of exchange that involve levels of differentia-

tion of the interest in utility short of what I am here calling the "market" level, namely, ascriptive exchange, the case of obligatory gifts, well known to anthropologists (cf. Marcel Mauss, *The Gift* [Glencoe, Ill.: Free Press, 1954]), and the case of barter. Both lack the involvement of a generalized medium that specifically symbolizes utility, namely, money.

6. The closest approach to this paradigm with which I am familiar from the literature is Herbert C. Kelman, "Processes of Opinion Change," *Public Opinion Quarterly* 25 (1961): 57–78.

7. This case, as well as the setting in which it fits, is much more fully discussed in my paper, "On the Concept of Political Power," *Proceedings of the American Philosophical Society,* Philadelphia, 1963. Generally, this is a companion piece to the present paper.

8. Ego can implement this threat through use of the *attitudinal* sanction of *disapproval,* and, in the case of compliance, by using influence he can reward alter with his *approval.*

9. The most important reason concerns the role of banking and credit, the bearing of which on the functioning of influence will be taken up later.

10. For reasons of space, no further attempt is made here to ground this statement. Cf. my paper on political power, op. cit.

11. To take an extreme example, a middle-aged man might stubbornly refuse to make a will because of a kind of phantasy of immortality. If, however, a physician informed him that because of incurable cancer he had only a few months to live, this might well be enough to persuade him to make the will. This treatment of information and intentions as the primary types of intrinsic persuaders has recently been modified.

12. For many purposes, economists have bracketed "goods and services" together as the two ultimate "want-satisfiers." For certain purposes of economic sociology, however, the distinction is vital, particularly because the concept of services constitutes one perspective on labor as a factor of production. (Cf. Talcott Parsons and Neil J. Smelser, *Economy and Society* [Glencoe, Ill.: Free Press, 1956], p. 157, for a preliminary discussion of the importance of the distinction.)

13. The term "justification" here refers to the level of norms. It seems useful to distinguish it from "legitimation," by which I would mean reference to the level of values. Cf. Talcott Parsons, part 2 of General Introduction, in Parsons, E. Shils, K. Naegele, J. Pitts, editors, *Theories of Society,* vol. 1 (Glencoe, Ill.: Free Press, 1961), pp. 43–44.

14. This, it should be noted, is independent of the assumption of formally binding obligation.

15. Berelson, P. Lazarsfeld, and W. McPhee, *Voting* (Chicago: University of Chicago Press, 1954).

16. Cf. Talcott Parsons, "'Voting' and the Equilibrium of the American Political System," in Eugene Burdick and Arthur J. Brodbeck, editors, *American Voting Behavior* (Glencoe, Ill.: Free Press, 1959).

17. Of course, for this analysis to be relevant, the association in ques-

tion need not be "fully" democratic, but this problem of ranges in degrees of democracy need not concern the present very limited discussion.

18. Incumbents of office, though they have power, are often very careful when pleading for certain measures to make clear that they will not directly bring their power to bear in the particular case. A good example is when officeholders who are adherents of a particular party lend their influence to strictly nonpartisan causes. Thus a state governor who is a good Republican may plead for *all* the people, regardless of party, to contribute generously to the Red Cross campaign.

19. For the collectivity as unit the relevant membership is that in more inclusive collectivities; e.g., a department is a subcollectivity in a university faculty.

20. Cf. Talcott Parsons, "Pattern Variables Revisited," *American Sociological Review* 25 (1960): 467–83.

21. This refers to a generalized paradigm of analysis in terms of four functional categories, elaborated more fully, for example, in the General Introduction to *Theories of Society* and in "Pattern Variables Revisited," as cited.

22. For example, this seems to be the position of Harold D. Lasswell and Abraham Kaplan, *Power and Society* (New Haven: Yale University Press, 1950).

23. For the concept of circular flow, cf. J. A. Schumpeter, *The Theory of Economic Development* (Cambridge, Mass.: Harvard University Press, 1934), chap. 1.

24. McCarthyism was a classic instance of a deflationary episode entering in the influence field, which at its culmination approached panic proportions: the demand for "absolute loyalty" was analogous to the demand for a return to the gold standard in the financial area. Cf. E. A. Shils, *The Torment of Secrecy,* and "Social Strains in America," chap. 7 of my book of essays, *Structure and Process in Modern Societies* (Glencoe, Ill.: Free Press, 1960).

Chapter 16

1. The concept of inertia is here used in the sense of classical mechanics, namely to designate stability in rate and direction of process, not a state in which "nothing happens." The *problem* then becomes that of accounting for change in rate or direction, including "slowing down." This of course runs counter to much of common sense in the field of human action.

2. Cf. T. Parsons and N. Smelser, *Economy and Society* (Glencoe, Ill.: Free Press, 1956), chap. 4. A considerably more developed version, applied to a case of special interest here, is given in N. Smelser, *Social*

Change in the Industrial Revolution (Chicago: University of Chicago Press, 1959), esp. chaps. 9–13.

Chapter 17

1. Raymond A. Bauer and Alice H. Bauer, "America, 'Mass Society' and Mass Media," *Journal of Social Issues* 16, no. 2 (1960): 3–66.
2. This part of the discussion is developed at greater length in Winston White, *Beyond Conformity* (New York: Free Press, 1961).
3. When we speak of market here in quotation marks we are generalizing the economic concept to cover several other related types. We hope no confusion results from this usage.
4. Cf. C. Wright Mills, *The Power Elite* (New York: Oxford University Press, 1956).
5. It is essential, in order to avoid ideological traps, to pay attention to both the "demand" and the "supply" sides, rather than explicitly or implicitly assuming that one determines the outcome of the other.
6. Cf. William Kornhauser, *The Politics of Mass Society* (Free Press, 1960); and Parsons, "Social Structure and Political Orientation," *World Politics,* October 1960.

Chapter 18

1. Robert N. Bellah, "Religious Evolution," *The American Sociological Review,* June 1964.
2. Cf. Talcott Parsons, "Evolutionary Universals in Society," *The American Sociological Review,* June 1964.
3. As archaeologists have emphasized, these developments usually also involve developments in urbanization. The comparative evidence on this point is summarized in *Courses Toward Urban Life,* edited by Robert J. Braidwood and Gordon Willey (Chicago: Aldine, 1962).

Chapter 19

1. George Wald, "Life and Light," *Scientific American* 201 (October 1959): 92–108.
2. Note that the species rather than the individual organism is the major system of reference here. See George Gaylord Simpson, *The Meaning of Evolution* (New Haven: Yale University Press, 1950).
3. Alfred Emerson, "Homeostasis and Comparison of Systems," in Roy R. Grinker, ed., *Toward a Unified Theory of Behavior* (New York: Basic Books, 1956).

4. Cf. Emile Durkheim, *The Elementary Forms of the Religious Life* (London: Allen and Unwin, 1915).

5. See W. Lloyd Warner, *A Black Civilization,* 2d ed. (New York: Harper, 1958), for an analysis showing that such boundedness can be problematic.

6. This analysis has been suggested in part by Charles Ackerman who bases himself on a variety of the recent studies of kinship systems, but, perhaps, particularly on Rodney Needham's studies of the Purums, *Structure and Sentiment* (Chicago: University of Chicago Press, 1960).

7. See Talcott Parsons, *Societies: Comparative and Evolutionary Perspectives* (Englewood Cliffs, N.J.: Prentice-Hall, forthcoming, 1964).

8. Cf. Gideon Sjoberg, *The Preindustrial City* (Glencoe, Ill.: Free Press, 1960), chap. 5.

9. Claude Levi-Strauss, *Totemism* (Boston: Beacon Paperbacks, 1963).

10. See "The Analysis of Formal Organizations," part 1 of my *Structure and Process in Modern Societies* (Glencoe, Ill.: Free Press, 1960); Peter M. Blau, "Critical Remarks on Weber's Theory of Authority," *American Political Science Review* 57 (June 1963): 305–16, and *The Dynamics of Bureaucracy,* 2d ed. (Chicago: University of Chicago Press, 1963); Carl J. Friedrich, ed., *Authority,* Nomos 1 (Cambridge: Harvard University Press, 1958), especially Friedrich's own contribution, "Authority and Reason."

11. Cf. Talcott Parsons, "On the Concept of Political Power," *Proceedings of the American Philosophical Society* 107 (June 1963): 232–62.

12. Max Weber, "The Financing of Political Bodies," in *The Theory of Social and Economic Organization* (Glencoe, Ill.: Free Press, 1947), pp. 310ff.

13. Weber, *The Theory of Social and Economic Organization,* op. cit., p. 377.

14. Weber, *The Theory of Social and Economic Organization,* op. cit., pp. 184ff. and *Max Weber on Law in Economy and Society* (Cambridge: Harvard University Press, 1954), chap. 8.

15. Weber, *Max Weber on Law in Economy and Society,* op. cit.

16. Weber, *The Theory of Social and Economic Organization,* op. cit.

17. Weber, "The Social Causes of the Decay of Ancient Civilization," op. cit.

18. See Roscoe Pound, *The Spirit of the Common Law* (Boston: Beacon Paperbacks, 1963); especially chaps. 2–4.

19. David Little, "The Logic of Order: An Examination of the Sources of Puritan-Anglican Controversy and of Their Relations to Prevailing Legal Conceptions of Corporation in the Late 16th and Early 17th Century in England," unpublished Ph.D. thesis, Harvard University, 1963.

20. Stein Rokkan, "Mass Suffrage, Secret Voting, and Political Participation," *The European Journal of Sociology* 2 (1961): 132–52.

21. Paul Hollander, "The New Man and His Enemies: A Study of the Stalinist Conceptions of Good and Evil Personified," unpublished Ph.D. dissertation, Princeton University, 1963. See also Allen Kassof's forthcoming book on Soviet youth.

Chapter 20

1. *The Principles of Sociology* (New York and London: D. Appleton and Co., 1924), vol. 2 (in three vols.), part 5, chap. 17, "The Militant Type of Society," and chap. 18, "The Industrial Type of Society."

2. Talcott Parsons, "Equality and Inequality in Modern Society; or, Social Stratification Revisited," *Sociological Inquiry* 40 (Spring 1970): 13–72.

2. Talcott Parsons," Equality and Inequality in Modern Society; or, Social Stratification Revisited," *Sociological Inquiry* 40 (Spring 1970): 13–72.

3. Robert N. Bellah, ed., "Introduction" to *Emile Durkheim*, Heritage of Sociology Series (Chicago: University of Chicago Press, 1973).

4. Talcott Parsons, "Christianity," *International Encyclopedia of the Social Sciences*, vol. 2, ed. David L. Sills (New York: Macmillan Co. and Free Press, 1968), pp. 425–47; Talcott Parsons, "Some Problems of General Theory in Sociology," in *Theoretical Sociology, Perspectives and Developments*, ed. John C. McKinney and Edward A. Tiryakian (New York: Appleton-Century-Crofts, Educational Division, Meredith Corporation, 1970), pp. 27–68; Parsons, *System of Modern Societies*.

5. Robert K. Merton, *Science, Technology and Society in Seventeenth Century England* (New York: H. Fertig, 1970); Joseph Ben-David, *The Scientist's Role in Society: A Comparative Study* (Englewood Cliffs, N.J.: Prentice-Hall, 1971).

6. Perry Miller, *Errand into the Wilderness* (Cambridge, Mass.: Harvard University Press, 1964).

7. Johannes J. Loubser, "Puritanism and Religious Liberty: A Study of Normative Change in Massachusetts, 1630–1850," unpublished dissertation, Harvard University, 1964.

8. The controversies over Weber's Protestant ethic thesis have recently been summarized in three works: *The Protestant Ethic and Modernization: A Comparative View*, ed. S. N. Eisenstadt (New York: Basic Books, 1968), Introduction, pp. 3–45; David Little, *Religion, Order and Law* (New York: Harper Torchbooks, 1969), "Bibliographical Essays: (A) Representative Literature Critical of the Protestant Ethic"; and Benjamin Nelson, "Weber's Protestant Ethic: Its Origins, Wanderings, and Foreseeable Futures," in *The Scientific Study of Religion: Beyond the Classics*, ed. Charles Y. Glock and Phillip E. Hammond (Harper & Row, 1973).

9. Parsons, *System of Modern Societies,* esp. chap. 6, "The New Lead Society and Contemporary Modernity," pp. 86–121, and "Conclusion: The Main Pattern," pp. 138–43.

10. See Lee Rainwater and William Yancey, *The Moynihan Report and the Politics of Controversy* (Cambridge, Mass.: M.I.T. Press, 1967); and Talcott Parsons and Kenneth Clark, eds., *The Negro American* (Boston: Houghton Mifflin, 1966).

11. One form is the nostalgia for *Gemeinschaft,* which has been a prominent feature of the sociological tradition, especially as portrayed by Robert Nisbet, *The Sociological Tradition* (New York: Basic Books, 1967).

12. The orientation of sociology is not toward restoring the societies that preceded the industrial and democratic revolutions, or even the educational revolution. Rather it has been toward a search for components of social systems that have accounted for the positive features of earlier societies with a view toward understanding how they can be re-shaped to meet the functional exigencies of emerging modern societies. See Edward A. Shils, "Mass Society and Its Culture," *Daedalus* (Spring 1960); and Winston White, *Beyond Conformity* (New York: Free Press, 1961).

13. One objection to this statement is obvious: The extreme student radicals of the 1960s resorted to the revolutionary tactic of confrontation, including the use of violence and deliberate disruption of academic discussions to deny what liberals consider a fair hearing for those whose positions they opposed. This behavior is a repudiation in practice of the procedural values of liberal society; it is often defended as necessary because of the repressive character of the Establishment. At the same time people who engage in such tactics repeatedly invoke *their* rights in a way that precludes their having repudiated these liberal values. Furthermore, this trait is common to *all* extreme radicals and not only to current ones. The Terror under the Jacobins was hardly democratic, yet it was perpetrated in the name of democracy. Communist tactics have been similar. This conflict between supposed ultimate values like equality and freedom and the tactics of radicalism is built into extreme radical movements.

INDEX